The Magic Egg
and
Other Tales from Ukraine

World Folklore Series

Folk Stories of the Hmong: Peoples of Laos, Thailand, and Vietnam. By Norma J. Livo and Dia Cha.

Images of a People: Tlingit Myths and Legends. By Mary Helen Pelton and Jacqueline DiGennaro.

Hyena and the Moon: Stories to Tell from Kenya. By Heather McNeil.

The Corn Woman: Stories and Legends of the Hispanic Southwest. Retold by Angel Vigil. Translated by Juan Francisco Marín and Jennifer Audrey Lowell.

Thai Tales: Folktales of Thailand. Retold by Supaporn Vathanaprida. Edited by Margaret Read MacDonald.

In Days Gone By: Folklore and Traditions of the Pennsylvania Dutch. By Audrey Burie Kirchner and Margaret R. Tassia.

From the Mango Tree and Other Folktales from Nepal. By Kavita Ram Shrestha and Sarah Lamstein.

Why Ostriches Don't Fly and Other Tales from the African Bush. By I. Murphy Lewis.

The Magic Egg and Other Tales from Ukraine. Retold by Barbara J. Suwyn. Edited and with an Introduction by Natalie O. Kononenko.

When Night Falls, Kric! Krac! Haitian Folktales. By Liliane Nérette Louis. Edited by Fred Hay, Ph.D.

Jasmine and Coconuts: South Indian Tales. By Cathy Spagnoli and Paramasivam Samanna.

The Enchanted Wood and Other Tales from Finland. By Norma J. Livo and George O. Livo.

A Tiger by the Tail and Other Stories from the Heart of Korea. Retold by Lindy Soon Curry. Edited by Chan-eung Park.

The Eagle in the Cactus: Traditional Stories from Mexico. By Angel Vigil.

Selections Available on Audiocassette

Hyena and the Moon: Stories to Listen to from Kenya. By Heather McNeil.

The Corn Woman: Audio Stories and Legends of the Hispanic Southwest. English and Spanish versions. By Angel Vigil. Spanish version read by Juan Francisco Marín.

Thai Tales: Audio Folktales from Thailand. By Supaporn Vathanaprida and Margaret Read MacDonald. Narrated by Supaporn Vathanaprida. Produced and with an Introduction by Margaret Read MacDonald.

Folk Stories of the Hmong: Audio Tales from the Peoples of Laos, Thailand, and Vietnam. By Norma J. Livo and Dia Cha. Narrated by Norma J. Livo and Dia Cha.

The Magic Egg
and
Other Tales from Ukraine

Barbara J. Suwyn

Drawings by the Author

Edited and with an Introduction by
Natalie O. Kononenko

1997
LIBRARIES UNLIMITED, INC.
Englewood, Colorado

Libraries Unlimited, Inc.
P.O. Box 6633
Englewood, CO 80155-6633
(800) 237-6124
www.lu.com

Production Editor: Kevin W. Perizzolo
Copy Editor: Brooke D. Graves
Proofreader: Eileen Bartlett
Indexer: Christine Smith
Interior Design and Typesetting: Judy Gay Matthews

Library of Congress Cataloging-in-Publication Data

Suwyn, Barbara J., 1949-
    The magic egg and other tales from Ukraine / [retold by] Barbara
J. Suwyn ; drawings by author ; edited and with an introduction by
Natalie O. Kononenko.
    xxxv, 230 p. 19x26 cm. -- (World folklore series)
    Includes bibliographical references (p. 207) and index.
    ISBN 1-56308-425-2
    1. Tales--Ukraine. I. Kononenko, Natalie O. II. Title.
III. Series.
GR203.8.S89 1997
398.2'09477--DC21   97-6734
                                                       CIP

This book is dedicated to my father,
who taught me to love stories,
and to my mother,
who taught me to seek the truth.

Contents

Part I
Animal Tales

Part II
How and Why Stories

Part III
Moral Stories

Part IV
Legends and Fairy Tales

Preface

"ONCE UPON A TIME."
When I was a child, those were the most magical words to me, for those were the words my father spoke as he began our bedtime stories. Each night, as the world outside gathered itself into darkness and silence, my three sisters and I lay tucked snugly into bed, enraptured by our father's tales of talking animals, good and powerful heroes, evil villains, enchanted castles, flying carpets, dragons, and fairies. My father's stories opened the doors to our imaginations and led us to our dreams. We loved stories more than any other form of entertainment; and when father told stories, we listened. No other words could so capture our attention as "Once upon a time."

As we grew older, my sisters and I turned to books. Throughout our childhood years we delighted in animal tales and fairy tales; we thrilled to adventure stories, mysteries, and tales of horror; and we swooned over romances. We shared our books and stories, as we still do, but it is my belief that our love of reading had its beginning in the bedtime stories we heard as children. I credit my father with instilling this love of stories and books in us.

Recently I asked my father where he had learned all the stories he told us as children. His reply was simple: "In school." Stories and learning are great companions. Stories are not just entertainment—they teach us. They teach us about ourselves and others, they illustrate great truths, and they illuminate the connectedness and meaning of our lives. It is therefore natural and good that stories be used to educate.

The stories in this book hold many opportunities for learning. They demonstrate the value of honesty, generosity, and kindness. They show us that animals can be great friends to people and that people have a natural place in the world. These tales also acquaint readers and listeners with the cultural roots of a country and people who have been too long forgotten. Ukraine, which has only recently emerged from the shadow of the Soviet Union, is a country rich in history and culture. Its folk literature is vast, and reading through it involves a bit of excavation. Here readers can find ancient pagan elements, Christian themes and characters, and modern populist influences. They will recognize parallels with tales from Western Europe as well as with those of Russia, Turkey, Poland, and other neighboring countries and groups. For example, some readers will note similarities between the character of Little Fox in this collection and the notorious Reynard of Germany and Eastern Europe. Many will recognize the Cinderella tale, which takes on some unique twists in the Ukrainian version ("The Golden Slipper"). These and other folktales of Ukraine have been shaped through history by a multitude of hearts and voices as they have been handed down from generation to generation. Through this process they have become richly layered with meaning.

& & &

Ukraine, which means "borderland," is situated between Europe, Asia, and the Mediterranean. Throughout its history, it has often been dominated by other nations, but Ukraine has also reaped cultural benefits from its associations. Ukrainian folktales illustrate the rich history of the country—depicting brave warriors, powerful princes, and poor but clever peasants. Educators can use these stories as springboards for further learning with extension activities that encourage research and study. Projects can range from having students write a report on the *cossacks* in Ukrainian history, listening to traditional *bandura* music, watching a film about the *Hutsuls* (an ethnic group from the Carpathian Mountains), or studying the geography of Ukraine with its mighty rivers, great plains, and wooded mountains. There are many opportunities for learning in this book—the possibilities are truly endless.

In the time it has taken me to assemble this collection, I have had the pleasure of working with stories that are highly entertaining and also rich in content. The tales have led me to learn more about the country, art, traditions, and people of Ukraine. In many ways, these tales have touched me.

There is an old tradition of welcome in Ukraine. When guests came to visit, they were offered bread and salt. Bread, the staff of life, is for Ukrainians the one essential food of life. Salt, a precious commodity and one of the first preservatives, is also a symbol of kinship and longevity. Offering salt to a guest meant the host was giving something precious and dear, and it was an invitation to live long in harmony. Life and kinship continue to be the sentiments that Ukrainians extend to their visitors. This collection of stories is extended to readers in that same spirit of welcome, of bread and salt, life and kinship. Perhaps they will sustain you or whet your appetite for more. My intent with the stories in this collection is to spark your interest and the interest of your students, children, or listeners. If you wish to learn more about Ukraine's history, geography, and culture, the publications listed in the bibliography will provide you with a good starting place. Above all, it is my sincere hope that these tales will touch and teach you as they have touched and taught me, and that through your sharing, these stories will live on.

Barbara J. Suwyn, 1997

Acknowledgments

I WOULD LIKE TO EXPRESS MY SINCERE APPRECIATION to the following individuals who supported and contributed to this endeavor: Dr. Bohdan Wynar, for giving me the opportunity to participate in the project, granting me the full use of his archives, and sharing with me his love for Ukraine; Dr. Bohdan Medwidsky and Dr. Robert Klymasz, for advice in the initial planning stages of the project; my editor, Prof. Natalie Kononenko, who contributed her time, expertise, and creativity to the project and guided me in finding sources, selecting and writing stories, and authenticating content; Dr. Eugene Petriwsky, for help in locating source material; Heather McNeil, Marilyn Hempstead, and Dr. Suzanne Barchers, for help with storytelling methodology and techniques; Dr. Larysa Onyshkevych, for sharing her version of "The Turnip"; Nadia Vynnych, for help with translation; Olha Yarema Wynar, for consultation on folk custom and tradition; Clark Richert, for technical help with maps, photographs, and illustrations; Kevin W. Perizzolo, my production editor, for his generous support and guidance throughout the production phase of the project; Judy Gay Matthews for her sensitivity in design and layout; Joan Garner for her outstanding cover design; the staff of Libraries Unlimited; and many others too numerous to mention.

Generous thanks go to the following people for allowing me to use their materials in this book:

Alexander Tkachenko: for use of his artwork *Ukrainian Christmas* (on the front cover) and *The Path to the Windmill.*

Myron W. Surmach: © Surma Book & Music Co. for use of *Christmas Is Here* (glass painting).

Natalie Kononenko: for use of photographs and stories: "Pea Roll-Along," "The Doll," "The Man Who Danced with the Rusalky," "The Christmas Spiders," "The Red Death," "How Evil Came into the World," "The Sun, the Frost, and the Wind," "Dnipro and Dunai," "St. Cassian," "Dovbush's Treasure," and "The Stranger.".

Bohdan, Marta, Virna, Danylo, Olena, Tamara, and Halina Koval: for use of Halyna Mazepa's artworks, "Girl with Buckets" (on back cover), "The Three Brothers," "Vasyl' and the Frog," and "The Two Daughters."

Bohdan S. Wynar: for use of photographs.

Introduction to Ukrainian Folktales

Natalie O. Kononenko

Tales and legends are but one small part of Ukraine's rich and varied folklore tradition. This tradition includes proverbs, riddles, dances, games, and songs of every kind, from long story songs about great battles to short lyric songs about love, from songs for adults to lullabies for children. The richness of Ukrainian folklore comes from many sources, but foremost among them is the Ukrainian people's intense feeling for the land and for all living things. Although Ukraine is a land of great cities, as well as towns, villages, and separate farmsteads, the heart and soul of the people and of their folklore are in the village. Villages depended heavily on farming and Ukrainian farming was wonderfully successful. In fact, Ukraine was known as the breadbasket of Europe and will probably resume that title someday.

The success of Ukrainian farming resulted not only from the fecundity of the soil, but also from a deep, centuries-old understanding of the land, the plants that grew in it, and of the animals that lived on it. We see that understanding here in the many stories about animals and the stories in which crops play a role. In "The Doll," "The Stolen *Postoly* and the Boiled Eggs," and "The Clever Maid," for example, understanding how crops are sown and reaped is central. In "Pea-Roll-Along," a vegetable as small as a pea makes a woman give birth to a great hero, one stronger than all of his brothers and mightier even than an incarnation of evil.

As for the animal tales, all folklore traditions have animal stories for the entertainment of children and for teaching virtues such as trustworthiness and generosity. Ukrainian folklore has this,too, along with a sense that animals are the kin of human beings. We see animals assuming human roles—farmer, midwife, village head—and interacting with people as if animals and human beings understood each other and lived on the same terms. In addition to all of the animals in specifically animal tales, we see many animals in tales outside this category. In "The Magic Egg," for example, there is an eagle who soars as high as the heavens, who can take people to the other world and also teach them respect for all life, animal as well as human. Respect for all life was important for, in many senses, Ukrainians did indeed feel that they were related to all living things, that they and animals were one. Should anyone forget this, stories such as "The Christmas Spiders" remind us that even the lowliest animals are blessed and can transfer their blessings to humankind.

As important as the feeling of being one with nature was the belief that the dead continue to interact with the living, protecting them, guiding them, making sure that they prosper and do all that is right and good. In our stories we meet old people who help young people and tell them what to do, offering counsel and guidance that is so wise it can overcome the devil himself. We learn that the gift of a dying relative, even something as small as a seed (perhaps a symbol for a bit of good advice) can protect the living, reward the pure of heart, and lead to prosperity. Even people who did some bad things during their lifetimes may become protectors and arbiters of justice after death. In the story of "Dovbush's Treasure," we see the Ukrainian Robin Hood supporting the poor and teaching good moral values, even though he himself did bad things as well as good while he was alive. In Ukraine, the presence of ancestors was always felt—past generations and traditions—with which people wanted to maintain contact, linking them to future generations through tales.

The perceived presence of ancestors led to great respect for old people. Unfortunately, it did not fully overcome the opposite tendency, a tendency to ignore elders or even mistreat them and cast them aside. Old people are often weak of body, even if they are strong of mind, and there is a certain temptation to avoid giving them their due. Certainly Ukrainians face this problem, as do peoples all around the world. Stories in every category remind us what folly it is to disregard the old. Whether it is an old dog or an old cat, who is cast out because of age and weakness but later triumphs over incredible adversity; an elderly father who seems stupid but outsmarts all his greedy and inattentive children; or a grandmother who seems ineffectual but can protect a child from beyond the grave, characters in folklore show us again and again that the old are valuable members of the community. The emphasis on old people in tales is probably not coincidental. Old people were the primary tellers of tales and conservers of the Ukrainian heritage. It is thanks to them, and to the triumph of the positive tradition of respecting old people, their wisdom, and their lore, that we have so vast a folklore tradition.

Another reason for the richness of Ukrainian folklore comes from the fact that Ukraine is such an ancient land. The area has been continuously inhabited since 5,000 B.C., and possibly longer. Archeological finds show that a well-developed culture existed several millennia before our era. They also demonstrate that the ancient culture is continuous with the culture of modern Ukraine, at least to a certain degree. Decorative motifs found on prehistoric pots, statues, and other artifacts are still used today.

Perhaps the two most interesting and most typically Ukrainian artifacts that are in use today and that can be linked to prehistory are *rushnyky* and *pysanky*. *Rushnyky* are embroidered towels. These are not towels used for drying hands or wiping the dishes; rather, they are decorative and sacred objects. They are hung around icons and around windows and doors. A newborn child is typically wrapped in a *rushnyk*; a *rushnyk* is placed on the body of a deceased person; a bride wears one as a belt on her wedding day. All these uses establish that the *rushnyk* is a sacred cloth used to protect people, especially people in transit, people moving in and out of a house, or people crossing from one stage of life to the next.

Pysanky are the famous Ukrainian batik Easter eggs. Unlike *krasanky* (which are Easter eggs all of one color, meant to be eaten to break the Lenten fast on Easter morning), *pysanky* are raw eggs, intricately decorated with beeswax and many colors of dye. They are not meant to be eaten, but are given as gifts to ensure health and prosperity and buried under houses and in fields to bring good crops and good fortune. Both *rushnyky* and *pysanky* have designs, such as the tree of life, soul birds, and votive female figures with upraised hands, that can also be found on prehistoric pieces unearthed in archeological digs. The *rushnyky* and *pysanky* show that motifs from an ancient belief system continue into today.

Ancient motifs are plentiful in our tales as well. In our stories we see magic trees, such as the tree that grows from a tiny seed to become the source of plenty, or the tree that speaks to the heroine and rewards her with apples while withholding gifts from her lazy and inconsiderate sister. There are magic birds that carry heroes out of the underworld, and many, many magical women—the Frog Princess and the *rusalky*, among others. It becomes obvious that there is a cultural heritage in the area of Ukraine that dates back many millennia: a rich heritage of artifacts paralleled by a rich heritage of legends and tales.

"Legend and tale" is a standard division of folklore. *Legends* are stories that are told as if they were true, though many contain fantastic elements such as ghosts, goblins, and sprites. *Tales* are make-believe stories, stories that happened once upon a time and three times nine kingdoms away. The legends in this book have been further subdivided into how-and-why stories and moral stories; the tales have been subdivided into animal stories and magic stories. Though these divisions are standard, they do not fully correspond to the place and uses of stories in Ukrainian folklore, nor do they fully reflect the degree to which the story categories blend into and influence one another. For example, "The Doll," which is now a fantastic tale, was probably once a mythical story told as if it were true. In it we encounter an old woman—called a witch in our version, but probably once a goddess figure—who controls the sun.

Prehistoric goddess figure (Photo by N. Kononenko)

Her horsemen of morning, noon, and night bring sunlight and then take it away as night falls. This was probably once seen as a true story explaining why night changes into day and back again.

The witch in this story also possesses a magical spindle and a magical loom with which she rewards the heroine for service. The fact that items used to make cloth come from a mythical woman who controls sunlight underscores the reverence that Ukrainians have for cloth even today. We see the sacred quality of cloth not only in the importance of the *rushnyk* (as discussed earlier), but also in the general regard for embroidery in Ukraine. In the past, all girls were expected to learn how to embroider by the time they were eight years old. By the time they married, they were supposed to have filled a huge dowry chest with embroidered pieces. Even now, many Ukrainians embroider and consider beautiful embroidery characteristic of a Ukraine home. Note also that the name of the heroine of "The Doll," Paraska, probably derives from the name of the patron saint of cloth and fiber arts, Paraskovia Piatnytsia.

The mythic background of tales and legends is extensive, and some of the peculiarly Ukrainian belief features that it lends to our tales need further explanation. One of these is the figure of the witch. Ukrainian witchcraft beliefs were quite complex and were probably influenced by ancient goddess worship as well as by more recent, western approaches. Thus, we have the more western idea that witches are bad and harmful, coexisting with the older, more native idea that witches are wise old women who can offer advice and guidance. In the Ukrainian village, there was a distinction between born witches and learned witches. *Learned witches* were bad. Their magic could harm people and they were most like what we associate with the term *witch*. The term *born witch* indicated a person who had magical powers but was not an evil person. The magic of born witches was almost never harmful; instead, they helped to heal sick people and sick farm animals and to restore crops. Many of the witches and wise women we see in our stories are of the born witch category. When we read about them, we should suspend some of the apprehension that the term *witch* arouses in us and try to adopt the Ukrainian perspective.

Witches were part of something called the *unclean force*. The unclean force is a huge category that comprises a great number and variety of beings. One of the ways in which Ukrainians expressed their feeling that the world around them was alive and that people could interact with any and all aspects of this world was a system of spirits. There were spirits for nearly everything in the farmstead (the house, the barn, the bathhouse, the shed) and everything outside (the field, the stream, the forest, and so on). Like witches, these spirits could be both good and bad. Although Christianity tended to view these spirits negatively, and the designation *unclean* probably comes from the time of Christianity, the spirits actually upheld many moral values. They made sure that people shared with the needy the fish they caught or the wood they cut; they rewarded those who were hardworking by tending their cattle for them or helping them with their spinning and weaving; they even punished those who did not go to church on Sundays. Among the stories presented here, we have a creation legend that tries to explain how these spirits came to be. We also encounter a very special version of the unclean force, the *klad* or treasure spirit, in the form of Oleksa Dovbush, who makes sure that people do not succumb to greed.

One unique member of the unclean force was the *rusalka*, sometimes also called the *mavka*. Often pictured as a mermaid because she made her home in a body of water such as a lake or a river, the *rusalka* was much more than that. *Rusalky* did indeed live in water, but they had legs and feet and they could come out of water, sit in trees, and even dance in fields. *Rusalky* are often described as sitting on docks, combing their green hair, and singing songs that were supposed to be the most beautiful, most entrancing songs in the world.

Like the witch, the *rusalka* probably evolved from an ancient goddess figure; thus, she was much more than a spirit of a building or a place. Also, like the witch, the *rusalka* could be good or bad. Often believed to be the spirit of someone who had died a bad death, such as a person who had committed suicide, a *rusalka* could harm people by leading them astray and tempting them to drown themselves. A *rusalka* could also do many good things. The goddess from which she developed was probably a crop and fertility deity who had control over water and rain and could make crops grow, as the *rusalky* were said to do. A typical legend tells of circles in forests or in fields where the grass grew particularly lush and green because it was a spot where the *rusalky* had danced. There is even a summer festival that, in certain parts of Ukraine, bears the name of the *rusalka* (though in other areas it is named for the seventh week after Easter). During this festival, girls do fortune-telling with trees, flowers, and water and try to act like *rusalky*, bringing fertility to the fields around the village so that the crops will grow.

Rusalky have captured the imagination of many generations. They appear extensively in both legends and tales, and stories about them are included in this collection. There are also many folk pictures of and songs about *rusalky*. *Rusalky* or characters based on them appear in modern Ukrainian movies, such as *Shadows of Forgotten Ancestors*; there is even a chocolate candy called a *rusalka*.

Tales and legends, along with other forms of folklore, have been extensively collected and very well documented in Ukraine. The reasons for the good documentation of Ukrainian folklore are both happy and unhappy ones.

The most positive is the love for Ukrainian folklore of people like this author, people who seek to collect and preserve Ukrainian traditions and to disseminate them as widely as possible. Systematic collection of Ukrainian folklore began early in the nineteenth century. The results of the many collecting efforts, both those made by individuals and those made by folklore expeditions, have been published in books, magazines, and journals. Many materials, however, remain in archives, unpublished. The wealth of Ukrainian folklore is great indeed!

The unhappy reason for the extensive recording of Ukrainian folk traditions is that folklore was often the only means of expression allowed Ukrainian authors and scholars. Ukraine is a rich and beautiful land coveted by many. It has almost never been free. Since the fall of the Kyivan state, it has suffered Turko-Tatar domination; domination by the Polish-Lithuanian Commonwealth, the Austro-Hungarian empire, and Poland; and rule by the Russian imperial and (most recently) Soviet empires.

When folklore began to be intensively collected, eastern Ukraine was part of the Russian Empire and western Ukraine was part of Austro-Hungary. In eastern Ukraine, activities that might encourage Ukrainian nationalist feelings were banned, but folklore was not. Russians saw Ukraine as a backward, border place: *Little Russia*, as Ukraine was so often called. They also saw folklore as ignorant, country literature, appropriate to their perception of Ukraine. Russians felt that the collection of Ukrainian folklore, by perpetuating the image of Ukrainian backwardness, would foster the subjugation of Ukraine. Therefore, they permitted the extensive scholarly activity from which we draw so much of our information today.

Ironically, when Ukrainian folklore was published, it was often published not as Ukrainian material, but as a subdivision of Russian folklore. Thus Aleksandr Afanas'ev's famous collection, *Russian Folk Tales,* is not strictly a collection of Russian tales at all, but one that includes Ukrainian and Belarusian tales alongside the Russian ones. Because Ukraine was labeled Little Russia and its language was considered a distant dialect of Russian, its folklore was seen as subsumable under Russian folklore. Russia supposedly consisted of three parts: Great Russia, what we call Russia today; Little Russia, or Ukraine; and White Russia, what we now call Belarus. The latter two could be—and often were—included under Great Russia. Some of the material drawn on here comes from books that nominally contain Russian folktales or Russian legends. We know that they are actually Ukrainian because we can easily distinguish the Ukrainian language from Russian. Sometimes Ukrainian tales appear in Russian translation to make them more accessible to a Russian reading public. In these instances we can discern their Ukrainian origin if the place where a tale or legend was collected is given in the index or the notes.

In western Ukraine, a similar situation prevailed, the major difference being that there was less of an attempt to assimilate Ukraine and Ukrainian culture into the politically dominant national group. A particularly productive period for folklore work in western Ukraine was the beginning and early part of this century, during which special folklore and ethnographic commissions collected information about and examples of all of the folklore forms listed at the beginning of this introduction, plus data on housing, clothing, and rituals such as funerals and weddings. Data gathered in western Ukraine have been used for the tales and especially for the legends, or "true" stories, presented in this book.

When the Soviets came to power, they controlled both eastern and (after World War II) western Ukraine. They took a less permissive attitude toward Ukrainian folklore than had Russian authorities during the tsarist period and Polish authorities in the west. Soviet government and other agencies soon recognized how effective folklore was in communicating information and ideas. It became Soviet policy to foster folklore, but not in its natural form. The old, classic collections disappeared. New ones, prepared following proper scholarly principles, were confiscated and destroyed. What we would consider true folklore was replaced with an artificial Soviet product. The job of folklorists was no longer to record folklore and present it in as accurate a form as possible; it was to remake folklore and turn it into an instrument that served the Soviet state. Thus folklorists went through stories and songs, taking out all references to religion, anything that might encourage Ukrainian nationalist feelings, and anything that might stimulate rebellious ideas. Only then were these reworked materials published. Folk forms that were considered particularly Ukrainian, such as *pysanky*, disappeared. Besides getting rid of all things that Soviet powers might find undesirable, folklorists were supposed to help folk artists create stories and songs to advance attitudes that would serve the Soviet state, such as submissiveness and collectivism. Instead of stories about ancestors, children listened to stories about Stalin. Instead of *rushnyky* with the tree of life or a goddess figure in the middle, people embroidered towels with portraits of Lenin and slogans to the glory of the Soviet Socialist Revolution.

Soviet rule has ended and Ukraine is now an independent country. In Ukraine, people are trying to reclaim their true folklore from the overlaid strata of Soviet influence. They are trying to recover truly Ukrainian stories, songs, and designs. Something quite different is happening in the United States. Though Americans of Ukrainian descent were always keenly aware of their heritage, Americans with no Ukrainian blood or ties often did not know that Ukraine even existed. So effectively had the Soviets presented Russia as the emblem of the Soviet Union that many people were unaware that the Soviet Union was indeed a union, that there were many non-Russian peoples living underSoviet rule. Now that the Soviet Union has fallen apart, all of the peoples hidden behind the Russian facade are being revealed, to the fascination of Americans who had never realized the richness and diversity trapped behind the Iron Curtain.

This collection is presented to respond to American interest in Ukraine and to Ukrainian Americans who want to read the lore of their land. It contains new versions of old favorites plus some stories that have not been routinely published in folktale collections. It has been our particular goal to include material that is little known outside Ukraine and material that has been mislabeled as Russian, as well as stories that appear in standard collections of Ukrainian folklore. This should help to make the picture of Ukrainian folklore presented here as accurate and as varied as possible.

With all our efforts, this collection just scratches the surface. There are many, many more stories out there, as well as songs, proverbs, charms, and other forms of folklore. We hope that you enjoy the stories in this book and that you get a chance to experience the rest of Ukrainian folklore as well.

Introduction

Barbara J. Suwyn

Folktales and History

THE FOLKTALES IN THIS BOOK reflect many elements from Ukraine's history—from ancient wedding and burial customs to the tradition of *pysanky* (elaborately decorated Easter eggs) and figures of *cossacks*, peasants, and princes. They also embody the country's cultural roots and values. Perhaps this is one of the reasons that storytelling still flourishes in many Ukrainian villages and towns. Although the Ukraine of today is very different from the Ukraine in these stories, the tales offer not only a map of Ukraine's past, but a portrait of the country's soul. Hopefully, this collection will extend the important tradition of stories beyond Ukraine's borders and into the future.

About the Tales

The tales in this book are as diverse as the people and countryside of Ukraine, yet together they show readers something of the spirit and unity of the land and its people. Under the guidance of my editor, I have sought to present tales that authentically represent the richness of the Ukrainian culture. I have also tried to create a collection that offers something for every reader. Tales such as "The Turnip," "Clever Little Fox," and "The Mitten," with their simple plots and repetitive lines, will delight very young listeners as read-alouds. Humorous animal stories, such as "Pan Kotsky, Sir Puss O'Cat" and "Old Dog Sirko," also appropriate for read-alouds, will appeal to children throughout the elementary grades; while stories with moral themes, such as "The Old Father Who Went to School" and heroic tales such as "The Flute and the Whip" will find audience with upper elementary students. There are even a few spooky stories—"The Man Who Danced with the *Rusalky*" "The Stranger," and "The Sorceress"— that will fascinate older students in middle and high school. But while there is something for everyone, not every story in this collection is for every reader or listener, and parents and educators should review specific tales before sharing them with any audience to see if the content is appropriate.

In re-telling these tales, my goal has been to present traditional stories in a style more accessible to readers and listeners. I have tried to keep the language and the sentence structure relatively simple, so that the tales lend themselves to read-alouds and re-tellings. At the same time I have tried to retain elements in the stories that encourage vocabulary development, make the tales appropriate for silent reading, and spark the interest of older readers. Finally, I have made a conscious effort to include heroes of both sexes and also sought to avoid negative stereotypes without destroying archetypes.

Sources of the Tales

The sources for this collection are varied and for each tale diverse sources were consulted. Many written collections, as listed in the bibliography, were used. Other stories were contributed by my editor. Most of these tales were handed down orally, but some are new conflations of traditional themes and materials. Tales that are the editor's original composites include "Pea Roll-Along," "The Doll," "The Man Who Danced with the *Rusalky*," "The Christmas Spiders," and "The Red Death." These originals are indicated with the editor's name at their endings. The editor has also shared her re-tellings of other tales. These include "How Evil Came into the World"; "The Sun, the Frost, and the Wind"; "Dnipro and Dunai"; "Saint Cassian"; "Dovbush's Treasure"; and "The Stranger." In addition, Larysa Onyshkevych wrote one of the versions of "The Turnip" on which I based my re-telling.

Historical Background

The history of Ukraine is long and complicated, and it is not my intention to describe it in detail here but to offer a simple summary that highlights certain historic events of interest to general readers. Those seeking a thorough history of Ukraine are encouraged to explore the sources in the bibliography.

Early Times

Evidence shows that human beings inhabited Ukraine in Paleolithic and Neolithic times. Even in prehistoric times the country's fertile soil and abundant wildlife supported pastoral, nomadic, and agrarian cultures—such as the Trypillians, the Seredosts, the Cimmerians, and Scythians. Later, Ukraine's position on the Black Sea connected the country and its people to Mediterranean cultures. In the late sixth and seventh centuries B.C. Greece established colonies on the Ukrainian coast, and Romans subsequently governed those colonies. Some scholars speculate that the Amazons and centaurs of Greek mythology were based on the people the Greeks saw in Ukraine. The horsemen galloping across the steppe of what later became Ukraine traveled so fast that they and their horses seemed to be one—thus the centaurs. Women in the territory fought and carried armor, as supposedly *cossack* women did when their menfolk went off to battle—thus the Amazons. The long-time absence of the men during the *cossack* period when the men would go off—to fight, fish, and tend flocks—leaving their wives behind to defend the homestead may be a remnant of an ancient practice of long-term segregation of the

sexes. This may also have given the illusion that there was a society of women and children only, where men were permitted to enter only periodically (Chubyns'kyi 1995).

The Kyivan Rus'

But Ukraine was not born as a nation-state until the ninth century A.D. At that time, the country was known as *Rus'* or *Kyivan Rus'* and it was ruled by the powerful princes of Kyiv. Situated at the crossroads of European trade routes, *Rus'* developed political and financial ties with the rest of Europe. Kyiv became a cultural center and Christianity was adopted as the official religion. Literature, chronicle writing, and law developed. It was also during this time

Wooden church

Ukrainian cathedral

that some of Ukraine's most beautiful art and architecture was produced. Between the tenth and thirteenth centuries, hundreds of churches (stone and wooden) were built and decorated with elaborate icons, frescoes, and mosaics. Many of these artifacts and buildings still exist. The famous Cathedral of Saint Sophia in Kyiv is one such treasure. This church housed the first Ukrainian library and became well known as a center of learning. A symbol of Ukrainian faith, the structure still stands. *Kyivan Rus'* lasted for four centuries, in what is often referred to as the princely era. Readers will recognize many elements of this medieval period, with its courts, castles, and royalty, in Ukrainian tales and legends.

Eventually, inner conflicts weakened Ukraine. After Asiatic nomads (particularly the Tatars, or Mongols as they are sometimes called) invaded and ransacked the country in the late Middle Ages, Ukraine became easy prey to foreign powers. Much of the nation came under Polish-Lithuanian rule and for generations many Ukrainians worked as serfs for foreign overlords. Increasing oppression led to a growing dissatisfaction among the population, culminating in the *cossack* uprising of A.D. 1648. This marked the next chapter in the country's history.

The Cossacks

The *cossacks* were a new class of Ukrainians who lived as independent frontiersmen, not unlike American cowboys. (The word itself is related to a term meaning "free person.") Many *cossacks* were serfs who had fled from their masters, but others were nobles and townspeople. By colonizing the wild southeastern plains of the country, the *cossacks* acquired land and wealth. In establishing new communities and fighting the Tatar nomads from the East and the Turks to the South, they also developed courage and military skills. Although the *cossacks* initially tolerated Polish domination, they eventually rebelled. Organized under the political and military leadership of elected rulers (called *het'mans*), the *cossacks* freed Ukraine from Poland and established an independent state based on democratic principles. They abolished serfdom, built schools, and restored Eastern Orthodoxy as the religion of Ukraine. *Cossacks* also made raids against the Tatars and Turks and they became well known as skilled and fearless warriors. There are many stories and legends about them. While generally depicted as honest and forthright heroes, occasionally (as in the story "Dovbush's Treasure") *cossacks* are of mixed repute.

Russian Imperialism

The *cossack* era was relatively short-lived and by the end of the eighteenth century, eastern Ukraine had been overtaken by the expanding Russian Empire. Peasants were again forced into serfdom, schools were closed, and speaking and writing the Ukrainian language was prohibited. All this was part of an effort called Russification, that is, making Ukraine subject to Russia. In the meantime, Austro-Hungary (under the Habsburg dynasty) forced its way into western Ukraine, and the Ottoman Empire of Turkey invaded the South.

In the late nineteenth and early twentieth centuries, Ukraine underwent a political and cultural revival. Secret societies conducted scholarly research of the history, language, and ethnography of Ukraine, and the arts began to flourish. Some of Ukraine's greatest literary figures—Taras Shevchenko, Ivan Franko, and Lesia Ukrainka—emerged during this vital and productive era. Unfortunately, the new feelings of Ukrainian nationalism only met with further repression and persecution from the tsarist government.

Lenin and the Bolshevik Revolution

After the collapse of the Russian Empire in 1917, the people of Ukraine established the Ukrainian National Republic. The Ukrainian parliament, named the Central Rada, was led by Ukraine's most highly respected historian, Mykhailo Hrushevs'kyi. Later that year, in the October Revolution, the Bolsheviks seized power in Russia. Soon after, they invaded Ukraine. For the next three years violence and terror reigned as Ukraine struggled for its independence. Meanwhile western Ukraine had declared itself a republic, only to be attacked by Poland.

After three years of strife, the Ukrainian republic collapsed and in 1920 Soviet Ukraine was established. In 1922 the U.S.S.R. (Union of Soviet Socialist Republics) was formed under the leadership of Lenin, Trotsky, and the communist party. Ukraine, along with Armenia, Georgia, and Belarus, was absorbed into the Soviet regime. After a brief reprieve that followed the revolution, Stalin and the Soviets began a reign of terror in Ukraine and elsewhere—attacking the intelligentsia (artists, writers, poets, professors, and other educated people); persecuting, imprisoning, and killing Ukrainian nationalists and other dissidents; and seizing farms and factories. Oppression from the Romanians and Poles only added to Ukraine's distress. Soviet persecution culminated in the great famine of 1932–1933, in which it is estimated that 3 to 6 million Ukrainians died of starvation. The famine was not the result of crop failure, but instead was caused by the policy of collectivization (i.e., the Soviet style of managing Ukraine's important agricultural economy), instituted by Stalin and the Soviet government. Having devastated and demoralized the Ukrainian population, the famine weakened resistance to Soviet rule. To this day, it remains not only a disastrous event in Ukrainian history, but one of the great tragedies of world history.

During World War II, Ukraine was invaded by Nazi Germany. Under Nazi rule the countless arrests of Ukrainian leaders and the mass deportation of citizens to forced labor camps provoked active resistance and guerrilla warfare led by the Organization of Ukrainian Nationalists (OUN). More Ukrainian lives were lost as Germany and the U.S.S.R. battled over Ukrainian soil. At the end of the war, the Soviets annexed western Ukraine, intensified their efforts at Russification, and tightened their control. Meanwhile, Ukraine began the long, slow process of rebuilding. Although the Ukrainian nationalist movement continued throughout the aftermath of the war and well into the 1950s, the Soviets repeatedly retaliated with imprisonments, torture, and death.

Under Soviet rule Ukrainian farms were collectivized; the Ukrainian language was suppressed and supplanted with Russian; travel to and communication with the West was severely restricted; religion was outlawed; priests, political leaders, intellectuals, and other so-called enemies of the people were persecuted and killed. Many churches and works of art were destroyed as well. Yet, the Soviets also initiated the rebuilding of Ukrainian factories and, as a result, Ukraine's industry expanded and its cities grew.

The Thaw

Stalin's death and the rise of Khrushchev marked a reprieve from terrorist executions and the beginning of a thaw in Soviet oppression. Ukraine's situation briefly improved as educational reforms were initiated and the country was allowed a more important role in the Soviet regime. In turn, the Ukrainian intelligentsia was revitalized and became more active and more vocal. Many Ukrainians, both intellectuals and the general public, continued to voice their opposition to Soviet rule throughout the '60s, '70s, and '80s.

Détente

Beginning in the late 1960s tensions between the Soviets and the West began to ease and a period of *détente* ensued. Trade with Western nations was reinstated and agreements were made between the Soviets and the West to limit nuclear arms proliferation. However, it was also during this time that the Soviet police (KGB) arrested many prominent Ukrainians (among others) and sent them to prisons and labor camps. Protests from within the country and around the world to some extent staunched the campaign, but in the 1970s repression continued to plague Ukraine.

Chornobyl

In 1986, an explosion and fire at the Chornobyl nuclear plant near Kyiv released large amounts of radiation into the atmosphere. Although the Soviet government downplayed the catastrophe, reporting only 35 deaths and 200 injuries, it is widely believed that the casualties were greater. New estimates indicate hundreds were killed and thousands were injured. Effects of radiation poisoning are still being reported today and the plant itself is an environmental hazard of lethal proportions.

The Diaspora

Throughout Ukraine's often harsh history, many people fled to other countries. Mass emigration from Ukraine began in the late nineteenth century—a reaction against adverse social and economic conditions. After World War II, motivations were more likely to be political. Waves of Ukrainians poured into Western Europe, North America, South America, and Australia, as well as into Siberia, Eastern Europe, and other parts of the world.

Glasnost', Perestroika, and Beyond

In the late 1980s Gorbachev instituted a new policy of openness in the Soviet Union. This policy, called *glasnost'*, lifted the old censorship in favor of public discussion of political and social issues and a freer dissemination of the news. In the meantime, Gorbachev's economic reform program, *perestroika* (or *perebudova,* as it was called in Ukraine), met with little success, and one by one the Soviet republics withdrew from the union. Ukraine remained a Soviet republic until 1991 when it declared itself an independent and democratic republic. It has since become affiliated with the Commonwealth of Independent States (CIS), a loose federation of former members of the Soviet Union. Having re-emerged as a nation, this urbanized, industrialized, and highly educated country enters a promising, if uncertain, future.

Kobzari (*bandura* players) with Ukrainian flags. A *bandura* is an asymmetrical lute that is considered the national instrument. (Photo by N. Kononenko)

Ukrainian Names and Words

Readers will see many Ukrainian words and names throughout this text. Parents and educators are encouraged to use the words as presented. This will acquaint listeners with the beauty of the Ukrainian language and will enhance the flavor of the stories. Ukrainian words are presented in italics and, if not explained within the text, are defined in footnotes. A glossary and pronunciation guide for Ukrainian and Russian terms and alternate spellings of words begins on page 201.

In traditional Ukrainian tales, characters are often unnamed or go by a common name, such as Ivan or Marusya (the Ukrainian equivalents of John and Mary). Because this book is intended to introduce readers to Ukrainian culture, a variety of common Ukrainian names have been used for the characters.

Readers may also notice that the term "tsar" has not been used. There were no tsars per se in Ukraine, although Russian tsars ruled the country for centuries. The leaders of old Ukraine were referred to as "princes" and "kings," and therefore these more generic terms have been used in place of "tsar." Some Russian terms have been used if they have been widely adopted in the English language.

About the Drawings

Many of the drawings that appear in this book are based on the motifs and designs of such Ukrainian folk arts as *pysanky*, wood carving, embroidery, and pottery. Thus, they serve to illustrate the culture as well as story elements.

—Barbara J. Suwyn, 1997

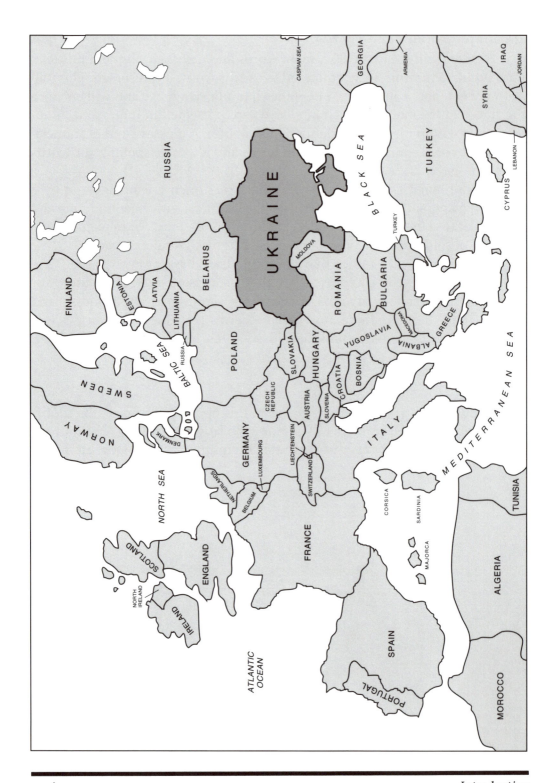

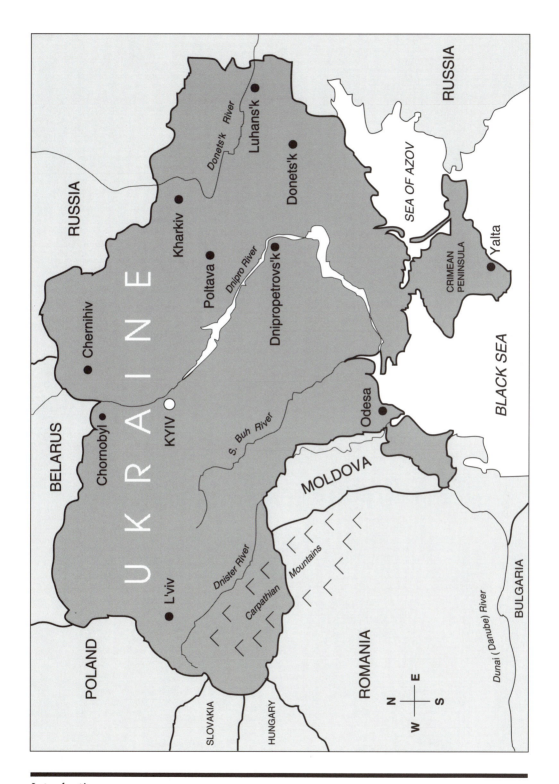

Part I

Animal Tales

Pan Kotsky, Sir Puss O'Cat

ONE DAY

when Little Fox was taking her daily stroll through the forest, she happened upon a strange creature. It was like nothing she had ever seen before. It was black, it was sleek, and it had long, white whiskers. Well, in truth, the creature was just a common house cat who had wandered from the farm and managed to get himself quite lost. But Little Fox didn't know that.

When the cat caught sight of the fox, his hair stood on end.

Little Fox's eyes widened. "How strange," she thought. "Who are you?" she asked.

The cat gathered his courage and straightened up. "I am Pan Kotsky, er—that is, Sir Puss O'Cat," he replied.

"And what, pray tell, is a Puss O'Cat?"

"Why, I am the fiercest animal that lives and I tear to bits anyone who crosses me."

"Oooh," said Little Fox, "I like you. Won't you come live with me and be my husband? I have a very nice house and I'll make you a fine wife."

Well, this sounded good to Sir Puss O'Cat, so off they went. When they reached Little Fox's hut, Pan Kotsky (Sir Puss O'Cat) made himself right at home. He found a nice warm spot by the fire and there he curled up to sleep.

The next morning Little Fox went out to hunt, but Pan Kotsky stayed home by the fire, licking his fur and napping. Little Fox brought home a big, juicy chicken. She let Sir Puss O'Cat have most of it, eating only the scraps that were left after he had finished his meal. The next day was the same: Little Fox hunted and Pan Kotsky stayed home. They lived together in this way for many days. Little Fox was happy and so was Pan Kotsky.

Then one day, while Little Fox was making her daily rounds, who should appear but Rabbit.

"Little Fox," he cried, "I haven't seen you for the longest time. Won't you have me for tea one of these days?"

"Oh no," Little Fox shook her head, "my husband, Pan Kotsky, is terribly jealous and I'm afraid he'll tear you to bits."

"Who is this Pan Kotsky?" Rabbit wanted to know.

"Why, he's the fiercest animal that lives and he tears to bits anyone who crosses him, that's who he is." Little Fox went on her way with her nose held high.

But Rabbit decided to see for himself, so he hopped over to Little Fox's house. He was just stretching up on his hind legs to peek through the window when a cinder from the fire landed on the sleeping Pan Kotsky.

"Mee-ow!" the cat screeched and jumped up all in a fright. When Rabbit heard the yowl he thought Pan Kotsky was screaming at him. He turned and ran as fast as he could back to the forest, his heart pounding.

The next day Rabbit called his friends together—Wolf, Boar, and Bear. He told them what Little Fox had said and explained what had happened when he tried to get a glimpse of Pan Kotsky.

"Hmm," said Wolf, "I have an idea." All the animals turned to him. "Let's have a dinner party and invite Little Fox and her new husband. That way we can protect each other and we'll get to see what sort of fellow this Pan Kotsky really is."

Everyone agreed and they planned to make a big soup—a *borshch*.*

"I'll get the meat," said Wolf.

"I'll get the beets and potatoes," said Boar.

"I'll get the cabbage," said Rabbit.

"And I'll bring some honey for dessert," offered Bear.

So they brought all the food together and soon a big pot of soup had been set to boil.

"Oh, one other thing," said Wolf. "Who will invite them?"

Bear groaned, "I don't think I should go, because I'm very slow and if this Pan Kotsky comes after me, I will never be able to escape."

---

* Borshch—*A hearty beet soup made with meat and vegetables.*

Boar piped up, "Well, I'm slow too, and clumsy as well."

"And I am old and blind," sighed Wolf. Everyone looked at Rabbit.

"Oh, all right," conceded Rabbit and off he hopped to Little Fox's to invite the two to dinner. Little Fox met him at the gate.

"I told you not to come here," she scolded. "Pan Kotsky will tear you to bits."

"But Little Fox, we—that is, Wolf, Bear, Boar, and I—would like to have you and your Pan Kotsky over for dinner. We have made a delicious *borshch*."

"Oh well, okay," said Little Fox, "but perhaps you had better hide until Pan Kotsky gets his fill. Otherwise, I can't say what he might do to you."

Rabbit agreed and then ran back to tell the other animals.

"Did you remember to tell them to bring their spoons?" asked Wolf.

"Oh, me!" sighed Rabbit and back he went again. This time he ran clear up to Little Fox's house. He stretched up to the window, tapped his little paw on it, and cried, "Don't forget to bring your spoons!" Without waiting for a reply, he was off.

Now the table was set and it was almost dinner time, so the animals had to hide. Bear climbed a tree and hunkered down among the leaves. Wolf hid behind a rock. Rabbit crawled into a hollow log and Boar crouched under the table. Everything was completely hidden from view except for Boar's little tail, which stuck out from under the tablecloth.

As Little Fox and Pan Kotsky approached, the wonderful smell of the soup wafted through the air. Pan Kotsky's tail began to twitch.

"Miaow, miaow," he cried. But the animals that were in hiding thought he was saying "More, more," and they thought to themselves, "How can he be demanding more already? He must have a huge appetite."

Pan Kotsky leapt onto the table and began gobbling up the soup, while Little Fox waited politely on the ground. The *borshch* was delicious! Then a tiny mosquito landed on Boar's tail and took a bite. Boar couldn't help himself—he flicked his tail. Pan Kotsky, thinking the tail was a mouse, grabbed for it, sinking his sharp claws into Boar's flesh.

"Yeow!" Boar jumped up and knocked the table over. Soup and plates and spoons flew everywhere. Pan Kotsky jumped to the tree where Bear was hiding. Bear, thinking the cat was after him, scrambled higher and higher until the branch broke and he fell right onto the hollow log where Rabbit was hiding. The log flew up in the air and crashed down, knocking Wolf on the head. The animals took off in all directions, running for their lives.

Later they came together.

"That was a close call," said Wolf.

"It sure was. Pan Kotsky grabbed my tail and threw me against the tree," exclaimed Boar.

Bear chimed in, "I know. He pulled me right out of the tree and banged me on the ground."

And Rabbit added, "He picked up the log where I was hiding and slammed it against a rock till I came out."

But Wolf shook his head, "That was no rock, it was my head he was hitting with the log. Why, look at the welt I have—it still hurts."

And they all shook their heads and muttered, "Tsk, tsk."

As for Pan Kotsky, he stayed up in the tree for a long, long time, trembling and wishing he had never left home. Why, if Little Fox hadn't coaxed him down with some honey, he might still be there. ॐ

Old Dog Sirko

WHEN SIRKO WAS A YOUNG DOG,
he worked hard on the farm and his master cared for him and fed
him well. But now Sirko was old. He couldn't run fast. He could
barely see. He was too tired to herd animals and too deaf to hear
intruders.

"What good are you?" the farmer yelled one day. "You're
nothing but a nuisance!" Then he took Sirko to the forest and left him
there to fend for himself.

Poor old Sirko! His heart was broken. He was too old and weak
to hunt for food, and even if he caught something, he had no teeth
to chew it. The old dog lay down with his head between his paws
and moaned. He thought about the warm farmhouse, about the
milk-soaked crusts of bread the farmer's wife used to give him, and
about how the master had praised him. Those times were over now.

"I might as well die," he thought to himself. He lay there for a
long time, feeling miserable. Then a wolf sauntered up to him.

"Hey, brother, what are you doing here? It's nearly nightfall.
Shouldn't you be getting back to the farmhouse?"

"I'm not welcome there anymore," Sirko replied dejectedly.
"The farmer says I'm old and useless. He's banished me to the
forest."

"Humans!" exclaimed the wolf. "What about all the work you
did for them, protecting their sheep and chickens? All those years of
service! Did they forget about that?"

"Well, as long as I was young and strong, they cared for me,"
said Sirko, "but now they say I'm good for nothing." And with that
the old dog began to weep.

"Hey, don't be such a baby," said Wolf. "I can't stand crying. Anyway, things may not be as bad as they seem. I have a plan—listen."

Sirko stopped sobbing and pricked up his ears.

"Soon it will be harvest time," began Wolf. "The farmer and his wife will have to work the fields and they'll bring their new baby along. Now, when the farmer's wife leaves her baby by the bale of straw, I'll run up and grab it. When I reach the edge of the forest, you run out, take the baby from me, and return it to your master. You'll be a hero—they're bound to take you back. Well, what do you say, old boy?"

"It sounds good," said Sirko. Already he felt better.

"Just don't forget whose idea it was," added Wolf.

"Oh, I won't," Sirko assured him.

The next few weeks were difficult. Sirko lived on mice and grasshoppers, but he managed to survive. Finally the harvest began.

Things happened just as Wolf had predicted. The farmer and his wife came to the fields, put their baby near a bale of straw, and set to work. Wolf sneaked up, seized the child, and took off running. The baby began to scream and when the farmer's wife saw what was happening, she too began to wail. She ran after the wolf, waving her arms in the air and yelling.

"Husband, husband, help!" she cried, "the wolf has stolen our baby!" The husband grabbed a pitchfork and he began to chase the wolf too. But the wolf ran faster and as he approached the woods, the farmer and his wife began to lose heart.

Just then Sirko leaped out at the wolf. Wolf dropped the baby and the two animals pretended to tussle with each other for a few moments. Then Wolf took off into the woods with his tail between his legs. Sirko picked up the baby and brought it to his master.

"Oh, Sirko, you have saved our baby," cooed the wife. She knelt down and gave the old dog a big hug.

"Such a brave dog," exclaimed the farmer. "I was wrong to turn you out, Sirko. From now on, we will treat you like a king."

So Sirko returned home with the farmer and his wife. They made him a new bed of goose down close to the fire, and every day the farmer's wife brushed the old dog until his coat glistened. At mealtime, Sirko sat on a chair next to the farmer and ate whatever the farmer and his wife ate. The farmer's wife even cut Sirko's food into tiny pieces so he wouldn't have to chew.

Being a loyal creature, Sirko remembered his debt to Wolf, and every day he brought scraps of food to the edge of the forest for his friend. But Wolf was not impressed.

"What? Stale bread again?" Wolf spit his food to the ground. "Don't you know it's almost winter? I need meat! It's getting harder and harder to find food in these woods. The least you could do is bring me a little piece of mutton or calf. After all, wasn't I the one who saved your life? You owe me one, pal—don't you forget it."

Well, at first Wolf's ingratitude disturbed Sirko. Then he had an idea.

"Perhaps I can repay you for your deed, my friend," said the dog. "Next week the master and mistress will have a christening for their young one. They have promised to prepare a huge feast. If I sneak you into the house, you can have your fill of whatever your heart desires."

"Now you're talking," said Wolf. His mouth began to water at the mere thought of all that food.

The feast day came. All week the farmer's wife had been preparing food—roast pork, stewed mutton with cabbage, smoked sausages, fresh loaves of bread, little sweet cakes for dessert, and bottles and bottles of wine. Soon the guests arrived and oh, what fun they were having! Nobody saw Sirko sneak the wolf into the house. Nobody noticed Sirko helping himself to the food and dragging it under the table where Wolf hid.

"Mmm-mm," the wolf smacked his lips and gobbled up all the food Sirko brought. Sirko went out for more, and more again. Wolf devoured it all. Finally, he was so full he could eat no more.

"Whew, I'm thirsty," said Wolf. "Can't you find me something to drink?"

So Sirko brought Wolf a bottle of wine. The wolf guzzled it down in an instant.

"More!" he bellowed.

"Shh! Not so loud, my friend," cautioned Sirko, "someone might hear you." Off he went to fetch another bottle of wine.

Wolf drained the second bottle as fast as he had drained the first, and now he was quite tipsy. The guests were too. Someone brought out a *bandura** and began to play. The others threw their arms round one another and began singing. When Wolf heard this, a tear came to his eye.

*bandura—*A stringed instrument somewhat like an asymmetrical mandolin; often used to play or accompany traditional folk songs.*

"Oh, such a beautiful song," he said, "I must sing along."

"No, no, please," begged Sirko, "they'll hear you."

But Wolf could not contain himself. When the guests got to the chorus, he burst out howling.

"What?!" The singing stopped and everyone started screaming, "A wolf, a wolf, kill him!" They grabbed brooms and mops and began beating on the furniture.

Sirko had to think fast. He snarled and pushed Wolf out from under the table and started wrestling with him. The guests gathered around them and raised their weapons.

"Please don't hurt our Sirko," cried the farmer's wife.

"She's right. Let Sirko handle it," said the farmer. "He knows what to do."

So the people backed away and Sirko pushed the wolf out the door and all the way to the woods. There they stood panting for a few moments. Then Sirko spoke.

"You saved my life, Wolf, but now I've saved yours," he said. "I think we're even." Then he ran back to the house. There everyone shouted, "Hurray for Sirko!" and patted him and stroked the old dog's head. The farmer and his wife were so proud. Sirko wagged his tail. Needless to say, they all lived happily ever after.

Clever Little Fox

L<small>ITTLE FOX</small>
was running down the road one day when she stumbled over a big log, stubbed her toes, and jammed a splinter into her foot.

"Oh dear," she cried, "my poor little foot."

She hobbled down the road, whimpering, "My poor little foot, my poor little foot." Little Fox thought about her cozy foxhole and how nice it would be to be there now. She headed toward home, but she couldn't move very fast, and soon it grew dark and cold. Little Fox was not even close to home.

"Now what will I do?" she thought to herself. Just then she saw the lighted window of a little hut. She limped up to the door and knocked—*knock, knock, knock.* An old man came to the door and peered out into the darkness.

"Who's there?" he asked.

"It's me, Little Fox," she said. "I hurt my foot and I'm far from home. Won't you please let me spend the night here?"

For a moment the man was quiet, then he answered, "Well, I really don't have room for you, Little Fox. My hut is small and there are no spare beds."

"Oh, please," begged the fox. "I don't need a bed. I can curl up in a corner, wrap up in my tail, and sleep quite peacefully."

"Well, all right then," the man agreed.

As soon as Little Fox stepped inside, she started moaning and groaning.

"Why, Little Fox, whatever is the matter?" asked the man.

"Oh, it's my poor little foot," whined the fox.

"Here, let me have a look. Sit on this chair under the lamp," offered the man. So Little Fox jumped up on the chair and the old man peered at her foot.

"Why, it's nothing but a splinter. Here, I'll pull it out."

But when the man reached for Little Fox's foot, she quickly drew it away, crying, "No, no, it will hurt."

"Nonsense," said the man, "just sit still and it will all be over in a jiffy." Little Fox gingerly extended her foot to him and he gave a quick tug. Out came the splinter and the man tossed it into the fireplace.

"There you are, you silly thing. Don't you feel better now?"

"Well, yes, but what did you do with my splinter?"

"Why, I put it in the fire so it can never harm anyone again," replied the man.

"But that was MY splinter," the fox protested. "I want it back."

"Well, it's burned to ashes now," the old man chortled, "and what good is a splinter to you anyway?"

"None of your business!" Little Fox shouted. "You had no right to burn my splinter. It was my only possession and you destroyed it. Now you must pay."

"That's ridiculous," said the man, and it was, but Little Fox would not listen. All night they argued, until finally the sun came up. Then the old man threw up his arms.

"Take one of my chickens, then, and be on your way," he said, "but don't ever show your face at my door again."

Little Fox wasted no time. She grabbed a fat hen, tucked it under her arm, and went running down the road. Oh, she was so proud of herself, she just had to sing a little song.

> Ho ho, hee hee,
> I'm clever as can be.
> I can outsmart the old man,
> and he can't outsmart me.
> Ho ho, hee hee!

Little Fox ran and ran, not paying any attention to where she was going. Then the sky began to darken and the air became chilly. Again, she was faced with the problem of where to spend the night. But when she spotted a farmhouse down the road, she knew just what to do. Up to the door she went—*knock, knock, knock.*

Clever Little Fox

"Who's there?" An old farmer and his wife came to the door.

"It's me, Little Fox, and I need a place to spend the night."

"We don't have room for you, Little Fox. As you can see, our house is small and quite full," replied the farmer.

"Oh, I can curl up in a corner, wrap myself in my tail, and I'll be just fine for the night."

"Well, okay," agreed the farmer and his wife.

As Little Fox stepped inside, she looked around and said, "Where should I put my chicken?"

"What's this, a chicken too? Well, put her in with the ducks," said the farmer.

"Will she be safe there?" asked the fox.

"Don't be silly. Of course she'll be safe—as safe as our ducks." So Little Fox set her chicken in the duck pen and curled up in a corner to sleep. As soon as she heard the farmer start snoring, Little Fox got up and tiptoed to the duck pen. She grabbed the chicken and gobbled it up. Then she scattered the feathers all around, cleaned her face and paws, and went back to her corner to sleep.

The next morning Little Fox got up and began looking all around the house.

"Here, chicky, chicky. Here, chicky, chicky." As she approached the duck pen, she gasped, "Oh, my poor little chicken!" The farmer and his wife came running.

"My chicken was eaten alive by your bad ducks." Little Fox pointed to the feathers that were strewn all over the duck pen and began to sob.

"That chicken was all I had in the world. Whatever will I do?" The old farmer and his wife looked at one another, baffled. The fox kept crying, though, until finally the farmer's wife whispered something to the farmer. Then the farmer took a duck from the pen and pushed it toward the fox.

"Here, take this in place of your chicken, then," he said, "but please be on your way now. We have a lot of work to do."

Little Fox was not crying now. She grabbed the duck, tucked it under her arm, and raced down the road, as happy as can be. Soon she was humming and singing again.

> *Ho ho, hee hee,*
> *I'm clever as can be.*
> *I trade a splinter for a hen and a hen for a duck.*
> *Ho ho, hee hee!*

Well, Little Fox was not running toward her foxhole but away from it. Once again, as night fell, she began to look for a place to stay. Ah, what luck! Another cozy farmhouse. Little Fox trotted up to the door—*knock, knock, knock.*

"Who's there?" called voices from inside.

"It's me, Little Fox. Won't you let me spend the night?"

"Our house is too small—we have no room for you," the farmer replied.

"I don't need a bed—I can curl up in a corner, wrap myself in my tail, and I'll be just fine."

"Well, if you're sure, I suppose that'll be all right." The farmer and his wife opened the door and Little Fox stepped in.

"Where can I put my duck?" she asked.

"Hmm. Perhaps your duck should sleep in the barn with our lambs," suggested the farmer.

"Are you sure my duck will be safe with the lambs?" asked Little Fox.

"Well, yes," replied the farmer, "why wouldn't she be?"

"One never knows," said the fox, shaking her head and rolling her eyes, "but if you say so, I believe you."

So the fox left the duck in the barn with the lambs. She went back to the house, curled up in a corner, and waited until the farmer and his wife were asleep. Then she tiptoed out to the barn, grabbed the duck, gobbled it up, and scattered the feathers all over the lambs' pen. She licked herself clean, ran back to the house, curled up in a corner, wrapped herself in her tail, and fell fast asleep.

The next morning Little Fox went out to the barn and began calling at the top of her voice, "Here ducky, ducky. Here ducky, ducky. Oh, where is my precious little duck?" Then she shrieked loudly and the farmer and his wife came running.

"Why, look! Your nasty lambs have eaten my dear little duck! Whatever will I do?" she cried. Then Little Fox began to sob. The farmer and his wife just looked at each other. Who ever heard of a lamb eating a duck? They didn't know what to say.

"That duck was all I had in the whole wide world and you must pay me for my loss," insisted the fox.

"We can't afford to pay you," said the farmer, "but perhaps you'd like to take one of our lambs in exchange."

So Little Fox grabbed the biggest, juiciest lamb and went running down the road, laughing and singing as she went.

Ho ho, hee hee.
I'm clever as can be.
I trade a sliver for a hen, a hen for a duck,
And a duck for a lamb.
Ho ho, hee hee!

Once again it grew dark and Little Fox looked about for a place to stay. When she spied a farmhouse, she quickly ran up to the door—*knock, knock, knock.*

"Who's there?"

"It's me, Little Fox. I need a place to spend the night." Little Fox peeked into the house and saw a warm fire burning in the fireplace. Mmmm, something smelled delicious, too. Little Fox had gone all day without food and now she was hungry. Her mouth watered.

"Sorry, our house is full." The farmer started to close the door, but Little Fox quickly stuck her foot inside.

"I don't need a bed—I'll just curl up in a corner, wrap myself in my tail, and spend the night that way. Please, please, please—it's so cold and dark out here."

"Oh, all right," said the farmer.

As Little Fox stepped into the house, she looked around and asked, "And where can I put my lamb?"

"Goodness, a lamb too? And a fat one at that! Well, I guess you can put him in the yard."

"Is the yard safe?" asked Little Fox.

"Oh yes, look how tall the fence is—and it's strong too. I built it myself," said the farmer.

So Little Fox put her lamb in the yard, went into the house, and curled up in a corner. But as soon as she was certain everyone had dozed off, she jumped up, tiptoed out to the yard, grabbed the lamb, and gobbled it up. Then she cleaned herself up and ran back to the house, where she slept quite soundly through the night.

The next morning, when she awoke, she immediately ran out to the yard and called, "Lambikins, where are you?" When the lamb did not appear, Little Fox began wailing at the top of her lungs. The farmer and his wife ran up and asked what had happened.

"My precious lambikins is gone!" Little Fox cried. "Nothing like this has ever happened to me before. I just can't believe it! That lamb was all I owned in the world and now, thanks to you, he's gone!"

The farmer and his wife protested, "But Little Fox, it's not our fault if your lamb ran away."

"Oh yes it is! Your daughter left the house early this morning to milk the cows. She must have let my lamb escape when she went out."

The daughter overheard what Little Fox said and she ran up and started arguing. "No, no! I didn't even see your lamb when I went out. And I was very careful to close the gate behind me when I left the yard."

"That proves it," yelled Little Fox. Then she demanded to be paid—this time with the farmer's daughter. What a ruckus! Little Fox yelled, the farmer and his wife cried, and the daughter screamed and stamped her foot on the floor. This went on for some time until the farmer finally calmed down and interrupted the shouting.

"Okay, Little Fox, you win. Take our only daughter. But you know she will try to run away. Let me put her in a sack for you, so you can carry her off easily."

"Well, that's more like it," said the fox. The farmer turned to his wife, patted her on the shoulder, and whispered something in her ear.

"Won't you have a cup of tea before your journey?" asked the farmer's wife, dabbing her eyes with her handkerchief. Little Fox agreed and they went to the kitchen, where they sat sipping tea and gazing out the window. Little Fox chatted about travel and the farmer's wife nodded quietly, sniffling from time to time.

After a while the farmer returned, carrying a large sack that he had carefully tied up at the neck. "Here she is, Little Fox," announced the farmer, "and now you had best be on your way. Half the day is gone already and you have a long way to go, I suspect."

Little Fox didn't even finish her tea. She jumped up and grabbed the sack. Oof, it was heavy! But she managed to throw it over her shoulder and start jauntily down the road. She was gasping a little, but she was so happy, she even sang her little ditty.

> *Ho ho, hee hee.*
> *I'm clever as can be.*
> *I trade a splinter for a hen, a hen for a duck,*
> *a duck for a lamb, a lamb for a girl,*
> *and now I've got the girl.*
> *Ho ho, hee hee!*

When she finished the song, she gave the bag a shake and said, "Isn't that right, my lovely dinner?"

"Grrr!"

"What a nasty thing you are," scolded Little Fox. "Why, you sound just like an animal. Come on, be a nice girl and sing with me." And she began her song again.

> *Ho ho, hee hee.*
> *I'm clever as can be—*
> *"Grr! Grr!"*

Little Fox set the bag down. "What is going on in there?" she demanded. "I'd better have a look." But as soon as she undid the tie, a big dog leaped from the bag and began chasing her. Little Fox ran and ran, with the dog nipping at her heels all the way. She finally reached her foxhole, hopped in, and lay panting in the dark. The dog stood just outside the door, sniffing and licking his chops, but he was too big to get in.

"How did I let myself get outsmarted like that?" thought Little Fox. She mulled over the day's events and wondered just what had gone wrong. Then she began to ask questions.

> *Little feet, little feet,*
> *what did you do when the dog chased me?*

And her feet replied,

> *We ran fast into the wood,*
> *so the dog couldn't catch you*
> *and make you his food.*

"Ooh, that's good, little feet. For that I will buy you some red leather boots." Her feet tapped against the burrow floor in delight. Then Little Fox spoke to her ears.

> *Little ears, little ears,*
> *what did you do when the dog came near?*

And the ears replied,

> *We listened carefully for the dog's hot breath,*
> *because we knew if he caught us,*
> *it was certain death.*

"Very good!" cheered Little Fox, "for that I will buy you a pair of beautiful golden earrings." Her ears twitched gleefully. Then she said,

> *Little eyes, little eyes,*
> *what did you do to keep the dog from my hide?*

And the eyes replied,

> *We looked keen and sharp and clear,*
> *because we didn't want the dog*
> *to eat our Foxy dear.*

"Ooh, yes! For that I will find you a pair of golden spectacles." The eyelashes fluttered and the eyelids batted and Little Fox turned to her tail.

> *Big, bushy tail, please tell me,*
> *how did you help me flee, flee, flee?*

But the tail just lay there. The fox cleared her throat and spoke louder.

> *Big, bushy tail, please tell me,*
> *how did you help me flee, flee, flee?*

Nothing. Little Fox repeated her question one last time.

> *Big, bushy tail, please tell me,*
> *how did you help me flee, flee, flee?*

Still there was no response.

"Traitor!' she shrieked, "for that I will let the dog bite you." And she thrust her tail out the door. The dog took one look at the fluffy red tail and sank his teeth into it.

"Yeow!" Little Fox yelped, but it was too late. The dog bit her tail off completely, and he went running home to show it to his master. Little Fox lay in her burrow whimpering all night long.

The next day she went out to hunt and came upon a family of rabbits. When they saw Little Fox without a tail, they burst into laughter. Even the baby bunnies pointed and laughed.

"Well, laugh all you like, you dumb rabbits," sneered the fox. "I may not have a tail, but I bet I know how to do the circle dance better than any one of you."

The rabbits looked at one another. "Circle dance? What's that?"

"What? You don't know the circle dance? Oh, it is so much fun! I can teach you if you like, but first I must tie your tails together." So the rabbits gathered around and Little Fox knotted all their tails together. Then she ran up to the top of the hill and yelled, "Run, rabbits, run! Wolf is on his way and he looks very hungry. He's going to eat you up!"

The rabbits tried to run, but they were all pulling in different directions. They pulled and pulled and pulled until—*POP!*—they pulled their tails right off.

Now it was Little Fox's turn to laugh, and laugh she did, but never again did she sing her clever song, and never again did she spend the night at a farmer's house. &

The Garden

O‌NE DAY
Little Fox and Brother Wolf were having tea together. As they sipped and chatted, their conversation eventually turned to their livelihoods.

"Ah," sighed Brother Wolf, "I'm getting too old for all this chasing around. Stealing sheep and hunting rabbits is very hard work and, to be honest, I have never felt quite right about it."

The fox nodded. "I know what you mean," she agreed. "It's getting harder all the time too. The farmers are constantly trying to outsmart us. Why, just the other day I went to steal a chicken and the farmer was there waiting for me. Would you believe he came after me with a pitchfork? I thought I would die!" Little Fox shook her head and took a big slurp of tea.

"Well, maybe we should try to make an honest living," said the wolf. Little Fox looked puzzled. "You know," he continued, "we could grow a garden like the farmers do. It's not difficult. I have watched them many times. I know how to do it."

"Oh?" The fox's ears pricked up.

"That's right," the wolf went on, "all we need is a shovel and a hoe and a few seed potatoes."

"Seed potatoes! Why, I have some potatoes sprouting in my den right now," cried the fox.

"Then we're all set." The wolf set his teacup down and smiled. "I have a shovel and I know where I can get a hoe. Er—uh, borrow a hoe, I mean."

That's how Brother Wolf and Little Fox agreed to grow a garden. The next day, they packed a picnic lunch of buns and butter and honey and set out to work. When they reached a clearing, they hid their picnic basket among some bushes, went to the field, and began to turn the soil.

After digging a few shovelfuls of dirt, Little Fox began to huff and puff. "Whew!" she said, "that sun is hot!" She wiped the sweat from her brow.

"Hmmph!" grunted the wolf, without looking up. He was intent on his hoeing.

Little Fox looked around. This honest work was very boring and it really wasn't easy as the wolf had promised. She was all out of breath and she was starting to get hungry too. Oh, to have a lick of honey!

Just then a crow that was sitting in the treetop made a loud, "Caw! Caw! Caw!"

Little Fox looked up quickly. "I'll be right there," she shouted, waving gaily. Then she set her shovel down and started walking away.

"What?" Brother Wolf looked up from his work. "Where are you going?"

"Oh, I must go to the crow's nest," the fox explained. "Mrs. Crow is having a baby and I promised I would be the midwife. Keep digging—I'll catch up when I get back." Then off she trotted.

As soon as the wolf's back was turned, though, Little Fox hurried into the bushes and helped herself to a big spoonful of honey.

"Ah," she sighed, happily licking her chops. She took a little nibble of a bun. Then quickly she put everything back the way it had been and ran back to the wolf, smiling and swishing her tail.

"What? Back so soon? Is the baby born already?" asked the wolf.

"Oh, yes," replied the fox.

"Was it a boy or a girl, then?"

"A boy."

"What did they name the boy?"

"Uh, Beginning." The fox picked up her shovel, fixed her eyes on the ground, and began to dig.

"Beginning," marveled the wolf, "what a strange name." But the fox made no reply and he went back to work.

After a while the fox started itching for more honey. Then the crow called out, "Caw! Caw! Caw!" Little Fox dropped her shovel and cried, "I'm coming!"

"Now what?" the wolf asked. He was getting irritated.

"It's another baby coming for the crows. I must help them."

"Well, don't be long," cautioned the wolf. "We still have a lot of work to do."

"Don't worry," the fox reassured, "I'll be back before you know it." And she hurried away.

Little Fox went straight for the bushes, where she feasted on honey and butter and buns. Then she put everything neatly back in the basket. There wasn't much left, but Little Fox felt much better. She returned to the garden.

"Back so soon?" The wolf looked surprised. "Has the baby come already?"

"Oh, yes," smiled the fox.

"What was it, then?"

"A girl."

"Ho," the wolf smiled, "and what did they name the girl?"

"Middle," replied the fox.

"Middle," repeated the wolf, "I've never heard of such a name."

The fox rolled her eyes. "Among crows such names are common," she retorted haughtily. "That's why they make so much noise."

The two friends resumed their work, but it wasn't long until the fox began thinking about the honey again. Her mouth watered and she looked around furtively for an excuse to leave. When she was certain the wolf wasn't looking, Little Fox picked up a stone and threw it at the crow. The crow squawked loudly and Little Fox threw her shovel to the ground and wiped her paws on her apron.

"You're not leaving again, are you?" asked the wolf crossly.

"Brother Wolf," the fox scolded, "didn't you hear the crow calling me? There's going to be another baby. I must hurry."

"Well, I never heard of such a thing," the wolf grumbled. "Why must you always be the one to help them out?"

The fox smiled, "I'm the only one they trust with their young. The crows are quite fond of me."

"Well, all right," said the wolf, "but don't dally. We still have a lot of work to do."

"Don't worry, I'll be right back." Then Little Fox rushed into the bushes, licked the honey pot clean, finished off the butter, and gobbled down the last of the buns. She left everything strewn about topsy-turvy and went back to the wolf.

"Is the birth over already?" he asked.

"Oh, yes," the fox smiled.

"And what did they have this time?"

"Another beautiful boy."

"What did they name this boy?"

"Finish," replied the fox.

"Well, I hope that means they're *finished* with these births for awhile and we can *finish* our work." Brother Wolf chuckled at his own cleverness. Then both animals got back to their gardening.

So the fox and the wolf worked. When lunchtime came, the wolf set his hoe down. He was famished. Actually, he had been hungry for some time, but he was too embarrassed to say anything. He waited for Little Fox to put her shovel down, but she just kept working. Brother Wolf tapped his foot, cleared his throat, and whistled, but the fox paid him no mind. Finally he said loudly, "Isn't it time for lunch?"

"Yes, of course," said the fox, but she kept digging, as though the work was more important than eating.

"Aren't you hungry?" asked the wolf.

"No, not really," Little Fox replied, "the crows fed me when I was there. You go ahead and eat."

So the wolf trudged into the bushes where they had hidden the picnic basket, but when he reached the spot, his mouth fell open. There was the empty, overturned basket, the honey pot licked clean, and the shiny, empty butter dish. Brother Wolf realized immediately that he'd been tricked. "So that's what Little Fox was doing," he thought to himself. "That's why those names were so strange—she made them up!"

Brother Wolf ran back toward the garden, shouting, "You scoundrel! So that's how you earn an honest living—while I slave, you eat all the food! Just wait, I'll make you honest yet, I'll get even with you!"

Waving his fists in the air, the wolf charged into the garden, but Little Fox was long gone. She had heard his rantings and ravings and had run into the woods. By the time Brother Wolf reached the garden, Little Fox was hiding in a tree hollow somewhere. There she lay, patting her stomach and moaning, for she had the biggest bellyache of her entire life! &

Further Adventures of Fox and Wolf

L ITTLE FOX WAS WALKING
down the road, hungry as can be, when she spied a pan of poppy-seed buns sitting on a windowsill to cool.

"Aha, fresh from the oven," she thought to herself, and she grabbed one and ran. Once she was far from the scene of the crime, Little Fox opened the bun and ate up the insides, leaving only the crusts. Then she filled the bun with straw, pieced it back together, and began walking down the road again, smiling and humming to herself.

By and by she passed a herd of cows. Two young boys were driving them to water.

"Hullo," she waved gaily.

"Hullo to you, too," the cowherds waved back.

Then Little Fox walked up to the boys.

"Look at my beautiful poppy-seed bun," she said, and she held the roll under their noses so they could smell it. "Wouldn't you like to have it? I bet you lads are hungry," she continued.

The boys laughed. "Of course," they replied, "but what do we have to do to get the bun?"

"Oh, I would take that little calf off your hands in a trade," Little Fox smiled coyly.

"I don't know," the oldest boy said, but the younger lad was ready to make the trade and he tugged on the other boy's sleeve anxiously. Little Fox continued her coaxing.

"These buns are really good," she said. "I ate one myself just a few minutes ago and it melted in my mouth." She waved the bun under the boys' noses again.

"Well, all right," the older lad agreed and he went to fetch the calf. When he returned with it, Little Fox handed him the bun gingerly, saying, "Be sure to say your prayers before eating. This is truly a bun to give thanks for." Then she took the calf and hurried away while the boys closed their eyes to pray. By the time they had finished their prayers, Little Fox had disappeared into the woods, so when they bit into the bun and realized it was filled with straw, there was nothing they could do but curse themselves.

In the meantime, Little Fox felled a tree, split the wood, and built herself a small sleigh. She harnessed the calf to the sleigh, hopped on, and went driving through the forest. Little Fox was very proud of herself and she held her chin up and smiled as she drove along.

By and by, who should appear but Brother Wolf. He came loping toward the sleigh, waving furiously, "Hello there!" Little Fox waved back and stopped to say hello.

"What a fine sleigh," exclaimed the wolf. "Wherever did you find it?"

"Find it?! Why, I made it myself," snorted the fox.

"Well, well," nodded the wolf, "and what about the calf? Don't tell me you made that too."

"I earned the calf, Wolfie," Little Fox retorted. "This is the kind of reward you can receive if you're willing to work for it."

"Oh, yes, I see." The wolf stroked his chin pensively, then suddenly brightened. "Hey, can I ride with you for a bit? I could use a lift."

"Oh no," Little Fox shook her head, "this sleigh is only built for one. If you get on, it will break."

"Don't be silly, Little Fox. You worry too much," the wolf scoffed. "If it will make you feel better, I'll just put one paw on the sleigh."

Little Fox scowled and said nothing.

"Oh, please, please, please," begged the wolf. Finally Little Fox gave in.

"See?" Wolf said, carefully placing his paw on the sleigh, "your sleigh is fine." Little Fox didn't say a word, but she whipped the calf and off they went.

After a time, the wolf spoke again, "I think I'll put another paw up."

"No!" shrieked the fox, "you'll break the sleigh."

"No I won't—I'll be careful. Just let me try it."

"Oh, all right."

The fox and the wolf rode along. Suddenly, there was a loud *creak*!

"Aag, there goes my sleigh," screamed the fox.

Brother Wolf just shook his head. "No, no, that was just my bones creaking," he said, "you know I'm very tired."

So the two rode on. Then the wolf said, "Perhaps I'll put my third paw up."

"No, no, no," the fox protested, "I told you this sleigh is only built for one." But again the wolf begged and Little Fox eventually gave in.

Along they went, and then, *c-r-e-a-k!*

"Oh, no! Now my sleigh is really breaking," cried the fox.

"Little Fox, I told you—you worry too much. I was just cracking a nut." The wolf worked his jaws as though he were chewing and the fox grew quiet again. Then she said, "Well, how about cracking one for me?"

"Well, I would, but that was my last one," replied the wolf.

So the two rode on for a bit.

"I think I'll put my fourth paw up," said the wolf.

"Oh no, you don't—you'll surely break my sleigh."

"Just let me try for one minute. I promise I'll be careful." The wolf pleaded and begged until the fox gave in.

As soon as the wolf put his fourth paw up, though, the sleigh groaned and buckled and fell to pieces.

Little Fox was furious. "Look what you've done to my beautiful sleigh," she fumed. "I told you not to get on. Now it's ruined." Brother Wolf hung his head while the fox shouted and screamed and scolded. Finally the fox threw her paws in the air and exclaimed, "I guess you'll just have to build me a new one. That's all there is to it."

"But foxy friend," the wolf protested, "I don't know how to build a sleigh. I'm just a poor uneducated wolf."

"Nonsense!" cried the fox, "I'll tell you what to do." Then the fox led the wolf to a tall stand of trees. Looking up, she said, "All you do is yell 'Fall down trees, crooked and straight.' You do that till you have enough lumber to build a sleigh. Get it?"

"Uh, I think so," the wolf mumbled. So the fox tied her calf to a bush and went to find some water while the wolf felled trees.

"Fall down trees, crooked and, uh, crooked?" Wolf spoke timidly at first. A big tree crashed to the ground. Seeing that he was getting results, Brother Wolf yelled louder, "Fall down trees, crooked and crooked!" More trees fell and the wolf kept shouting. Soon the ground was covered with trees, but they were all crooked and not suitable for sleigh building. When Little Fox returned, she was shocked.

"What have you done now, you big oaf?"

 "I did just as you told me—I said 'Fall down trees, crooked and crooked.'"

"Oh, you nincompoop! You're supposed to say 'Fall down trees, crooked and *straight*.' " The wolf hung his head in shame. "You had better try again," the fox continued, "I'm going to try to find some dinner. When I get back that wood better be ready." Little Fox stomped off in a huff.

This time Brother Wolf got it right. "Fall down trees, crooked and straight," he yelled. As soon as there was enough wood for the sleigh, he stacked it into a pile and sat down.

"Whew!" the wolf wiped his brow and sighed. "Chopping wood is hard work. Now I'm hungry." Brother Wolf looked around to see if Little Fox was coming, but she was nowhere in sight. Then he glanced around to see if there was anything to nibble on. His gaze fell on the little calf. Well, he knew it wasn't right, but hadn't Little Fox been cruel to him? The wolf went over to the calf, tore a hole in its side, and ate all the meat. Then he stuffed the hide with sparrows, sealed the hole with straw, propped the calf against the bush, and ran off.

By and by Little Fox returned. She hadn't found any dinner, but she was glad to see all the wood. Quickly she built herself a new sleigh and tied the calf's rope to it. Then she sat in the sleigh and yelled, "Giddyap!" The calf did not move.

"Giddyap!" she shouted louder and whipped the calf. Still it did not move.

Little Fox got out of the sleigh and marched up to the calf, ready to give it a licking. But as she approached, she noticed a little tuft of straw sticking out of the calf's side. Little Fox tugged on the straw and out flew the birds. What was left of the calf toppled to the ground.

Now Little Fox was really mad. She knew exactly what had happened and she vowed to get even with Brother Wolf.

Meanwhile, she was hungrier than ever, so she set off down the road in search of food.

It was not long before she saw some *chumaks* (that is, cart drivers) driving a wagon filled with fish. Quickly she ran ahead of them and lay down in the road, pretending she was dead.

When the driver saw the fox, he stopped his wagon and got off.

"Well, well, well," he said, "what have we here? A dead fox?" He gave the fox a little nudge with his foot, but she didn't move.

"I think this pelt will make some fine fur caps for my children," he said, and he threw the fox onto the wagon and drove on.

As soon as Little Fox knew the *chumaks* weren't looking, she grabbed a fish and tossed it to the side of the road. Then she grabbed another and did the same thing. She kept doing this until she had thrown about half a dozen fish off the cart. Then she jumped out too. She gathered up all the fish and began feasting on them, for she was famished.

As she was eating, who should come walking up but Brother Wolf.

"Hullo, there," he cried, grinning.

"Hullo to you, too." The fox scowled and did not look up from her dinner.

"What are you doing, Little Fox?" the wolf asked.

"What does it look like?" she snapped back, "I'm eating fish."

"My, they certainly look tasty."

"They are tasty, Wolfie, but don't think I'll give one to you. I know what happens when I share my things with Brother Wolf." The wolf looked away, embarrassed, but those fish smelled good.

"Well, won't you at least tell me how to catch my own fish then?" he pleaded.

"Oh, all right," the fox replied, chomping and smacking her lips. Then she wiped her mouth and paws and pointed to the river, which was frozen over with ice.

"See that river?" she began. "What you need to do is go over there and cut a hole in the ice. Then stick your tail down the hole and swish it about in the water, yelling, 'Bite, fish, bite, big and small.' Keep yelling that over and over until you get all the fish you need."

Brother Wolf quickly thanked the fox and ran to the river. He chopped a hole in the ice, just as Little Fox had told him, then stuck his tail into the water and swung it back and forth, yelling, "Bite, fish, bite, big and big only."

Little Fox watched the wolf from the corner of her eye and chuckled softly.

"Freeze, wolf tail, freeze," she said.

"Did you say something, Little Fox?" the wolf called.

"Oh, I was just saying, 'Bite, fish, bite, big and small,'" she replied.

Further Adventures of Fox and Wolf

"Thanks for your help, friend, but my tail is getting very heavy now. In fact, I can hardly move it."

"Then you must pull it out." Of course, when the wolf tried to pull his tail out of the river, it was frozen fast.

"Come help me, Little Fox," he cried. Little Fox ran up and together they pulled and pulled and pulled until—*Pop!*—the wolf's tail was pulled off.

"Oh, dear," Brother Wolf whimpered.

"Why did this happen?" Little Fox scolded, "what were you saying?"

"I said, 'Bite, fish, bite, big and big only,'" confessed the wolf.

"Well, no wonder!" exclaimed the fox. "That's why your tail was so heavy!"

The wolf felt foolish without a tail. "What will I do?" he whined.

"Mm," Little Fox scratched her head. "I know—I'll go to the village and see if I can find some brandy and a bandage." She went scurrying off, leaving the wolf behind.

When the fox reached the village, she sneaked into one of the houses, where some bread dough had been left to rise. She ate several handfuls, then took some more and smeared it on her head. Then, she returned to the wolf.

Brother Wolf was still lying by the side of the river, sobbing.

Little Fox held her head as if she were in great pain. "Oh me, oh my," she moaned.

The wolf looked up. "What happened?" he snuffled. "Did you find the brandy and bandages?"

"No, no," wailed the fox, "the villagers saw me and they beat me so hard, they cracked my skull. Now I'm losing my brains."

"What?" The wolf squinted and pulled a face. "Ugh, that looks awful."

"If you think it looks awful, you should know how it feels," said the fox. "I think you're going to have to carry me home."

"But, Little Fox, I have been wounded myself."

The fox began wailing even louder. Brother Wolf stood up and hobbled over. Little Fox climbed on his back and sighed deeply. Then they started for home.

As they went along, Little Fox stretched out and smiled. Ah, this was a fine way to travel! Finally the wolf was paying for his bad behavior. Little Fox mumbled under her breath, "The loser carries the winner," and she chuckled softly.

"What was that, Little Fox?"

"Oh, I was just saying 'The loser carries a loser,'" she replied.

"Oh."

On and on they went until they came to the fox's den. Then Little Fox jumped down and yelled out, "The loser carried the winner home!" and she laughed and laughed.

"What?!" Brother Wolf's eyes bulged out and his fur stood on end.

"Why, you, you—" he snarled. He turned to pounce on the fox, but she was too fast. Into her den she flew, quick as a wink. As the wolf stood snapping and growling at her door, she giggled and repeated, "The loser carried the winner, because he's such a sinner!"

Well, the wolf stood there for awhile, but soon realized that he was only making a fool of himself. So he left, cursing and muttering that he would never, ever trust Little Fox again. And after that, why, Brother Wolf and Little Fox had many more adventures together, because that's how wolves and foxes are. 🦊

The Donkey and the Wolf

A DONKEY WAS GRAZING
in his pasture one day when he noticed that the fence had broken
down in one spot.

"Aha," he thought, "here is my chance for freedom!"

He stepped over the broken fence and trotted down the road.
When he came upon a lovely meadow at the edge of the forest, he
stopped.

"This will be my new pasture and home," he announced to no
one in particular. Moments later he was nibbling on the sweet clover
and rolling in the long, silky grass.

"This is the life!" he thought. He patted his full belly and smiled.
Just then he noticed a lean wolf lurking at the edge of the woods.
Now, this wolf was well known in the village for stealing and eating

lambs. The donkey shuddered just to think of it. The
wolf had noticed the donkey too, and he was already
smacking his lips. His eyes gleamed as he strode
boldly toward his prey. As he neared, the donkey
started bowing and scraping the ground with his hoof.

"Thank goodness! Here you are at last!" shouted
the donkey. "I've been waiting for you for three days."

"What are you talking about, you old fool?" said
the wolf. "Don't you know I'm here to eat you?"

"Ah, that would be a shame under the circumstances," Donkey
replied, shaking his head slowly from side to side. "The townspeople
would be very disappointed indeed."

"What are you getting at? Explain yourself," the wolf barked
back, "but make it snappy. I am in no mood for chitchat."

"Well, it's quite simple," replied the donkey. "There's been a
terrible fight between the two candidates for mayor and the townspeople agreed that you are the only one who can manage things now.
They want you to run for mayor of our village."

For a moment the wolf stood with his mouth open and his mind reeling. He could see it all—a luxurious home in the village, banquets and feasts without end, power. Ah, how fine it would be to be mayor!

"Me, mayor?" he beamed, "well, what do you know? I suppose the townspeople have finally come to their senses about me."

"Yes, but we have no time to waste," said Donkey. "The election is today. Hop on my back and I'll take you to town immediately."

So the wolf jumped on the donkey's back and they headed for the village at a brisk trot. What a strange sight! When they reached the town's edge, Donkey brayed loudly. Everyone came out of their houses and, seeing the wolf, picked up sticks and stones and ran toward him. They knocked the wolf off the donkey's back and beat him soundly. Wolf finally managed to get away and dragged himself to a haystack to rest awhile. As he lay there, he began thinking.

"My father was not a mayor," he mused aloud to himself. "My grandfather was not a mayor either. Whatever made me think I could be a mayor?" Then the wolf sighed deeply, "Oh, I am so foolish, I deserve a good licking!"

Now, it just so happened that a young farmhand was resting on the other side of the haystack. When the boy heard the wolf talking to himself, he grabbed a pitchfork and went after the wolf. Wolf jumped up and ran down the road. The boy chased him all the way to the forest's edge, and after that, the wolf was never seen or heard from again.

As for the donkey, word has it that he went back to the farm and lived in the farmer's field for the rest of his life. And whenever the fence broke, he told the farmer immediately. &

The Little Round Bun

THERE ONCE LIVED AN OLD FARMER
and his wife, who were so poor they didn't know what to do. They
were too old to work, and each day they grew poorer, sadder, and
hungrier, until one day there was no more food left in the house.

"Why don't you bake us some bread, old woman?" said the
farmer.

"Because we have no flour," replied his wife.

"Can't you find even a little?" asked the old man. So the old
woman scraped out the very last bits from the flour bin and added
a few dry crumbs and got just enough to make a little round bun, or
a *kalach*, as they say in Ukraine. She found two dried-up currants and
a leathery strip of apple peel and these she pressed into the dough
so that they looked like two little black eyes and a crooked little
smile. The old woman popped the bun into the oven. She was so
proud of herself that she began to sweep the hut and hum, beaming
brightly as she worked. As the little bun cooked, the house filled with
the smell of baking bread, and the old man began smiling too.

When the old woman pulled the *kalach* from the oven, it was so
perfect that she and the old man both gasped, "Ahhh!" She set the bun
on the windowsill and the two of them waited eagerly for it to cool.

 Suddenly the *kalach* jumped from the windowsill down
to the ground. There it started rolling down the road. The
old couple jumped up from their chairs and chased after it,
waving their arms wildly and shouting, but the *kalach* kept
rolling. As it rolled, the little bun sang:

I'm a little round bun straight from the oven
and I roll all day beneath the golden sun.
If you want to catch me, you can run, run, run,
but I'll just roll away, 'cause I'm a little round bun.

The old man and old woman ran and ran, but the bun rolled much faster than they could run and eventually they gave up and went back home. The little bun kept rolling down the road. By and by it met a rabbit.

The rabbit took one look at the *kalach* and said, "What a tasty meal has rolled my way!" But just as he started to reach for the bun, the little *kalach* spoke.

"Don't eat me yet," said the bun, "wait till I sing my little song." So the rabbit sat back on his haunches while the little round bun sang:

> *I'm a little round bun straight from the oven*
> *and I roll all day beneath the golden sun.*
> *I rolled from the farmer and I rolled from his wife,*
> *and I'll roll from you for my life, life, life.*
> *If you want to catch me, you can run, run, run,*
> *but I'll just roll away, 'cause I'm a little round bun.*

As it sang, the little round bun rocked to and fro. When it reached the end of the song, it quickly rolled away. The rabbit hopped after the bun, but the little *kalach* rolled very fast. It wasn't long before the rabbit tired of the chase and gave up. The little round bun rolled on.

By and by the *kalach* ran into a lean and hungry wolf.

"Aha!" said the wolf, "that bun looks like a tender bite." Drooling, he reached for it, but when he did, the bun spoke.

"Don't eat me yet, Mr. Wolf. Listen to my little song first."

"Hmm," thought the wolf, "I do like music." So he lay down on the road and closed his eyes while the little bun sang:

> *I'm a little round bun straight from the oven*
> *and I roll all day beneath the golden sun.*
> *I rolled from the farmer and I rolled from his wife,*
> *and I rolled from the rabbit for my life, life, life.*
> *If you want to catch me, you can run, run, run,*
> *but I'll just roll away, 'cause I'm a little round bun.*

Again the little bun rocked to and fro as it sang, and when it reached the end of the song, it quickly rolled away. The wolf opened his eyes and saw what was happening, and he jumped up and began chasing the *kalach*. But the little round bun rolled faster and faster down the road and soon the wolf could not even see it. Panting, he turned around and went home. The little round bun rolled on.

By and by the little round bun ran into a huge brown bear. The bear was busy picking blackberries, but when he saw the little bun, he dropped the berries and swung a mighty paw toward it. The little bun managed to dodge the bear's paw and, shaking with fear, it cried out, "Please don't eat me yet. Wait till I sing my little song."

"Oh, who cares about your stupid song," grumbled the bear, but he groaned and sat down to listen to the little bun sing.

> *I'm a little round bun straight from the oven*
> *and I roll all day beneath the golden sun.*
> *I rolled from the farmer and I rolled from his wife,*
> *and I rolled from the rabbit for my life, life, life.*
> *I rolled from the wolf—I rolled right away,*
> *'Cause I'm a little round bun and I'm made that way.*
> *If you want to catch me, you can run, run, run,*
> *but I'll just roll away, 'cause I'm a little round bun.*

Rocking to and fro, the *kalach* sang and sang. When it reached the end of its ditty, it quickly rolled away.

"Hey, wait!" roared the bear, and he staggered to his feet, but it was too late. The little round bun was rolling down the road as fast as the wind, and the old bear could not catch up. Finally the bear gave up and went back to the blackberry patch. And the little round bun rolled on.

By and by the *kalach* ran into a sleek red fox.

"You look just like my dinner," said the fox, but as she reached for the bun, it spoke up once again.

"Please don't eat me yet," it begged, "wait till you hear my little song."

So the fox sat down and arranged her fluffy tail around her. Then she perked up her ears while the little bun sang:

> *I'm a little round bun straight from the oven*
> *and I roll all day beneath the golden sun.*
> *I rolled from the farmer and I rolled from his wife,*
> *and I rolled from the rabbit for my life, life, life.*
> *I rolled from the wolf—I rolled right away,*
> *and I rolled from the bear, 'cause I'm made that way.*
> *If you want to catch me, you can run, run, run,*
> *but I'll just roll away, 'cause I'm a little round bun.*

As it sang, the little bun rocked to and fro. When it reached the end, it started to roll away, but the fox called after it, saying, "Oh, please don't go—your song is so lovely. Sing it for me again, but this time come closer, so I can hear it better."

The little round bun grinned and rolled up so close to the fox that it could feel her breath. The fox closed her eyes and sighed blissfully as the little bun sang:

> *I'm a little round bun straight from the oven*
> *and I roll all day beneath the golden sun.*
> *I rolled from the farmer and I rolled from his wife,*
> *and I rolled from the rabbit for my life, life, life.*
> *I rolled from the wolf—I rolled right away,*
> *and I rolled from the bear, 'cause I'm made that way.*
> *If you want to catch me, you can run, run, run,*
> *but I'll just roll away, 'cause I'm a little round bun.*

When the *kalach* finished, the fox clapped and cried, "Bravo, bravo!" The little round bun smiled its crooked smile. Then the sleek red fox begged, "Oh, your song is so lovely! Can I hear it just one more time? Please? If you sit on my nose and sing, I'll be able to hear it very well."

So the little *kalach* jumped onto the fox's nose and began to sing: "*I'm a little round bun straight from the oven,*" it began, rocking to and fro, "*and I roll all day beneath the golden—.*" SNAP! The fox opened her mouth, clamped her jaws around the little round bun, and gobbled it right up. Then she licked her lips, smiled, and sauntered down the road, singing:

> *There was a little round bun who came straight from the oven*
> *and it rolled all day beneath the golden sun.*
> *If you want to catch a meal, you can run, run, run,*
> *but it's your wits that will get you a little round bun.* ✑

The Mitten

IN A HOUSE
at the edge of the forest, on a day when fresh snow covered the earth
and the air tingled with ice crystals, a young boy named Misha sat
talking by the fire with his mother.

"Look, son," said the mother, "we are almost out of firewood.
Will you run out to the forest before it gets dark and fetch an armful
of wood for the night?"

"Okay, mama," replied Misha. He pulled on his tall boots, slipped
into his heavy winter coat, and buttoned it up to his chin. Then he
grabbed his cap, pulled it down over his ears, and headed out the door.

"Not without your mittens," Misha's mother called after him,
and she handed him a pair of red wool mittens.

Misha took the mittens and ran outside. He came to a clearing
in the woods, stuffed the mittens into his pockets, and began gathering wood. Soon he had a big armful—almost more than he could
carry—so he turned around and headed for home. When one of his
mittens fell from his pocket into the deep white snow, Misha didn't
notice. But Maid Meadow Mouse did.

Out she skittered from under a log, and ran right up to the
mitten. She sniffed all around and peeked inside. It looked so cozy,
she decided to spend the night there. Maid Meadow Mouse had just
settled in for a nice winter nap in her new home when she heard a
strange noise: *Boing! Boing! Boing!*

"Yoo hoo," came a voice from outside.

Maid Meadow Mouse peered out. "Who's there?" she asked.

"It's me—Flippety Frog," came the reply.

Sure enough, a frog stood shivering at the door. "Mind if I join you?" he asked.

Maid Meadow Mouse did not really want to share her new home, but the frog seemed nice and, brrr, it was cold out there, so she invited him in.

No sooner had the frog settled in then there was another strange sound: *Hip, hop. Hip, hop.*

"Hello there, anybody home?"

Maid Meadow Mouse and Flippety Frog peered out and saw a rabbit crouched at the door.

"Why, it's Hoppity Hare!" exclaimed Flippety Frog. "Won't you join us?"

Maid Meadow Mouse scowled, but she didn't want to be rude, so she didn't say anything.

"Don't mind if I do," said the rabbit, and with that he burrowed deep into the mitten with the frog and the mouse. Everyone wriggled and squirmed until they had settled into their places. They were all about to doze off when they heard another noise: *Whoosh! Flap, flap, flap.*

"Who, who, who is in there?" called a voice from outside. Maid Meadow Mouse, Flippety Frog, and Hoppity Hare exchanged glances and looked out the door. A big owl stared back at them with two round yellow eyes.

"I'm Wide-eyed Old Owl," he announced. "It's awfully cold out here. Could I come in?"

The three animals inside fidgeted and cleared their throats and glanced at each other, but no one wanted to argue with the old owl, so they let him in. The owl flapped his great wings and the mitten billowed out just enough for him to squeeze inside.

"There now," sighed Maid Meadow Mouse, "let's all get some sleep." But she had no sooner finished saying it than another sound echoed through the forest: *Stamp! Stamp! Stamp, Stamp, Stamp!*

"Open up and let me in!" The animals inside the mitten all quivered a little.

"Who is it?" they asked.

"It's me—Bristly Burly Boar," came the answer, "and I need a place to sleep."

When the animals heard who it was, they immediately made room. Bristly Burly Boar had long tusks and sharp hooves. No one wanted a quarrel with him! So he climbed in. Everyone snuggled up together and fell asleep. Suddenly another sound wakened them: *Pitter, patter. Sniff, sniff, sniff.*

The animals looked outside. There stood Slyboots the fox.

"Brrr!" she shivered, "can I come in?"

"Well, okay," said Maid Meadow Mouse, "but you're the last one. We're simply out of room." Slyboots squeezed in and everyone settled in once more for a nap.

Sluff. Sluff. Sluff.

"Dear friends, please don't forsake me. I need a place to stay—just for one night." It was Woeful Wolf.

"Can't you see there's no room?" squeaked Maid Meadow Mouse, who was now feeling rather cross. But the wolf began to howl, and everyone felt sorry for him. They wiggled and squeezed, and Woeful Wolf climbed in.

Ka-boom! Ka-boom! Ka-boom! Heavy footsteps thundered through the forest.

"Oh dear, that sounds like Big Bully Bear," said Woeful Wolf.

"Oh no," everyone gasped. Without even waiting for him to ask, they all scrunched together as close as they could. Big Bully Bear crawled in and the mitten stretched and stretched and stretched. It seemed as though it would have to burst, but it didn't, and all the animals breathed sighs of relief. Then they finally nestled down to finish their warm nap.

By then night was falling and the first stars began to tremble against the dark sky. Misha arrived home with the firewood. His mother saw that his hands were red and raw with the cold and she shook her head, asking, "Where are your mittens, son?"

"In my pockets," Misha answered, but when he reached for them he found only one.

"You must have dropped one," said the mother. "You must look for it in the morning." Then she rubbed Misha's hands and held them between her own to warm them.

Meanwhile, in the lost mitten, the forest creatures were fast asleep, breathing slowly and dreaming animal dreams.

Just before dawn there was a light scratching at the entry. Songster Sparrow, who had been out singing all night, was ready to go to bed.

"Anyone home?" he chirped. The animals inside the mitten stirred and sighed.

"A-hem. Can I come in?" asked the sparrow. No answer.

"Well, I won't take up much room. I can't imagine that I would bother anyone," the bird continued. He was so tired that he swayed a little as he carefully put one skinny foot into the mitten. Where should it land but in the middle of Big Bully Bear's soft wet nose!

"Ah, ah, ah-CHOO!" The bear sneezed so hard that all the animals flew from the mitten and tumbled helter-skelter into the snow.

Just then Misha arrived at the clearing and saw the animals running off in all directions. Puzzled, he blinked his eyes and shook his head. Then he saw his mitten. He picked it up—it seemed warm. When he put the mitten on, it seemed bigger, too. Misha looked all around, but the animals were nowhere to be seen.

"Oh well," he said, "I'm glad I found my mitten." And he shrugged and walked home. &

The Turnip

O<small>NCE THERE WAS A FAMILY</small>—
a grandpa, a grandma, a mama, a papa, a boy named Sasha, and a little girl named Lala. They all lived together in a little house. They were very poor, but even though they didn't have much, they always had each other and they never lost hope.

No, they never lost hope—that is, until one day when Grandma opened the cupboards and found that they were empty.

"Grandpa, the cupboards are empty," she cried.

"Look harder," he replied, and the whole family gathered around while Grandma looked into every corner of every cupboard.

Grandma searched and searched and searched and finally she said, "Aha!" She opened her hand for everyone to see. In the middle of her palm lay a tiny black speck.

"It's a *ripka** seed," she beamed.

"Ah, a *ripka* seed," everyone murmured and smiled.

"I will hoe the garden," said the grandpa.

"I will plant the seed," said the mama.

"I will water the seed," said the papa.

"I will pull the weeds," said Sasha. Everyone looked at Lala.

"What will I do?" she asked.

"Oh, you'll think of something," they all answered together, "you'll think of something."

So the grandpa hoed the garden, and the mama planted the seed, and the papa watered the seed, and Sasha pulled the weeds. And Lala watched as the *ripka*—that is, the turnip—grew and grew and grew. By the end of the summer it was HUGE!

Then one day Grandpa said, "It is time to harvest our *ripka*. I'll pull it out so we can eat it." With both hands he grabbed hold of the turnip stem and gave a big tug, but the turnip stuck. It wouldn't budge!

* ripka—*turnip*

"Come help me, Grandma," he called. When Grandma came, Grandpa took hold of the stem again, and Grandma grabbed hold of Grandpa's waist. Together they tugged and tugged, but still the turnip would not budge.

"Come help us, Papa," they called. When Papa came, Grandpa held the turnip by its stem, Grandma held Grandpa by the waist, Papa held Grandma by her apron strings, and together they tugged and tugged and tugged. Still the turnip would not budge.

"Come help us, Mama," they called. When Mama came, Grandpa held the turnip by its stem, Grandma held Grandpa by the waist, Papa held Grandma by her apron strings, Mama held Papa by his belt, and together they tugged and tugged and tugged and tugged. Still the turnip would not budge.

"Come help us, Sasha," they called. When Sasha came, Grandpa held the turnip by its stem, Grandma held Grandpa by the waist, Papa held Grandma by her apron strings, Mama held Papa by his belt, Sasha held Mama by her skirt, and together they tugged and tugged and tugged and tugged and tugged. Still the turnip would not budge.

"Come help us, Lala," they all called. When Lala came, Grandpa held the turnip by its stem, Grandma held Grandpa by the waist, Papa held Grandma by her apron strings, Mama held Papa by his belt, Sasha held Mama by her skirt, and Lala held Sasha by the hand, and together they tugged and tugged and tugged and tugged and tugged and tugged. Still the turnip would not budge.

Then a little kitty cat walked by. "Come help us, kitty cat," they all called. When the kitty cat came, Grandpa held the turnip by its stem, Grandma held Grandpa by the waist, Papa held Grandma by her apron strings, Mama held Papa by his belt, Sasha held Mama by her skirt, Lala held Sasha by the hand, and the kitty cat held Lala by her boot, and together they tugged and tugged and tugged and tugged and tugged and tugged and tugged. Still the turnip would not budge.

Then they saw a wee little mouse scurry by. "Come help us, wee little mouse," they all called. When the wee mouse came, Grandpa held the turnip by its stem, Grandma held Grandpa by the waist, Papa held Grandma by her apron strings, Mama held Papa by his belt, Sasha held Mama by her skirt, Lala held Sasha by the hand, the kitty cat held Lala by her boot, and the wee little mouse held the kitty cat by his tail, and together they tugged and tugged and tugged and tugged and tugged and tugged and tugged until—POP, the turnip finally came out.

Then the wee little mouse fell to the ground. And the kitty cat fell on the wee little mouse. And Lala fell on the kitty cat. And Sasha fell on Lala. And Mama fell on Sasha. And Papa fell on Mama. And Grandma fell on Papa. And Grandpa fell on Grandma. And the turnip fell on Grandpa. Everybody laughed and laughed and laughed.

They all carried the turnip to the house and cooked it up in a big pot. Lala looked into the pot. Mmm, the turnip smelled good. She dipped a spoon in and took a taste. Mmm-mm, the turnip tasted good.

"Now I know what I can do," she said. So she filled her plate with turnip and ate it all up.

Pysanky (Ukrainian Easter eggs) are made with wax, dyes, and a writing tool called a *kystka*. The tradition hearkens back more than 2,000 years.

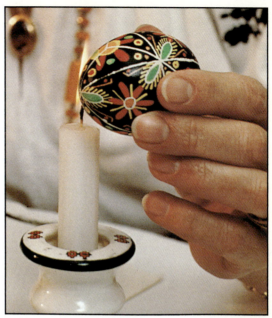

Photograph by N. Kononenko

Photograph by N. Kononenko

(Upper left) Herbs and hand-painted pottery are displayed in a traditional Ukrainian home.
(Upper right) Traditional hearth.
(Below) For Ukrainians, bread comes in many shapes and sizes.

Rushnyky (embroidered towels) shown with a wooden cradle (right) and draped around religious icons (below).

Photograph by N. Kononenko

Photograph by N. Kononenko

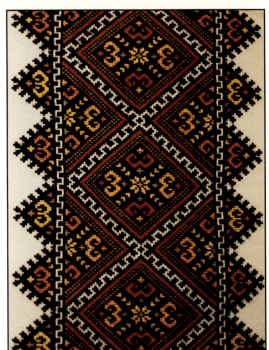

Details of Ukrainian embroidery.

Blessing of the fruit on *Spas* holiday at the *Lavra* or Cave Monastery in Kyiv.
Photograph by N. Kononenko

Medieval castle at Uzhhorod.

Adobe houses with thatched roofs were once common in the Ukrainian countryside.
Photograph by N. Kononenko

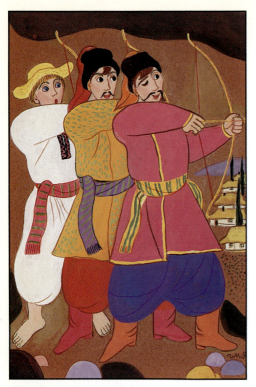

"The Three Brothers"   "Vasyl' and the Frog"

Two (above) of Halyna Mazepa's illustrations of "The Frog Princess."

"Christmas Is Here" from an original glass painting by Yaroslava Surmach-Mills.
Courtesy of Surma, New York. © Surma Book & Music Co., MCMLXXVI.

One of Halyna Mazepa's illustrations of "The Two Daughters"

Halyna Mazepa, a well-known Ukrainian artist, also illustrated a number of children's folktale books. Works featured in this collection (above, preceding page, and back cover) were executed in tempera and ink on paper. Illustrations courtesy of Bohdan, Marta, Virna, Danylo, Olena, Tamara, and Halina Koval.

"Path to the Windmill," a mixed media painting by Alexander Tkachenko.
Courtesy of the artist.

Alexander Tkachenko, a Ukrainian born artist, combines contemporary painting techniques with traditional Ukrainian folk themes and motifs. Another of his recent works appears on the front cover.

Part II

How and Why Stories

How the Earth Was Made

BEFORE ALL AND EVERYTHING,
there was a creator, and this creator floated on a white stone in a sea
of water. Day after day he floated, musing about all and sundry
things. One day as the creator was thinking, he began to choke. He
coughed and coughed until he coughed up a gob of spittle. As the
creator tried to catch his breath, out from the spittle stepped *Hohol'*,
that is to say, Satan.

The creator pointed his finger to the sea of water around them
and commanded, "*Hohol'*, dive to the bottom of the sea and fetch me
some sand so I can show you something grand. And be sure to repeat
my name as you do this or your venture will fail."

Hohol' plunged into the water, diving deeper and deeper until
he touched the bottom of the sea. But he did not repeat the creator's
name, so when he came back to the surface, his hands were empty.
Hohol' sputtered and gasped and, seeing that he had failed, he
cursed. Then he dove again. This time, as he swam toward the
bottom, he did not say the creator's name, but he did think it. So
when he surfaced, lo and behold, there were a few tiny grains of sand
under his fingernails.

The creator took the grains of sand and sowed them in the
garden of the heavens, and from the sand grew a blue and
beautiful earth.

As beautiful as this earth was, though, it was completely
covered by water, so the creator said to *Hohol'*, "Let's shape this
earth into something better. You go west and I'll go east, and
when I say the word, push with all your might."

So each went his own way and when they were opposite
from each other on either side of the earth, the creator spoke.

"Now," he said and they both began pushing as hard as they could. As they squeezed, the earth groaned and buckled. Land appeared, mountains rose, and valleys and rivers formed beneath them. Now the earth was part water and part land, and it was a beautiful thing to see. So the creator and *Hohol'* came together to admire their work.

After *Hohol'* looked upon the earth, he frowned and scratched his head.

"What are the mountains for?" he asked. The creator grinned.

"You see how steep those mountains are?" he said. "When man climbs down the mountain he will call my name for help. But when he reaches the bottom and turns back to see where he's been, he will say, 'Oh what a devilish hill!' So you see, we will both be remembered for our work." The creator laughed heartily and so did *Hohol'*, and the whole earth shook with thunder. ⌘

How Evil Came into the World

LONG, LONG AGO,
before there was an earth to stand upon and before there were people to remember and tell, there was a vast aching darkness. The darkness was surrounded by water and above the water flew two spirits—one made of light, the other made of shadow.

One day the light spirit said to the dark spirit, "Let's make something." The dark spirit agreed, so the light spirit said, "Let there be light." And there was light.

But all this light made the dark spirit feel small and unhappy.

"There's too much light," he grumbled. "Can't I have just a little darkness?" The light spirit consented, so the spirit of shadow made night.

Sky, sun, moon, stars, and all the heavenly planets—these were created by the spirit of light. Earth, animals, plants, and other visible things were made by the light spirit and the dark spirit together. Then the light spirit went off and began creating on his own, carving figures with his sword. These he called human and they looked like the spirit of light himself. The spirit of light also created angels to fly in the heavens.

When the spirit of shadow saw what the spirit of light was doing , he became very jealous. He too wanted to make beings in his  own likeness, but he did not have the power to create by himself. So he waited until the light spirit fell asleep, sneaked over to his side, and stole the light spirit's sword, hiding it under his robes. Quietly, quickly the dark spirit ran. When he was sure he could not be seen or heard, he took the sword out and struck a rock with it. Out poured multitudes of dark things, and sickness and sorrow too. Turning away from the spirit of light, the spirit of shadow ruled over these dark beings. He ordered them to renounce the light and because he was their master, they obeyed.

When the light spirit awoke and saw what had happened, he was troubled. Out of goodness itself he created a friend—a holy spirit who spoke with the spirit of light. But the spirit of shadow grew envious again and once more he stole the light spirit's sword. Then the dark spirit created many more dark beings and sent them after the creatures of light, to seduce them and carry them away.

When the light spirit awoke and saw what had happened, a great anger seized him. He called out to all creatures, both light and dark, saying, "I am Lord." In a thunder he cursed the spirit of darkness, naming him Satan and his followers devils, and he cast them all from his presence.

At first Satan resisted. He did not want to leave, but the Lord chased him and his regiments out with the sword. Then the Lord made an oath upon the sword that from then on it belonged to him alone; no one else could command it or even touch it. "Amen, amen," his followers agreed.

The Lord of light sent his angels to guard against the dark ones' return, but the dark ones fought viciously, singeing the angels' wings so that they could not fly. Quickly the angels ran back to the Lord. He created new wings for them and he gave his sword to the angels, saying, "Only to defeat evil may you use this sword."

At that, the sword burst into flames and the angels took it. With new wings they flew into the face of darkness. There they fought Satan and his forces until one by one the dark ones fell to Earth. Some fell into the water, and some fell into the forest, and some fell into other places, until there was not a place on Earth where darkness had not been.

Today these dark creatures still exist—*mara* and *vodianyk, domovyk* and *pol'ovyk.**

It is true that some tell of the dark ones and their tricks, but others do not believe. That is because the dark ones cannot be seen by the human eye. Always they must live beneath the light, cast away and hidden. ༀ

* mara—*the specter.*
* vodianyk—*the water dweller.*
* domovyk—*a house spirit.*
* pol'ovyk—*a field demon.*
These are various types of spirits and demons from pagan beliefs. According to folk belief, these spirits can protect their domains or make mischief and cause trouble for humans.

The Sun, the Frost, and the Wind

ONE DAY
the Sun, the Frost, and the Wind came down to Earth and strolled along the roads of old Ukraine. As they walked, they came upon a simple peasant who was walking the other way.

"Greetings, oh great sir!" the peasant hailed. "May God's blessing be upon you. Long may you live and long may you prosper. May all good things come to you and yours, now and forevermore. May God bless you and keep you, you and all your kin." The peasant bowed deeply and went on down the road.

"What a good and decent fellow!" exclaimed the Sun, beaming brightly. "He may be but a simple peasant, but he certainly knows how to give a proper greeting. I am touched and honored that he greeted me so respectfully."

Frost bristled and scowled. "What makes you think the peasant was greeting you? When he said 'great sir,' surely he was addressing me."

"Oh, you cold and silly fool," scoffed the Sun, "of course it was me he greeted. I warm the poor man and make his crops grow. I can also burn his crops with my searing rays. His prosperity and his downfall are my doing. It's quite obvious that the peasant greeted me."

"You are mistaken," said Frost. "I can freeze the peasant's crops. I can kill his livestock. Why, I can even kill him!" The Sun looked askance.

"It's true," Frost continued. "All I need to do is wait until everything sprouts in springtime and then dance across the peasant's fields. All of his crops will die and he will die too, only slowly and miserably. It is me the peasant fears and respects and it is me he greeted."

Then the Wind interrupted the other two. "I'm afraid you are both wrong," he said, "and I can prove it."

"How?" the Sun and the Frost replied in unison.

"We must ask the peasant himself," answered the Wind. So the Sun, the Frost, and the Wind hurried down the road, chasing the peasant. When they caught up with him they asked, "Good man, you gave a good and proper greeting, but you addressed it to only one of us. Which one was it?"

"Why, the Wind," the peasant replied without hesitation.

Then the Sun reddened with anger. "Insolent fool! I'll teach this peasant to insult me! I will blast him with my heat. I'll burn him to the ground for this!"

"Oh no, you won't," said the Wind, "I won't let you burn him. I'll fan the peasant with a cool breeze. As long as I blow, you will not be able to kill him."

Meanwhile, Frost turned white with rage. "Stupid man. He'll not get away with offending me. I will bury him in frost until he freezes to death."

But again the Wind silenced his companion's anger. "You can do nothing without me, Frost. Unless I add my force to your cold, the peasant will not freeze—he will live."

At that, the Sun and the Frost turned to leave, and the Wind followed them. The peasant lived on and continued to pay homage to the Wind, although he never forgot to respect the Sun and the Frost also.

We too pay homage to these great forces—the Wind, the Sun, and the Frost. For it is the Wind that carries in springtime and chases away the cold. It cools us in the summer and brings clouds heavy with rain. If the Wind is angry, it spreads sickness and disease. It can penetrate everywhere, through the cracks of a house and the seams of our clothing. That is why people repeat the riddle:

> *In and out the windows,*
> *Through each and every crack,*
> *It travels through the household,*
> *And never leaves a track.*

The answer, of course, is "the Wind." 🍃

Dnipro and Dunai

LONG, LONG AGO,
in times before we remember and before there were stories to tell, two great rivers of Ukraine—the Dnipro and the Dunai (or the Dnieper and the Danube)—were not rivers at all, but people. In fact, they were husband and wife and they served in the court of the mighty prince of Kyiv. Dnipro and Dunai loved each other very much and always did everything together.

One day the two attended a feast at the court of Kyiv. Many, many people were there, all eating, drinking, and making merry. There was every kind of food, every kind of drink, and every kind of entertainment—jugglers, minstrels, singers, and tale-tellers of every sort. Everyone was having a wonderful time. Toward the end of the day, though, some of the young men who had drunk too much began boasting.

"I can shoot an arrow from here to the next village," said one.

"Ha!" cried another, "You'd be lucky to shoot past your own nose. I can shoot over a mountain." They all laughed and teased and boasted until someone noticed that through all this Dnipro had sat silent. So they turned to the mighty warrior.

"What do you say, oh great and mighty Dnipro?" The young men suddenly feigned seriousness. "Have you no comment to make? Are you willing to admit that we are your superiors?"

Dnipro smiled and shook his head. "Why should I join in this silliness?" he said. "My wife, Dunai, can shoot further than any of you."

This made the young men angry. "Oh, really?" they challenged Dnipro. "We'll see what your wife can do!" Everyone insisted that their archery skills be put to the test right then and there. The whole entourage went out to a field, set up a target, and began to shoot. At first, all the men could hit the target, but as it was moved further and further away, fewer and fewer remained in the competition. Finally, Dnipro was the only man left. He was about to take his leave when someone remembered what Dnipro had said about his wife.

"What about Dunai?" the men began clamoring. "Make her shoot too!"

So Dnipro called his wife forward and handed his bow to her.

"Please don't make me shoot, dear husband," pleaded Dunai. "You know I am carrying our child and nothing good can come from a competition between the two of us."

But Dunai's protest angered her husband. "Shoot, woman," he commanded. So Dunai took aim and shot. Her arrow hit the center of the target, splitting Dnipro's arrow in two. The target was moved back further. Dnipro's arrow hit the center, and again Dunai shot and split her husband's arrow in two. So it went until Dnipro said they needed a more challenging target. The crowd cheered and howled for more.

"Whoever can shoot through my wedding ring will be the winner," Dnipro said, laughing. But when he shot his own arrow, for the first time that day it missed its mark.

Dnipro scowled and handed the bow to his wife. "Shoot now, woman," his voice boomed over the crowd.

Dunai began to weep. "Oh, my dear husband, please don't make me shoot," she begged. "Nothing good can come of a competition between husband and wife."

Dnipro's face turned red with anger, "Shoot!" he bellowed, "or you will live to regret it."

Stung by her husband's threat, Dunai took the bow in her arms and lifted it to shoot. Her hands trembled with fear as the sound of the crowd thundered in her ears, and tears streamed from her eyes.

"SHOOT!" Dnipro roared. And so Dunai shot. Her arrow flew straight through the ring, so clean it did not even leave a scratch. The crowd stood as silent and still as statues—they were awestruck, but Dnipro whitened with rage.

"How dare you beat me?" he bellowed, and he drew his sword and charged toward his wife.

Dunai fell to her knees. "Please forgive me, my husband, and spare my life—if not for my own sake, for the sake of our child." Dnipro stood above his wife, ready to plunge his sword into her as she pleaded for mercy.

"Our child is a magical child," Dunai continued. "His arms are golden to the elbow and his legs are silver to the knee. On his forehead is a great golden star and on the nape of his neck is a silver moon. Our child will grow to be a great champion, a defender of our land."

But Dnipro's rage was so great that he could not hear the words of his wife, let alone listen to reason. As Dunai reached desperately for her husband's hand, Dnipro's sword struck deep. The crowd moaned. Some began weeping.

As Dunai lay bleeding, a child was born. His arms were golden to the elbow and his legs were silver to the knee. He had a golden star on his forehead and a silver moon on the nape of his neck. But the magical child did not move and did not breathe. He lay stillborn upon the ground. Only then did Dnipro hear the words his wife had spoken. Only then did he realize what he had done.

Dnipro's anguish was so great that he could not contain it. He fell on his sword beside his dear wife, his blood flowing swiftly from his wounds as his wife's had flowed swiftly from hers. On and on the blood flowed. Rivulets joined to form streams and streams joined to form rivers.

So it is that from the blood of this mighty warrior flows the river Dnipro and from the blood of his valiant wife flows the Dunai. Today Ukraine has two great rivers, but their foolishness destroyed their own child, the promised defender of the land, the champion of Ukraine. ✎

Saint Cassian

Long ago,
but not so very long ago, a poor peasant set out to sell his crops at the market. He loaded his old wagon with as much grain as he could, because he needed money to buy salt and sausage for the winter. Without the food, he and his family might starve. As he drove, the rickety old cart heaved and creaked under the load, bouncing precariously along the bumpy road. The peasant hadn't gone far when the cart hit a stone and lurched off the road into a muddy rut. There it settled, stuck in the mire. The poor man pushed and pulled and shook his fist. He prodded his horse, then whipped his horse, and then begged the horse to pull the cart out, all to no avail. Just as he was about to give up, St. Cassian came down the road.

"What are you doing, my good man?" he asked.

The peasant fell to his knees. "Oh, please help me, sir," he begged. He explained what had happened and why he had to get to town that very day to sell his grain.

"If I don't sell the grain, I won't be able to buy food for winter," he said, "and my family will go hungry. Won't you help me pull my cart back onto the road?"

Cassian grimaced. "What? Me get down in the mud and soil my robes to help a peasant? You must be crazy. Don't you know who I am?"

The peasant began blubbering and assured Cassian that he had no idea who the saint was. He had only begged for help from a passing stranger because he was so desperate to get to town. Cassian sniffed, dusted off his mantle, and continued on down the road, while the peasant sat down by the cart and wept.

The poor man was so distraught that he did not see St. Peter approaching. Only when the saint spoke did the peasant look up from his hands.

"Why do you weep, my good man?" St. Peter asked. The peasant hesitated to explain, because of the treatment he had gotten from St. Cassian, but St. Peter's face looked so kindly and concerned that he repeated the story once more.

"And now I have insulted a saint!" he concluded.

"You poor man!" St. Peter exclaimed. "Let me help you." Then St. Peter got down in the mud with the peasant. Together they were able to dislodge the cart and push it back onto the road. The peasant got into the cart, expressed his thanks for the assistance, and drove down the road. His cart went so smoothly that it seemed as though it were new. In no time at all he reached town, sold all his grain, bought all the provisions he needed, and even got a new pair of shoes for his little son. When he returned home, he and his family rejoiced and gave thanks for their good fortune.

Now, all this time, as the peasant struggled and pleaded for help, God was watching. He saw how uncharitable St. Cassian was and how generous and kind St. Peter was. He called the two saints to his side and said, "St. Peter, your kindness pleases me. You shall have two festival days every year. All the people will remember you and celebrate in your honor. But as for you, Cassian, you would not stoop to help a poor peasant. Therefore, you will have a festival day only once every four years. Your day will be the 29th of February, and only in a leap year will the people remember you. Furthermore, you shall live under the earth, in the mud that you so disdained. When you emerge from the soil on your festival day, your precious robes will be covered with dirt and grime. Your gaze will be terrible. If you cast your eyes upon a beast or small child, that creature will sicken. Your breath will be as cold and damp as the soil in which you live, and it will carry the sickness of your gaze."

And so it is. Only in a leap year does Cassian have his day, and, as God decreed, it is not a day of celebration, but a day of fear and loathing. People hide their children and their cattle on St. Cassian's day. Some won't even go out themselves until February 29th has passed. ৶

The Christmas Spiders

ONCE THERE WAS A poor peasant family. They were so poor that they had almost nothing at all. The children wore tattered clothing and ran about barefoot, even in winter. Many, many times there was not enough to eat and they all went to bed hungry. Through the seasons they somehow managed to survive, but one year was especially difficult. The summer was hot and windy, and the little patch of dirt they called their garden dried up. Fall came, then winter. Christmas was on its way.

As the holiday season approached, the parents talked to one another. They wanted to make the day special for their children, and more than anything they wanted to give the little ones a treat to celebrate Christmas. But how could they? They had no money. They could not even afford warm clothes or shoes for the children. No, there would be no gifts.

"Let's at least put up a Christmas tree," said the father. "Maybe if we have faith, everything will work out. Maybe I'll find work and we can buy some candy and nuts to put on the tree. Then we could let the children have them as their presents on Christmas morning."

The father grew excited and happy as he spoke, but the mother shook her head sadly. "Don't get their hopes up," she said. "A tree will only remind the children that we have nothing. You know they'll be getting no presents. It's better not to disappoint them."

The father's smile quickly faded. "Maybe you're right," he conceded.

Days passed and the snow piled high outside the door. The closer they came to Christmas, the more anxious the father became. Finally he decided that the family could not celebrate the holiday without a tree. Taking his ax in hand, he ventured out into the snow toward the forest. He walked and walked, his breath clouding before him in little puffs. When he reached a clearing, he saw that there in the middle of it stood a small, perfect tree.

"This tree was meant to be ours!" the man exclaimed and excitedly he chopped it down. Then he loaded the tree on his shoulder and carried it home.

When he arrived, the children met him at the door.

"Daddy, Daddy," they cried, clapping their hands, "does this mean we're going to have Christmas after all?"

"Well, I suppose so," the father mumbled sheepishly. But when the mother heard this, she ran to the kitchen to hide her tears in her apron. Her husband followed her.

"Now, now," he said, taking her gently by the shoulders, "we will have a Christmas. Surely we can find a few coins around here."

So together they scoured the house, searching for a few pennies to buy presents with. First they checked the money box. It was empty. Then they looked into all the secret places where they might have hidden money, or where a stray coin might have fallen. But everywhere they looked they found nothing.

Finally the father said, "There is not a cent in this house. I will go into town to see if I can find work. Maybe someone will hire me to chop wood or carry coal. I am strong and there are many that need help. Maybe I can earn a little change to buy Christmas presents for our family." The wife said nothing, but sighed and nodded in agreement.

The next day the father went to town, asking for work, but it was too close to the holiday. Everyone was busy with Christmas preparations and no one was thinking about routine tasks. Even if they had been, money was tight at holiday time. Again and again the man was rejected.

While the father searched for work, the little Christmas tree stood alone in the corner. No one decorated it, no one admired it, no one even gave it a

second thought. In the silence of the little house's dark corner, tiny spiders moved into the tree, one by one, spinning their webs on this branch and that, from one branch to another.

Then Christmas Eve came. As night fell, the father became cold and discouraged. He gave up looking for work and trudged home. When he entered the house, he saw that the tree was filled with spider webs. His mouth dropped.

"Our tree has been infested with spiders," he gasped. "Clean it up at once! We can't have bugs in our home."

The family came running and gathered around the tree. They too stared open-mouthed, for it was indeed covered with webs.

"But Daddy," piped up Oksana, the youngest daughter, "aren't spiders God's creatures too? Look how beautiful their webs are! Can't we leave them on for one day as Christmas decorations?"

The other children chimed in, begging and pleading, so the father and mother agreed to leave the tree as it was for the night. Then the whole family went to bed.

The next morning the children awoke early and ran to the tree. The mother and father were still in bed, but they heard their children pattering about.

"Poor darlings," said the mother. "I told you they would expect something."

"Yes," agreed the father, "I guess you were right." He had no sooner said the words than they heard the cries of little Oksana.

"Mommy! Daddy! Come quick! Come and look at the tree! The spider webs are even more beautiful today."

The mother and father roused themselves from bed and hurried to where the tree stood. As they approached, they saw the spider webs glistening in a strange, vivid way. They touched the webs. They were hard! Then the father reached for one.

"They're silver!" he marveled, turning the web over in his hand. "In the night they turned to silver!"

The children clapped and jumped up and down. "Thank you! Thank you for our Christmas present," they all cried. Their mother hugged them all and smiled through her tears.

That Christmas turned out to be the most wonderful Christmas of all. The parents took the webs from the tree and sold them. They bought their family food, warm clothes, shoes, and even warm boots for winter. Together they gave thanks for the blessings of God's creatures.

That is why we do not kill spiders anymore, and why many will not even sweep their webs from their houses. For it is true—even the lowliest creature on earth is a gift from above.

–Natalie O. Kononenko

The Red Death

IN A TIME SO LONG AGO that it is now barely remembered, it was the custom to kill old people. That's right—it seems unthinkable, but what we now consider a natural death was then considered bad and shameful. If someone died in his sleep, people believed that his soul had been stolen by an evil spirit. To avoid a bad death, an old person would ask her son or daughter to give her a good death—what they then called a *red death*. A red death was an honorable death. It meant you could help those you left behind. People believed that those who died a red death could make the crops grow and the rain fall and their families prosper. Some claimed that those who died a red death could even intercede on behalf of the living in the land of spirits. A person who left this life willingly could return to it willingly and help all those left behind, or so it was said.

Everyone partook in this strange practice. Petro knew this, but he could not bring himself to give his father a red death. The old man was well on in years and each day his hair turned whiter and his body grew weaker. The neighbors told Petro that his father's time had come, but Petro kept procrastinating. He did not want to take his father to the cabin in the woods where old people were left to die. Petro loved his father deeply and enjoyed his company, and he had no other family left. The old man did not really want to die either, for although his body was feeble, his mind was alert and his heart was strong. But the neighbors kept pushing. They told Petro that if he did not follow the traditions, they would all suffer. Droughts, untimely frosts, crop failures—these were only a few of the ways in which they could be punished. Again and again, Petro agreed to do his duty, but when the time came, he could not.

One day the neighbors banded together and came knocking on Petro's door. They raised their fists and shouted, insisting that Petro act immediately. Petro realized that he could no longer put them off. He bundled his father onto a sleigh and headed toward the forest as night began to fall.

The sky darkened, Petro's heart began to ache, and then he began to cry. He could see that his father was unhappy too and this only made him feel worse. Finally he stopped the horses, turned the sleigh around, and headed back toward the village. There was no moon that night and by the time Petro got back to his house, it was so dark that no one saw them return.

Petro lifted his father out of the sled and hid him in the root cellar among the beets and cabbages. He covered the old man with a heavy blanket and then went to bed.

The next morning, Petro announced to the neighbors that he had done the deed—his father had died a red death. The grumbling stopped.

From then on Petro went to the root cellar with food for his father every day. He spent hours visiting with the old man, chatting about this and that. Time passed and winter changed to spring. Like everyone else in the village, Petro turned to his farming, but he still visited the root cellar as well. The spring was mild that year and the planting season went well, but when summer came, troubles began.

First there was no rain. Then the winds rose up and blew across the land, drying everything in their path. People began to worry and fret. What if the crops failed? What if there wasn't enough food for winter? Petro worried too and he started thinking that his neighbors might have been right about the punishment of the gods. But he said nothing.

One day when Petro was visiting his father, the old man said, "What's bothering you, son? You've hardly spoken a word all week and your eyes are full of worry."

Petro told his father what was happening with the crops. "I'm afraid it's all my fault," he added, hanging his head.

"Ah," replied the father, wagging his finger, "I have seen this before, this drying wind. You must shield your crops and conserve the water in the soil." Then Petro's father told him how to build fences and cover the soil so the water wouldn't evaporate.

Petro did exactly as his father had told him and his crops began to flourish. So he went to his neighbors and told them how to save their crops too. By the end of the season, there was a big harvest and plenty of food for all.

Throughout the winter, the villagers ate well. When spring came, they all went out to plant again. This time there were fierce rains right from the start. Day after day water poured from the sky. The fields began to flood and everyone said they'd be lucky if any seedlings at all sprouted from the soggy soil. Again the fear of hunger and famine took hold in their hearts.

So, again Petro went to his father. This time he didn't wait for his father to ask; he simply told the old man what was happening and asked what he should do. Petro's father listened closely, his eyes brightening.

"Yes, of course, I know what to do. You must dig drainage ditches. That will save the seeds." Petro did as his father had told him, and soon his fields were flourishing again. As before, he went from house to house, telling his neighbors how to save their crops.

So it was that there was another bountiful harvest. Everyone was happy and the village celebrated with many harvest festivals. At one such festival, a group of men sat discussing their good fortune.

"It's all because of Petro," said one man. The others agreed. "Yes, Petro showed us how to farm. He saved the day." The talk continued on like this for some time.

Later, when they saw Petro at the festival, they called to him, "Ho, Petro!" Then they all gathered around him, slapped him on the back, shook his hand, and thanked him for his good advice.

"But there is one thing we can't figure out," said a man named Ivan. "How did you know how to conserve water? Where did you learn to build shelters from the wind and to dig drainage ditches?"

Petro's face reddened. He made up one story after another, but the men could see he was not telling the truth, and they kept pressing him.

Finally, when Petro could bear it no longer, he burst out, "It wasn't me at all. It was my father who saved us," he said. "You see, I did not kill him; in fact, he lives today. He has advised me about everything—drainage ditches, wind fences, mulching—everything. They were all his ideas, not mine." Then Petro confessed how he had only pretended to kill his father, how he had brought the old man back to the house and hidden him in the root cellar, and how he had kept him there for two years. He told them how his father had guided him in growing and preserving his crops.

"What?" Everyone was shocked. Some of the men became angry and started yelling at Petro. They demanded that he kill his father immediately.

"Wait, wait," said Ivan, "don't you see? Petro's father saved us all from starvation." The group grew quiet.

"You're right," another agreed. "We owe Petro and his father an apology."

With that, they all went to Petro's house and brought the old father up from the cellar. They shook his hand and thanked him for his advice and told him of their good fortunes. Then they apologized for saying that he should die. Petro's father wept with relief and so did Petro. After that, no one in the village ever died a red death again.

And so it is everywhere today. The red death disappeared from all of Ukraine. We do not kill old people anymore. We respect them and use their wisdom to guide us in living, for we know that their experience can be our salvation. 🐌

–Natalie O. Kononenko

Part III

Moral Stories

The Stolen Postoly and the Boiled Eggs

BONDARCHUK WAS UP TO NO GOOD.

This rich farmer was always plotting ways to get peasants to work his land for next to nothing and now he had his eye on Danylo, a big, strong man. He wanted the peasant to help with the year's crop, but how to enlist him? Bondarchuk stewed and schemed and twirled his long black mustache until he came up with a plan. Then he sent one of his servants to steal something from the peasant.

In the dark of night, Bondarchuk's servant sneaked into Danylo's hut. Careful not to wake the sleeping man, he tiptoed about, rummaging through the peasant's belongings. All night he searched for something worth stealing, but Danylo was so poor that he couldn't find anything. Just before dawn, the servant realized that Danylo had no real valuables, so he grabbed a pair of *postoly** (shoes) and ran out the door.

When Danylo awoke, he yawned and stretched and rubbed his eyes, as he did every morning. But when he reached for his *postoly*, they were gone! He scratched his head and tried to remember where he had put them, but he was certain that he had left them under the bed as always. Well, what to do? Outside the frost lay thick on the ground. Winter was on its way and Danylo wondered how he would survive without his shoes. As he sat sulking, the door swung open. It was Bondarchuk, the wealthy farmer who lived nearby.

"Why so glum, Danylo?" Bondarchuk asked.

"Why shouldn't I be sad?" the peasant replied sourly. "Some scoundrel has run off with my *postoly*, winter is on its way, and I haven't a cent to buy a new pair."

* postoly—*shoes; cheap peasant footwear.*

Bondarchuk feigned sympathy. "Oh, my dear friend, that is indeed terrible. But listen, don't worry. I'll buy you another pair of shoes and you can pay me back by working on my farm for a year."

The peasant thought this offer was ludicrous, but what else could he do? He agreed and went to work for Bondarchuk. Day in and day out he slaved, but Danylo was a big fellow and the boss fed him so little that he was always hungry. He soon became so weak that it was difficult for him to do his work. Finally he went to Bondarchuk.

"How can I work when my stomach rumbles and aches with hunger all day?" he complained.

Again the landlord pretended to feel sorry for Danylo.

"I'll tell you what, my friend," he said. "I'll have my wife give you a boiled egg every morning. That way you'll have more strength and you'll be able to work off all your debt by the end of the year. All right?"

"All right," agreed the peasant, relieved that at last his hunger would be eased.

For an entire year Danylo worked like a dog—plowing, planting, threshing— just to pay for a pair of shoes. The landlord's wife gave him a boiled egg every morning, and although he was still hungry, at least he had the strength to work.

From Danylo's sweat, the rich man prospered with bountiful crops and a big harvest. When the year was up, he saw how much Danylo had done for him and he sorely wanted the peasant to stay longer, so he summoned the man to his house.

"So you finally paid for the shoes," he said, stroking his long mustache.

"That's right," nodded Danylo.

"And did you get an egg to eat every day, too?" Bondarchuk furrowed his bushy eyebrows.

"Yes, I did," the peasant answered.

"Oh!" Bondarchuk gasped and rolled his eyes as though he were in great pain. "Do you know how much you have cost me?"

"What are you talking about?" cried Danylo. "What have I done?"

"What have you done? What have you done? Why, you have devoured three hundred eggs, that's what you've done," said the landlord. "If my wife had put those eggs under brood hens, I would have gotten three hundred chicks. And if those chicks had grown, they would have laid a thousand eggs. Those thousand eggs would have hatched into a thousand more chicks. I could have sold them at the fair for a sack of money." Bondarchuk paused for a moment and shook his head. "So you see, Danylo, you have cost me a sack of money. If I take this case to court, they'll make you work for me for at least another year to pay off your debt."

As the landlord spoke, Danylo became enraged. When Bondarchuk finished his tirade, Danylo blurted out, "Have it your way then, you cheat—take it to court. But I'll not work for you again—not even for another minute!" And he stomped off angrily.

Once he had cooled off, though, Danylo was filled with despair. How could he possibly win against a rich man? The poor peasant roamed aimlessly along the roads, agonizing over his fate, until he ran into an old *Hutsul** who lived in the area.

"What troubles you, friend?" the old *Hutsul* asked. Now, this *Hutsul* was not only old, but also wise. He carried a blue mirror in his pocket and when he looked into it, he could see where the rabbits slept, how the stars fell into the sea, and what made the sun smile. He understood the languages of trees and why the moon spread her skirts of melancholy over the hills.

"What's there to be happy about?" Danylo replied, downcast. He spilled out the whole story and ended by saying, "Bondarchuk has fixed me for good. I worked for him for a full year and now he's dragging me to court. What can I do?"

"A rich man's greed knows no bounds," the *Hutsul* said, "and he who becomes a sheep makes easy prey."

"So there's no hope?" Danylo whimpered.

The *Hutsul* continued, "Might makes right and beggars can't be choosers. The judge is a learned man, but in my mirror he would see nothing, for a judge's heart is always clouded."

 Then the old man took his mirror from his pocket and gazed into it. He glanced down to the ground and looked up into the sky. He looked all around to the mountains and forests. Suddenly, he smiled and called Danylo to come closer. He whispered something in the peasant's ear. Danylo nodded, smiled, and went on his way.

---

* Hutsul—*highlander or mountain dweller of the Carpathian region of Ukraine.*

When the day of the trial came, Bondarchuk arrived at court in full regalia. He strutted in like a peacock, dressed in a fine velvet suit. His face was flushed with excitement. The judge and the clerk took their places, and all three waited for Danylo's arrival. Minutes turned into hours, and as time passed, the three grew more and more agitated.

"Where is that fool?" Bondarchuk fumed and pulled on his mustache. The judge snorted and looked at his pocket watch and the clerk tapped his fingers nervously. Just when they were about to give up, Danylo burst into the room, heaving and panting.

"Excuse me, your honor," he said breathlessly, "but I have been very busy."

"What do you mean?" the judge responded brusquely.

"Well, I boiled some potatoes and planted them, boiled some barley and planted it, boiled some oats and planted them—"

Before he could finish, the judge interrupted, "What are you talking about? You can't get a crop from boiled potatoes or boiled barley!"

"Oh yes," said Danylo, "just as Bondarchuk says he would get thousands of chicks from the boiled eggs that his wife gave me."

"What?!" The judge turned to Bondarchuk. "What kind of eggs did your wife give to Danylo?" he asked.

"Well, uh, uh, boiled eggs, your honor," the landlord stammered.

The judge looked at the clerk, then at Danylo, and then at Bondarchuk. Then he burst out laughing. The clerk started laughing too, and so did Danylo. But Bondarchuk did not laugh. He stood there tugging on his mustache and looking bewildered. Suddenly he grabbed his coat and hat and rushed from the court. As Bondarchuk's carriage clattered down the road, he could still hear them laughing. And that's the last time the rich farmer tried to take a peasant to court. ⚘

The Two Daughters

Once there was a widow
and a widower who married. Each had a daughter and now the four lived together. The widow's daughter, Larysa, was a quiet, serious girl, but her stepsister, Marusia, was just the opposite. The truth is, the widower had spoiled his daughter, but he could not see that. In fact, he constantly criticized his wife's daughter.

"Why doesn't she work harder?" he would say to his wife. Whenever Larysa cooked dinner, the old man would say it was too hot or too cold, or seasoned poorly. Whenever she cleaned, he would point out a place that she had missed. Meanwhile, her stepsister, Marusia, did nothing, for although the girls were only a year apart in age, Marusia's father said she was too young for chores.

All this made Larysa grow more distant from her family. Her stepfather and stepsister accused her of being snobbish and only her mother remained loyal to her.

One day the two girls went to a village gathering. Larysa sat in a corner spinning her flax while her stepsister gossiped and flirted. Marusia left her flax near a candle, where it caught fire and burned up. By the end of the evening, Larysa had finished her spinning, but Marusia had accomplished nothing.

The two sisters walked home together in the moonlight. When they came to a fence, Marusia quickly climbed over it, but Larysa struggled because of the large spindle of thread she was carrying.

"Let me hold your spindle so you can get over the fence, sister," Marusia offered. Larysa handed her the flax and climbed over, but by the time she reached the other side, her stepsister had run on ahead. Marusia arrived home well ahead of Larysa and she told her parents that she had spun the flax and Larysa had burnt hers.

The father shook his head. "See how irresponsible your daughter is?" he exclaimed.

The next day, Larysa's stepfather suggested she go off to find work. His wife objected at first, but tensions were running so high in the household that she finally gave in.

So mother and daughter set out for the forest. They walked and walked until the sun began to sink.

"Mother, perhaps you should go now," said Larysa, "so you can get home before dark."

"But what about you, my daughter?" her mother asked.

"Don't worry about me. I'll find a place to sleep and look for work in the morning."

So the mother turned homeward and Larysa found a hollow treetrunk where she spent the night.

The next morning the girl continued her journey. She passed by an apple tree that was overgrown with weeds. The tree called out to her, "Please help me. If you pull these weeds and make me look nice, I'll repay your kindness one day."

Larysa quickly set to work. She pulled all the weeds, pruned the tree and watered it, and then went on her way.

After she walked a bit further, Larysa became thirsty. She saw a well in a field and went over to it for water. The well was old and crumbly.

"Please make me look nice again, miss," the well said. "I'll repay you someday if you do." Larysa rolled up her sleeves, scrubbed the well, and patched it. Then she took a drink of water and went on her way.

By and by she saw an old dog approaching her. His fur was dirty and matted. As he neared the girl, he gazed at her with his sad eyes. "Please clean me up," he pleaded. "I will certainly repay you for your kindness."

Larysa took pity on the dog. She washed him and brushed his fur till it glistened. Then she continued her journey.

After a time she came to an old oven that stood, cracked and peeling, by the side of the road. As the girl neared, the oven called out to her, "Please fix me. I promise I will be of service to you one day."

Larysa knelt to scrape and scrub the old oven. She mixed clay from the earth around it and patched all the cracks. When she had finished, she straightened up, brushed the dirt from her hands, and walked on.

Now the day was growing old and Larysa wondered where she might spend the night and where she might find work. Just then she saw an old woman approaching from the opposite direction.

"Hello, young lady," the old woman waved.

"Hello," replied Larysa. The old woman stopped to chat with the girl.

"What brings you this way, then?" the woman asked.

"I'm looking for work," Larysa explained.

"How fortunate. I'm looking for help," the old woman beamed. "Would you like to work for me?"

"Certainly."

The old woman took Larysa to her house. It was a small hut tucked deep in the woods and it was filled from top to bottom with marvelous things, like giant pine cones, rocks that looked like animals, and animal bones.

Larysa looked about wide-eyed, marveling at each new thing she saw. Then the old woman took her aside.

"Listen, what you need to do for me is quite simple. Every morning and every evening you must feed my forest friends. Here are some pots. Fill them with water and warm them on the stove, but don't let the water boil. Add flour to the water and stir it well. Then pour the mash into the feeding trough outside. Whistle twice. All manner of creatures will come—snakes, toads, lizards—but don't be afraid. They will simply eat their food and leave."

"As you say, then," said the girl. "I'll begin tonight."

When evening came, Larysa filled the pots with water, lit the stove, warmed the water, and stirred flour into it. She emptied the mash into the trough, whistled twice, and watched in amazement as snakes and toads and all manner of creatures slithered and crawled up from the woods. When they had finished eating, they crawled away.

This is how Larysa spent her days with the old woman in the forest. After a year had passed, the old woman said, "It has been one year since you began working for me. Now you must decide whether to stay another year, or leave. Either way, you have been a great help."

Larysa thought for a few moments. She was fond of the old woman, but she missed her home and her family. So she thanked the mistress for all her kindness and made ready to leave.

"Since you are going, please take this horse and cart," offered the old woman. Then she filled a chest with embroidered towels and shirts and many other fine things and gave it to the girl. Larysa thanked the old woman and they bade farewell to each other. As the girl drove off, the old woman waved tearfully.

It wasn't long before Larysa came to the oven that she had once cleaned. It was filled with fresh pies and warm bread. "Take some, my friend," said the oven, "for you have helped me." Larysa took some of each and drove on.

No sooner had she had gotten back on the road than a dog came running up to the cart. It was the same dog she had cleaned and brushed a year ago. Now it was carrying a beautiful bead necklace in its mouth. The dog ran up to Larysa, wagging his tail. He dropped the necklace at her feet and spoke.

"Take it," he said, "you have earned it with your friendship and good deeds."

"Why, thank you," cried Larysa, and she tied the necklace around her neck. Then she patted the dog and continued her journey.

On and on she went until she came to the well. Because she was thirsty, Larysa went up to it for a drink. Beside it stood a water jug and cup, both made of solid gold. Larysa filled the cup and drank from it. The water was sweet and cool.

Then the well spoke. "Take the jug and cup, miss. It's the least I can do to repay your kindness." So Larysa filled the jug with water, placed her new treasures in her cart, and drove on.

When she arrived at the apple tree, the girl could not believe her eyes. The tree stood lush and laden with fruit, as beautiful as can be imagined. "Help yourself," the tree said, "for you have helped me." Larysa guided her cart under the tree and filled it with apples. Then she drove home.

When she arrived, she called out to her family and everyone ran to meet her. They could not believe what they saw: a cart filled with treasures of all kinds—food, garments, gold—and Larysa wearing a lovely necklace.

"Where did you get these things?" her mother asked, "and where have you been all this time?"

"Working," the girl replied, "but please help me unload the cart now."

After Larysa's return, the family lived happily together for a time, but Marusia grew more and more jealous, especially because of the necklace. She told her father that it was unfair for only Larysa to have had the opportunity to work. She begged him to allow her to leave home as her stepsister had done.

Marusya's father finally consented. He asked his wife to take the girl to the same place she had taken her own daughter. "Very well, then," the wife agreed.

The Two Daughters

The next morning Larysa's mother took Marusia down the same path she had walked with her own daughter one year before. When they reached the spot where she had left Larysa, she said, "Well, here is where I turn around." And the two parted company.

Marusia found the same hollow tree where her stepsister had slept and she spent the night there. She slept late, though, and the sun was high by the time she began walking. The girl rushed along, knowing that she had little time to reach her destination. When she passed the apple tree, it was again all overgrown with weeds. The tree cried out to her, but Marusia pretended not to hear and walked quickly away.

Soon she became thirsty. When she saw the old well in the field, she ran to it. "Ugh, it's dirty," she complained. All the same, she drank from it.

"Please scrub me and make me look nice again," the well entreated. "I will repay your kindness."

"Hah!" cried the girl. "What could you ever do for me?" She ran quickly down the path.

By and by, Marusia ran into an old dog, all dirty and matted. The dog gazed at the girl with his sad eyes and said, "Please wash me and brush my coat. I will do a good deed for you one day."

"Ick," cried the girl, "I wouldn't touch you if you paid me in gold, you filthy thing!" Then she kicked the dog out of her way and ran down the road.

On and on she ran, until she passed an old oven at the side of the road. "Please clean me and patch me," the oven pleaded.

"Can't you see I'm in a hurry?" the girl snapped, and on she went with her nose in the air.

By then the day was growing old and Marusia wondered where she would spend the night and if she would find work as her stepsister had. Just then she saw an old woman approaching.

"Hello, young lady," the old woman called brightly.

"Hello," replied Marusia.

When she got a little closer, the old woman asked, "And what brings you here?"

"I'm looking for work," the girl replied.

"Would you like to work for me?"

"I suppose so."

So the old woman took Marusia to her home in the forest. When the girl arrived, she looked about suspiciously, and wondered if the old woman was crazy because she had such strange things in her home.

"What you need to do for me is quite simple," the old woman said. "You must feed my forest friends every morning and every night. First, take these pots and fill them with water. Warm the water on the stove, but don't let it boil. Then mix flour into the water, empty the mash into the trough out front, and whistle twice. All manner of creatures will come crawling up—snakes, lizards, and the like—but don't be afraid. They will simply eat the food and leave."

Marusia nodded as though she understood. "I'll start tomorrow," she said. Then she ate a big dinner that the old woman fixed for her and went to bed.

As usual, Marusia slept late. She woke with a start, quickly filled the pots with water, and set them on the stove to warm. Then she went back to bed. When she woke again, the water was boiling over. She hastily took the pots from the stove and stirred in the flour, but it all stuck together in a big lump. Marusia shrugged as if to say, oh well, better luck next time. Then she emptied the glop into the trough out front and whistled twice. All manner of creatures came in from the forest.

"Oooh!" Marusia wrinkled up her nose and went running back into the house. The poor forest creatures ate the hot porridge and died. When Marusia came back, they were all lying still on the ground.

"Mistress, come quick!" she yelled. "You said these creatures would eat and leave, but here they are all lying about."

The old woman came running and when she saw what had happened, she clutched her heart and wailed. "You've killed them—my precious forest friends," she sobbed.

But Marusia only shrugged. "They're just vermin," she said, and went back into the house.

Later the old woman came to her and said, "Since I won't be needing your services any more, you may leave. You can take the old horse tied out back." With that, she walked away.

Well, Marusia didn't know what to do, but with the old woman gone, the house seemed creepier than ever. Anyway, there was no one to fix her dinner and she didn't know how to cook, nor did she have any desire to learn. So she got on the horse and started for home.

By the time she reached the oven, she was getting hungry. "Perhaps there's some bread in the oven," she thought to herself. But when she looked inside, it was empty. She turned away, discouraged.

Then she saw the old dog running down the road, carrying a beautiful necklace in his mouth. It looked just like the necklace Larysa had worn. Marusia chased after the dog, but he growled and backed away from her. "You did not help me when I asked, and now you will not get the necklace," he said.

So the girl continued her journey. By and by she grew thirsty. When she saw the old well in the field, she jumped off her horse and ran to it. The water was very low, though, and there was nothing to draw it with. "You refused to help me, young lady," said the well. "You don't deserve even a drop of my water."

On and on the girl traveled, all the while growing hungrier and thirstier. When Marusia came to the apple tree, she knew she was almost home, but the thought of a nice, juicy apple made her mouth water. To her dismay, though, she found that she could not reach the fruit. It was all too high in the tree. Marusia grabbed hold of the trunk and shook and shook the tree, but no apples fell.

"None of my apples for you," said the tree. "You did not help me when I asked you." So Marusia kicked the tree angrily and left.

By the time she reached home, Marusia was exhausted, hungry, and thirsty. She dragged herself into the house.

"My daughter, what has happened?" cried her father, alarmed to see the girl looking so tired and disheveled. So Marusia recounted her story. When she finished, her father sighed and shook his head.

"You're lucky you weren't killed," he said. He was silent for a moment and then continued, "Perhaps you weren't made to be wandering out in the world. I think you should stay here from now on." Marusia just nodded.

And that's what Marusia did. She stayed home with her parents and became a bitter and cranky old woman. But Larysa had many more adventures. She learned how to do many things and she married a fine lad who worked just as hard as she did. Together they had a wonderful family and lived happily all their lives. ❧

Honesty and Dishonesty

ONCE THERE WERE TWO COUSINS,
one rich and one poor. Often they would chat together about life, or this and that, and almost always they disagreed about things. One day as they were walking together, the poor cousin asked, "Do you think it pays to be an honest man, cousin?"

At this the rich lad laughed, "Oh, cousin, you are so foolish. It is only with lies and deceit that you can ever become rich!"

But the poor cousin disagreed, "Surely it pays to be honest. Many would agree with me."

"Well, I'll make you a wager they don't. We'll ask the first three people we see. If they agree with you that honesty pays, I'll give you everything I own. If they agree with me, you give me everything you own."

The poor cousin thought for a moment. He could not afford to give away any of his possessions, but oh, what might he accomplish if he had his cousin's livestock and home! Surely people would agree with him that honesty pays.

"All right, it's a deal," he said. They continued down the road. On and on they walked, and soon they came upon a laborer who was walking the other way. As the man approached, the rich cousin started waving.

"Good day!" he shouted.

"Good day to you too," replied the laborer.

"Listen, we have a question for you," said the rich cousin. "Does it pay to be honest?"

"Ho!" the laborer snorted, "if it paid to be honest, I'd be a rich man. Why, I just worked the entire year—long and hard, too—and what do I have to show for it? My boss even cheated me out of three weeks' wages. No, I would say honesty definitely does *not* pay."

"That's one point for me," the rich cousin gloated. The poor cousin looked downward and grimaced, but said nothing.

They continued walking. By and by they met up with a wealthy merchant.

"Good day, sir," they greeted him.

"Good day to you too," he replied.

"I wonder if you could settle our dispute," began the rich cousin.

"Yes, yes, we want to know if it pays to be honest," the poor cousin quickly chimed in.

The merchant rolled his eyes. "What a question!" he exclaimed, "how do you think I became rich? To sell, you must trick your customers. A little lie here, a little lie there—it does no harm. In my line of work, I'm afraid it's not honesty that pays, but dishonesty." The merchant walked away, chuckling and muttering to himself.

"You see, cousin? That's two for me," said the rich lad. "There is no way you can win the bet now, but I tell you, if the third person we meet says honesty pays, we'll call it a draw." The poor cousin agreed and the two walked on.

By and by they came upon a priest. "Ah," thought the poor cousin, "surely the priest will agree with me," and his hopes were renewed.

"Good day, father," he greeted the priest eagerly.

"Good day to you too, my sons," replied the priest.

"Father, tell us, does honesty pay?" the poor cousin asked.

"Honesty?" The priest looked surprised. "Where can you find honesty in this day and age? All around I see only lies and deceit. The ways of the world are wicked, my sons. Honesty does not pay—only dishonesty." The old priest walked away, shaking his head sadly.

"You see?" cried the rich cousin. "Everyone agrees with me—even the priest! Now all your possessions are mine!" He rubbed his hands together and began making plans for his new property.

The poor cousin was so sad that he left his cousin without saying a word. He went home and said goodbye to his animals, then left his hut and wandered out into the world.

Soon the poor lad grew hungry. Thinking he might find some blackberries to eat, he went into the forest. He spotted a big thicket and had just started picking berries when he saw a bear. Before the bear could see him, he climbed a tree and hid among the branches. There he fell asleep, only to be awakened in the middle of the night by a strange ruckus. It was the evil spirits flying and they came to roost in the tree right next to the one where the poor cousin crouched.

The poor man could see that there were four spirits, one of which was the ringleader. After perching in the tree branches, the spirits began to speak with one another.

"What did you do today?" asked the ringleader.

"I wrecked a dam," replied the first spirit. "The overlord is cursing and whipping his laborers like mad, but there's nothing they can do. Many will die and others will fall into our clutches." He cackled loudly and jumped up and down in the branches, shaking the leaves, and the other spirits did the same.

"That's good," said the ringleader, "but not good enough." The spirits fell silent. "The three large pines at the edge of the forest could be felled into the river to start a new dam. The rest would be easy."

"Ah, but they don't know that," replied the evil spirit, and his brother spirits agreed.

Then the second evil spirit spoke. "I drained the village wells, my lord. It's a great hardship. Now the townsfolk have to walk thirty miles just to get water. Many will die of thirst and others will fall into our clutches." He clapped his hands and gave a shrill laugh, and again the tree shook with evil.

"That's good, but not good enough," said the ringleader. Again the spirits fell silent. "The villagers can make another well. All they need to do is move that big rock at the edge of town. There they will find all the water they could ever need."

"Ah, but they don't know that," said the second spirit. His evil brothers glanced furtively at one another and nodded in agreement.

Then the third evil spirit spoke. "I did a very nasty thing," he boasted. "I made the king's beautiful and beloved daughter fall ill with a terrible disease. Soon she will die. Surely the king will then fall into our clutches." All the spirits gasped at the thought of having the king himself within their power. Once again the tree rattled with evil.

"Yes, yes, that's good, but it's still not good enough," said the ringleader. The evil spirits fell silent once more. "If anyone were to sprinkle the princess with morning dew, she would recover."

"Ah, but they don't know that," replied the third evil spirit, and all his brothers agreed.

"True enough, but we still have work to do," said the ringleader—and off they flew into the night.

Overhearing all this, the poor cousin was astonished. He slept the night in the tree and when he woke, he told himself it was a dream.

"But what if it's not a dream?" he thought, "what if it's true?" He decided to go see if the dam was still standing.

As he approached the river, he could hear the angry shouts of the overlord and the groans of the workers. He saw the overlord standing with a whip in his hand. He saw the laborers sweating and struggling. They had welts on their backs. But the river flowed swiftly—they could not fix the dam quickly enough to stop it.

The poor cousin stepped up to the overlord and said, "Whipping your workers won't accomplish anything."

For a moment the overlord stood with his mouth open, and then he bellowed, "Do you have a better idea? You insolent fool, you!" He snapped his whip upon the ground.

"As a matter of fact, I do," the cousin replied calmly. "Give me your best man and we'll stop the river."

"Fine," snorted the overlord. He pulled a strong man off the line and shoved him toward the poor cousin. Together they felled the three trees into the river. Quickly the other workers finished the new dam. The overlord stood amazed.

"I am grateful to you, lad," he said. "Take this horse and 100 *rubles** for your trouble." The poor cousin took the money, mounted the horse, and rode off toward the village where the wells had been drained.

On his way there, he saw an old woman straining under a yoke strung with two buckets. She stumbled along awkwardly, water spilling everywhere.

"Good woman," he greeted her, "might I trouble you for a sip of water? It would lighten your load." The old woman sighed and set her buckets on the ground.

"How can I give you water when I don't even have enough for my own family?" she said.

"Don't worry," replied the young man, "I can show you a place near the village where there is water enough for everyone." So the old woman gave the

---

* ruble (rouble)—*Russian (Ukrainian) monetary unit. 100 kopecks equals 1 ruble.*

poor cousin a drink and then followed him to the village. As they neared the town's edge, the old woman ran ahead, telling everyone about the lad and his promise. Soon a crowd had gathered.

"This young man will save us all," the old woman announced. The villagers swarmed around the poor cousin and his horse, following them to the big rock.

"Now, if someone will just help me move this rock," said the lad, and several people joined him to push the rock away. Beneath it was a gushing spring of cool, clear water. The villagers laughed and danced and splashed themselves with water.

When the young man prepared to leave, all the villagers pressed money and food and gifts on him. Thus the poor cousin became richer than he had ever imagined.

He then rode off to the castle where the sick princess lay dying. On his way he stopped in the forest to collect dew. When he arrived at the castle, the young man demanded to speak to the king.

"Your majesty," he said, "I understand your daughter is gravely ill." The king nodded sadly and the lad continued, "I believe I can cure her."

The king shook his head. "What can *you* do?" he asked. "I've had the finest physicians in the land trying to cure her and they can do nothing." The king sighed deeply. "But if you insist, go to her. We will see what happens."

So the lad went to the princess's chamber. There she lay, pale and thin. It was plain to see that she was on the brink of death. He took out a small vial of dew and sprinkled it over the princess. Instantly she opened her eyes and smiled. At that the servants rushed in, exclaiming, "She's alive, she's alive. It's a miracle." They began feeding her, stroking her hair, and murmuring with happiness, for everyone loved the young princess. Soon she was walking about as rosy-cheeked and beautiful as ever.

The king was overjoyed. "You may have my daughter's hand in marriage, if you so choose," he said, "and when I die, you shall inherit the kingdom."

So it came about that the lad married the princess, and when the king died a few years later, the former poor man became king. He was a kind and just ruler, and the people loved him.

He had ruled for a number of years when a rich merchant came asking for permission to trade in the kingdom. The merchant was none other than the new king's rich cousin. When the king saw who it was, he ran to the man and embraced him warmly, saying, "Cousin, tell me about your life."

The rich cousin told the king of all his travels. When he finished, the king said, "When you and I were young lads, you told me that honesty does not pay. But it is through honesty that I became king, and you are just a merchant." Then he recounted the whole story of how he came to be king. When he ended his tale, the two cousins feasted together and drank wine. Before the cousin left, the king gave him many gifts and told him to remember that honesty pays.

Once the merchant left the palace, though, he was seized with jealousy and greed. "I deserve to be as rich as my stupid cousin," he said to himself, and he decided that he would go to the forest where his cousin had seen the spirits. Perhaps he could do the same as his cousin had done.

When he came to the tree that his cousin had told him about, he did not know what to do. He did not want to leave his possessions behind, lest he lose them, but it was difficult to climb the tree encumbered by heavy robes, jewelry, and sacks of gold. Well, he thought, perhaps these things would come in handy with the spirits. Certainly they would earn him some respect, and perhaps he could use his gold and jewels for bargaining. The merchant struggled and panted and finally got up the tree with all his possessions. He made himself as comfortable as he could among the branches. There he lay, draped with his jewels and furs, with bags of gold hanging from the branches around him. Just as he began to doze off, a great ruckus arose. It was the evil spirits flying to their roost. The merchant stirred and his sacks of gold swayed, jingling noisily. One of spirits heard the noise and saw the merchant.

"Look over there," he shouted, pointing to the tree where the merchant sat.

"Why, it's a rich merchant, loaded with jewels and gold," said another. At once they pounced on the man, taking everything from him—even his clothes. Then they flew off shrieking. The spirits left the merchant without a stitch or a penny. Now he was as poor as a church mouse, and that is how he lived the rest of his life. ☟

The Clever Maid

ONCE THERE WAS A
poor peasant who had nothing to his name. But he did have a daughter, and her name was Natalka. Through the years they managed to scrape by, but as the man grew older, he wanted to provide for his daughter so that she would have something when he was gone. He went to his landlord and asked if there were something he could work toward, perhaps a horse or a cow.

"Why yes," said the landlord, "I'll give you a cow and if you work for me for a year, you can keep it." He showed the peasant a rather sickly, thin cow. It didn't seem like a very good deal, but the peasant had no other choice, so he accepted the offer.

The peasant took the cow and went to work for his landlord. Day in and day out, he slaved in the fields, never allowing himself even a short break. In the meantime, Natalka cared for the cow and the cow became healthy and fat. When harvest time came, the peasant worked even harder and longer hours. In fact, he worked so hard that just before his year was up, he became ill. He missed three days of work and then reported back to the landlord to make up for the time he had missed.

"I'm sorry," said the landlord, "but you broke your promise. I want the cow back."

"Sir, I am willing to make up the time," the peasant protested, but the landlord would have none of it.

"A promise is a promise," he said, "the cow is mine."

The two men argued for hours, but they could not reach an agreement. Finally, the landlord suggested that they take the matter before the king, who was said to be a wise man. The peasant was tired of arguing, so he agreed.

Now, the king, as wise as he was, did not want to listen to this argument. When the two men began explaining the situation, he put up his hand and said, "Before you go any further, let me ask you three questions. Think about them and bring your answers to me tomorrow. Whoever has the right answers can keep the cow."

The two men looked at each other and shrugged.

"The first question is, what best fills a man's stomach? Next, what gives a man most pleasure? And finally, what travels fastest? Now go and think on it. Tomorrow you will bring me your answers."

So the two men departed. As they walked, the landlord started jabbering.

"I can't believe he asked such simple questions. Everyone knows it is meat that best fills a man's stomach and money that gives the most pleasure. As for what travels fastest, why, what else could it be but hunting dogs? Those are my answers and they are right. I know the cow will be mine."

The poor man said nothing, for he was deep in thought. The landlord was right, but surely the king was not looking for such obvious answers. He thought and thought. Still, he could not come up with anything, and by the time he reached home, he was confused and disheartened. He walked into the house, sank into his chair, and sighed.

"What's troubling you, father?" his daughter asked, for she could see he was distraught. The peasant explained what had happened and complained that he could not think of the right answers to the king's questions. Natalka smiled.

"That's easy, father. What best fills a man's stomach is our mother earth, for the earth feeds us throughout our lives. And it must be sleep that gives the most pleasure. Why else would we leave everything for it? What travels fastest? I say it is thought. Thought takes us anywhere in no time at all."

The girl's father chuckled, "You're right, Natalka. I will tell this to the king."

The next day the landlord and the peasant went to the king. "Have you the answers, then?" the king asked.

"Yes, yes," the landlord blurted out impatiently. "It's meat that best fills a man's stomach, gold that gives most pleasure, and hunting dogs that travel fastest. Now can I take the cow?"

"Wait just a moment," the king replied, and he turned to the peasant. "What have you to say?"

"I say Mother Earth best fills a man's stomach, for she nourishes him throughout his life. And it is sleep that gives most pleasure, for we give up everything for it."

"Hmm," the king stroked his chin pensively. "And what about the third question?"

"Nothing travels faster than thought," the peasant replied. "It can travel anywhere in no time at all."

"Well said," the king exclaimed. "The cow belongs to you. You are indeed a clever man!" The landlord stomped off in a huff, while the peasant stood there beaming.

"Actually, it was my daughter who came up with the answers," said the peasant, shrugging.

"What? A young girl who pretends to be as wise as royalty?" The king scowled with displeasure. He handed the peasant a basket of boiled eggs.

"You give these eggs to your daughter. She must put them under her hens to hatch. When the chicks are grown, the girl will roast three for me. I'll have them for breakfast tomorrow morning or you will go to prison."

The peasant stood with his mouth open, stuttering with dismay. "But, but, how can I ... how can she ... ?" he protested weakly.

"That's enough!" boomed the king. "Come back tomorrow morning with the roasted chickens."

The poor man was really discouraged now. He left in a quandary. Why had he agreed to let the king decide his fate? It had only made things worse. Maybe he should have let the landlord keep the cow. At least then he wouldn't be faced with prison. So he thought as he walked home with the eggs.

By the time he reached home, the peasant's eyes were filled with tears. His daughter met him at the door.

"What's wrong, father? Did my answers displease the king?"

"Oh, Natalka, now we have a real problem," the old man replied. Then he recounted what had happened, adding, "I'm supposed to bring him three roasted chickens tomorrow morning. What can I do?"

But his daughter just laughed. "That rascal!" she said, handing her father a pot of porridge. "Take this porridge to the king. Tell him we need millet to feed the chicks when they hatch. He should prepare his field and plant the porridge. As soon as the millet is ripe, he must reap it, thresh it, and send it to me, so I can feed the baby chicks."

The father did as his daughter had instructed, but the king was not amused. He took one look at the porridge and threw it to his dogs. Then he took a stalk of flax and handed it to Natalka's father.

"Tell your daughter to soak and dry and dress this flax, then spin it into a hundred yards of cloth. If it's not done, I'll put you both in prison for the rest of your lives."

The peasant stumbled home, crying. When Natalka saw him coming down the road with his head hanging, she ran to meet him.

"Father, father, what is it now?"

Her father handed her the stalk of flax. "The king says you're to make a hundred yards of cloth from this, or we'll both go to prison. What shall we do?" The old man buried his face in his hands.

Natalka shook her head as her father spoke. Then she went out to the apple tree in the yard, broke a tiny twig from it, and handed it to her father.

"You tell the king that if he wants cloth, I must have a spinning wheel. He can fashion it from this. Then I will spin his flax."

So the peasant trudged back to the castle and spoke again to the king. He told the king what his daughter had said and handed him the little twig.

The king threw the twig to the floor angrily. "This girl is a tough one," he thought to himself. Then he said aloud, "Go tell your daughter to come here. She must neither walk nor ride, be neither barefoot nor wear shoes, and come neither with a gift nor without one. If she cannot do as I have requested, you will both be hanged."

Hanged! Now the king was threatening him with death! The peasant returned home, sadder than ever. He told his daughter of the king's new demands and threw his arms into the air. "We are doomed," he lamented.

But Natalka comforted him, saying, "No, father, I will go to the king and everything will be fine. But first you must catch me a live rabbit."

So the father went to catch a rabbit while his daughter prepared for her trip. She harnessed a goat to a sled, caught a sparrow, and put a shoe on one foot but not the other.  When her father brought the rabbit, she put it under her arm. Then she placed one foot on the sled and, with the sparrow in hand and the rabbit under her arm, she left for the castle.

The king was waiting for her. As the girl approached, he saw that she had once again outwitted him, so he sent the dogs after her. Natalka saw the dogs coming, though, and released the rabbit. Immediately the dogs started chasing the rabbit.

Then the peasant's daughter entered the castle. "I brought this for you," she said as she held the sparrow out to the king. The bird flew from her hand and out the window.

Just then, two men arrived to have the king settle their dispute. It seems they had spent the night in a field, and during the night one of their mares had foaled. Both wanted to claim the colt as their own. They presented their case to the king, who said, "Tie the mares to two different trees. The foal will go to its rightful mother."

So the men tied their horses to two trees and then both began calling to the colt. The poor colt became terribly confused and ran off. Everyone stood staring, not knowing what to do next, until Natalka spoke up.

"You would have better luck if you did it the other way around," she said.

"What do you mean?" snapped the king.

"If you tie the foal to the tree, its rightful mother will go to it," she explained.

The men did as she suggested and as soon as the horses were free, one ran straight to the colt.

The king saw that the girl was wiser than he was and he shook his head. "You are truly a clever woman," he sighed. "Go home now. Go to your father and live in peace."

So the peasant's daughter returned home. Her father was overjoyed to see her, and from then on they had no problems with the landlord or the king. In fact, whenever the king needed advice on a difficult problem, whom did he send for? The clever maid, Natalka. &

The Gossip

TWO BROTHERS,
honest and hardworking men, lived on the outskirts of a small
village. They made a decent life for themselves by farming, hunting,
and fishing. But the younger brother had a weakness—he was a
gossip! Time and time again the older brother would confide in him
only to find out later that the whole town knew the secret. Now, this
troubled the older brother, but what could he do? After all, he only
had one brother, and there was no one else in the world for him to
turn to.

One day when the brothers went to check their traps in the
forest, they found a small sack of gold coins. Happily they exclaimed
at their good fortune, but the older brother immediately began to
worry, "Now my brother will tell the whole village and everyone
will want to get their hands on our money." He thought and thought
until he came up with a plan—yes, he would teach his brother a
lesson!

So the older brother went to the river and caught a pike. Instead
of bringing it home, he placed it in the garden among the peas. Then
he took a hare from one of their traps in the forest and put it in one
of his fish traps in the river.

Later that day, when the two brothers went out to check their
fish traps, the older brother said, "I've been hearing strange rumors
lately."

"Oh?" The younger brother immediately became interested.

"Yes, they say the fish are now living on the land and the forest
animals have moved into the river. What do you think of that?"

"Oh, what nonsense!" scoffed the younger brother. The older
brother agreed and said no more as they walked on toward the river.

When they pulled the fish trap from the river, though, there was the hare. The younger brother stood with his mouth agape for a moment and then said, "What if that rumor is true?"

"Oh, it can't be," the older brother assured him, and the younger brother agreed.

As they walked home, the older brother said, "Let's stop at the garden and get some peas for dinner." So they did, but as they were picking the peas, the younger brother suddenly cried out, "Th-there's a p-p-pike in the p-p-peas!" Sure enough, the older brother came and marveled at the fish, then lifted the pike into their basket and said, "Well, perhaps those rumors are not so far-fetched after all." Amazed, the younger brother agreed again.

After dinner the two brothers went to their parents' grave. On the way they saw two shadowy figures tussling at the side of the road. It was actually a bear killing and eating a cow, but because it was getting dark, the younger brother could make neither head nor tail of it.

"What's that?" he asked.

"Why, that's a dead man wrestling with the devil," replied the older brother.

The younger brother shuddered and said, "Let's get out of here." So they turned and went home without visiting the graveside.

A few days later, the two brothers went to the village. As soon as they arrived, the younger brother started grabbing people and blabbering, "We found a sack of gold coins at our traps in the forest." A crowd started gathering as the younger brother launched excitedly into his story, but the older brother looked at the younger as if he were crazy.

"Have you lost your mind? When did such a thing ever happen to us?"

"Why, just the other day," exclaimed the younger brother, "the same day we found the hare in the river and the pike in the pea patch." But the older brother just looked more puzzled.

"You remember," the younger brother went on, "it was the same day we tried to go to our parents' grave, but we ran into the devil wrestling with a dead man and we had to turn back."

The villagers began to snicker and the older brother took his younger brother by the arm, saying, "I think perhaps we should leave now. It sounds like you're getting tired."

The younger brother protested vigorously. "No, it's true," he insisted, but the townspeople were no longer interested. They shuffled away, chuckling and shaking their heads.

So the two brothers went home and from then on no one ever believed the younger brother's stories. Eventually, he just stopped telling them. And that is how the older brother taught his younger brother not to gossip.

The Old Father Who Went to School

ONCE THERE WAS A MAN
whose wife died and left him with three children to raise—two boys
and a girl. The man lived many years, his children grew, and eventually they married and moved into separate homes to start families
of their own.

The time came when the man could no longer care for himself,
and the old fellow thought to himself, "I will spend my remaining
days with my children." He packed his bag and went to live with the
oldest son and his family. The family met him at the door with smiles
and open arms. At first they treated him with respect. His shirts were
always mended and the wife made sure he had plenty of food at the
dinner table; she even cut his meat for him. But after a time, the bliss
wore thin and the son and his family became resentful. The wife
forgot to mend the father's shirts and the children poked fun at their
old grandpa. Even his own son was cruel—sometimes he would
glower angrily or fly into a rage over what seemed to be a minor
detail.

"You sound like a hog! Can't you eat without snorting?" Then
the children would snicker and the wife would tighten her lips, but
no one would say anything in the old man's defense.

Disheartened, the father thought to himself, "I am a burden to
my son and his family. Perhaps I should stay with my second son."
He packed his belongings and went to live with the second son and
daughter-in-law. At first they were happy to see him and there was
no end to their graciousness, but the old man soon realized that he
had only traded wheat for straw. Every bit of food he took was met
with angry glares from around the table. Then one night the old man
overheard the son and his wife talking.

"Things were hard enough before your father came. Now we have to take care of a helpless old man on top of everything else," the wife chided.

Much to the old man's dismay, his son agreed, adding, "But what can we do with the old fool?"

"There's nothing for me to do but go live with my daughter," thought the father. In the middle of the night, he packed his bag and left without even saying good-bye.

But things were no different at his daughter's. Everyone was kind at first, and they called him *didus'* (that is how they say grandpa in Ukraine), but things soured quickly.

"Must you eat so much?" the daughter scolded. And the son-in-law rolled his eyes at every word the old man uttered, as if to say, "What an old fool!" The old man realized that none of his children wanted him and he had nowhere to go. What could he do?

Then one day the children got together for a meeting to decide what to do with their father. As they sat around the table arguing, their voices grew louder and louder. So it was that their father, who sat in the next room, heard every word they said.

"But we have four little children to feed," said the eldest son's wife.

"Our home is so small, we have no room for an extra person," said the second son.

"You know we have no money," said the daughter, "we cannot afford to care for him."

And so it went on into the night. Tears rolled from the old man's eyes as he listened to his children discuss his fate. When he finally fell asleep, they were still arguing.

The next morning at breakfast, everyone seemed quite pleased and they told their father that they had a wonderful plan for him.

"Oh?" The old man brightened and his bleary eyes widened a little.

"Yes, father, we've decided to send you to school."

"To school?! But I am old. I'm almost blind. How can I go to school at my age?" he protested.

But the children insisted, "Oh father, don't be so difficult. You'll have your own desk to sit at, and we'll take turns packing your lunch. You'll be fine."

The old man hung his head, but kept silent. What else could he do? He did not want to go to school, but he didn't want to stay where he wasn't wanted, either. Finally he agreed, and he set off for the school, which was in a neighboring village.

Stunned by what had become of his life, the old man stumbled down the road. He turned things over and over in his mind, but he just could not make sense of it. After walking for some time, he saw a nobleman approaching.

"Hello there, good fellow," the nobleman greeted him.

"Hello to you too, kind sir," he replied.

"What takes you down this road?" the nobleman asked as he dismounted from his horse. The old man motioned the noble to come closer, and opening his lunch bag, offered some food.

"Uh, well, I am going to school in the next village," he shrugged.

"What? To school? Why, at your age you should be taking it easy and enjoying life! Why go to school?" So the old man poured out the whole story, and as he did the tears again began to stream down his cheeks.

"There, there now." The nobleman put an arm around the old man's shoulders. "Don't fret. School is not the place for you, but I have something here that might help." He took out a silk purse—the kind that only a nobleman would have—and took something from his saddlebag to fill it. Then he put the bag into a carved wooden box and handed it to the old man. Ooof, it was heavy! The old man shook the box, listened to it jingle, and smiled.

"Now, here's what you do," began the nobleman. And they ate bread and cheese together as the nobleman laid out his plan for the old father.

When the old man returned home, his children saw him coming. At first they were upset, but then they saw the box.

"What do you suppose the old duffer has there?" said one.

"Who knows? That box looks heavy though. Look how he's carrying it." said another.

Still another added, "Perhaps it's money or jewels." At that they all ran out to meet their father.

"*Didus', didus',*" they cried. Oh, they all acted so happy to see him, as they hugged and kissed him and patted his back. Then their gazes all fell to the box.

"Ah, you're wondering about the box," the old
man began. "Well, the strangest thing just happened. You see, when I was a young lad, before I married, I knocked about the world a bit and made a little money. I didn't want to spend it all, so I buried this box beneath an oak tree down the road. I guess I just forgot about it then. But I happened to pass by the old oak on my

way to school, and I thought to myself, 'Aha! I wonder if my little box of goodies is still under that tree! I dug and dug, and sure enough, here it is!' " He held up the box for his children to see and they all smiled and clapped their hands in anticipation.

"Let's have a look inside," said the eldest son, but the father shook his head.

"Oh, you'll get it all right, but only after I die. And the one who gets it will be the one who treats me the best." He turned and walked into the eldest son's house as the family stood with their mouths gaping. Then they all rushed after him, begging him to stay at their own houses or at least to have dinner with them. And did he have any shirts that needed mending? Oh yes, now there was no end to their kindness.

So it went. For the rest of his days, the old man was treated like a king, but he never let the box out of his sight. When he finally died, the children had an elaborate funeral for him, each trying to outdo the next with flowers and prayers and tears. The funeral lasted for days, but when it ended the children began to quarrel with one another. Each thought he or she alone deserved the box. They talked and talked, but they could not agree, so they asked the townsfolk to vote.

The whole village gathered together and each of the children made their case. Well, after all the speeches and hours of deliberation, the villagers decided that the children had all been equally good to their father and that they should divide the contents of the box evenly amongst themselves.

The eldest son ran to fetch the box. He returned, holding the box high and beaming from ear to ear. He set the box carefully in front of his siblings and the second son carefully opened the lid. The daughter lifted out the beautiful silk purse and gingerly shook it. Jingle, jingle, jingle—a sigh went through the crowd. Then the daughter slowly poured the contents onto the table. But—what did they see? Glass, glass, and more glass! The brothers and sister glanced nervously at each other and began desperately rummaging through the pile. Finally the eldest son exclaimed, "Why, our father left us nothing but glass!"

It was then that the villagers began to snicker. One after another they put their hands to their mouths as the laughter bubbled out. A little girl piped up, "You see what happened when you sent your father to school?"

An old man added, "I'd say he learned his lesson well—and now perhaps you'll learn yours!" &

Dovbush's Treasure

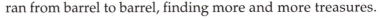

THINGS WERE NOT GOING WELL FOR IVAS'—
first a bad harvest and now his youngest son lying in bed sick with
fever. Winter was approaching, and as the days shortened, the poor
peasant wondered how his family would survive. Perhaps, he
thought, he could gather a little wood to sell in the village.

So Ivas' ventured into the forest, his head filled with worries.
With his eyes fixed on the ground, he scrambled about picking up
small scraps of wood. Hours passed but he still had only a small pile.

Farther and farther he wandered. Finally it started getting dark.
Ivas' looked around and realized that he didn't know where he was.
He was lost! What could he do? He kept walking in hopes that he
would find a familiar spot, but he recognized nothing. By then it was
almost too dark to see anything, so when the poor man spied a cave,
he crawled in, covered himself with leaves, and went to sleep.

Outside the cave the owls hooted, the wolves howled, and
darkness seeped over the earth. Ivas', dreaming strange dreams,
slept fitfully.

When he awoke, it was light. Ivas' looked around and saw that
the cave was full of barrels. Brushing the leaves from his clothes, he
crept over to one of the barrels, timidly lifted the lid, and peered inside.
Gold coins and jewelry! He went to another and looked—silver! Yet
another was filled with precious gems. With his heart pounding, Ivas'

ran from barrel to barrel, finding more and more treasures.

Suddenly he stopped in his tracks. He looked around.
Wasn't anyone here to guard the treasure? He had a strange
feeling that he was being watched, but he saw no one. Ivas'
called. No one answered. He called again. Still no answer. He
began scurrying from barrel to barrel, stuffing as much loot

into his pockets as he could. When his pockets were full, Ivas' jammed some into his boots and still more into his shirt. As he did, he kept looking nervously over his shoulder, but he saw nothing. Then, just as he was about to leave, he heard a voice.

"Put it back." Ivas' spun around. There stood the most horrible-looking man Ivas' had ever seen. His long, tangled hair and beard were filled with twigs and bits of leaves. His sunken eyes flamed wildly. His clothes, which had obviously been very fine once, were now ragged and covered with moss. Ivas' stood with his mouth open.

"Put it back, I said," thundered the old man.

"Wh-who are you?" stammered Ivas'. He was shaking so hard that the coins in his pocket jingled.

"I am Oleksa Dovbush* and this is my treasure," was the answer. And the old man went on, bellowing like a bull. "I shed innocent blood for this treasure and now there is a curse on me and my riches. The earth will not accept my body and God will not accept my soul. I cannot die."

Still shaking, Ivas' stood rooted to the ground, his eyes wide.

"Take only what you need and put the rest back," Dovbush continued, "or you too will suffer eternal damnation."

"Yes, yes, of course." Ivas' smiled weakly as he emptied first his pockets, then his shirt, and lastly his boots. When he finished, he picked up two gold pieces and put the rest back in the barrels.

"Now go," shouted the old man, pointing his gnarled finger toward the cave entrance. "Follow the stream until you come to a large rock, then climb the hill and you will be at the road to the village."

Ivas' wasted no time leaving. He followed Dovbush's instructions and soon found himself at the road to the village. As he walked, he kept thinking about what had happened and wondering if it was really true. Again and again Ivas' thrust his hand into his pocket and rubbed the two coins together to reassure himself. When he finally arrived home, Ivas's wife, who thought he had perished in the night, threw her arms about his neck and sobbed with joy.

---

* *Oleksa Dovbush is a historical figure. This* cossack *(independent warrior, frontiersman) was the leader of the* opryshky *(a band of outlaws) and, like Robin Hood, he fought against injustice and robbed from the rich to give to the poor. But he purportedly also ambushed and killed many people, keeping a lot of the riches for himself.*

It was not long after this day that Ivas' and his family began to prosper. The peasant used his gold pieces wisely. First he bought medicine for his son. Then he bought grain for the planting season. He planted the grain, tended his crop carefully, and reaped a good harvest. Ivas' had enough to feed his family and a little left over to sell. With his profits, he bought more grain and in the next season he again made a profit. Then he repaired his house and bought farm animals. First he bought a goat, the next year a cow, the next a horse, and then another horse. In the meantime, Ivas's wife expanded the garden. She grew more and more vegetables. She planted fruit trees. She bought hens and sold the eggs. The children too grew healthy and strong. Even the youngest, who had always been sickly, stopped catching cold after cold.

But all this prosperity did not go unnoticed. The neighbors began to talk, first a little, then more. Some whispered about sorcery and buried treasure. Others said Ivas' was a thief. Some even thought Ivas's wife was up to something.

Then one day Ivas' made the mistake of going to the tavern with some of the other villagers. He made an even bigger mistake by drinking too much *horilka* (that is, vodka). The men began to question and tease him.

"What's your secret?" demanded Ihor the blacksmith, pounding his big hairy hand on the table.

"Yes, tell us," the others chimed in. "How did you get so rich?"

"Are you a magician or did you steal it?" wheedled Dmytro, another peasant farmer like Ivas'.

At first Ivas' denied everything and said he had earned his money by hard work and careful planning. But the villagers kept pestering him. "All right, all right, I'll tell you," said Ivas', giving in at last. He recounted the whole story of how he had gotten lost in the woods and stumbled upon Dovbush's treasure. That only made the teasing worse.

"You really think you saw old Dovbush?" laughed the tailor they called Danylo. "Why, he's been dead for a hundred years. You don't believe in ghosts now, do you?"

"I can't believe you left behind all that treasure," Ihor said incredulously. "You must be crazy."

"Yes," taunted Dmytro, "no wonder you were always the poorest man in the village. You're too stupid to take advantage of opportunity."

"And he never even went back to check." Ihor shook his head sadly and everyone roared with laughter.

When Ivas' left the tavern, the men were still talking and their laughter rang in his ears. He tried to go back to work, but their words kept gnawing at him. What if he was a fool as they all said? Was he really so stupid?

Ivas' lay awake all night, tossing and turning, thoughts churning through his mind. Perhaps Dovbush had not been a man at all, but just a moss-covered stump. Maybe he had been so tired and frightened in the woods that he had dreamt Dovbush. Why not go back just to see? The children were getting older; they needed things, and his wife deserved nicer things too. Ivas' was tired of scrimping and saving. Surely a barrel of gold would solve all his problems.

By morning Ivas' knew exactly what to do. He set out for the forest, retracing his steps, walking along the same road on which he had returned years ago. When he reached the hill, he climbed down it. There was the rock and the stream. Ivas' followed the stream to the cave's entrance, then crawled inside. His heart was pounding so hard that his ears rang, but as his eyes grew accustomed to the light, he saw the barrels. Barrels and barrels and barrels! Ivas' ran to one and excitedly wrenched off the lid, only to recoil in horror. The barrel was full of writhing vipers and snakes! Gasping, he stumbled to another barrel and opened it—bats flew out. Underneath them rats squirmed and squeaked noisily. He staggered to a third barrel, bumped into it, and tipped it over. Out poured fleas, ticks, and other blood-sucking vermin. They scattered in all directions.

The wind howled, "Take only what you need."

The Man Who Danced with the Rusalky

THEY SAY
*rusalky** are girls who died before their time. It is never a good death, for these are young women who end their lives with broken hearts, because they have been rejected by their lovers. They throw themselves into a river and drown, but their spirits live on to torment men. During the day they swim in the river, dark shadows beneath the shimmering surface of the water. At night they emerge and sit on the riverbanks to comb their long, green hair and sing in the moonlight. It is said that *rusalky* are more beautiful than humans and that their voices hypnotize those who hear them. Sometimes the *rusalky* dance in the fields or climb trees and sing strange songs to entice men. A *rusalka* will hide among the branches so that she cannot

be seen—only her reflection in the water below is visible. If a man hears her singing and approaches, he sees only the reflection, not the spirit herself. When he bends to take a closer look, the *rusalka* jumps down from the trees onto his back and drags him under the water. There she wraps her long hair around his body and tickles him to death. There are many stories about *rusalky*. This is one.

There once was a young man named Oleksandr. All his life he had been hearing stories about the *rusalky* and he somehow got it in his head that he wanted to see one. It was all he could talk about or even think about—how to see a *rusalka* and live to tell of it. Everyone told him not to do it, but when they warned him of the dangers, Oleksandr would just nod and say, "I know, I know," and quietly continue his scheming. Thus his desire completely possessed him.

Rusalky (plural of *rusalka*) means water nymph or mermaid.

Now, there was an old woman in the village who was older than anyone, and she knew more than anyone too—more than anyone else could learn in an entire lifetime. Her name was Baba Vasylykha. Everyone said she was born with a sixth sense and that she had many powers. Some called it white magic, because she used it only for good. One day Oleksandr went to her and told her of his desire to see a *rusalka*.

"How should I do it?" he asked. "What do you advise?"

The old woman shook her head gravely. "No," she said, "this is a bad idea." Then, like everyone else, she tried to discourage the young man, recounting the stories and warning of the dangers. But this only fanned the flame of his desire. Oleksandr kept insisting until the old woman realized that she could not dissuade him.

Finally she said, "Well, if you must go then, at least take this precaution. Remember, *rusalky* always strike from behind. They cannot attack a Christian man from the front because he wears a cross. But if they jump onto the man's back or shoulders, his body shields them from the cross and they can do what they wish. If you wear two crosses, one in front and one in back, the *rusalky* will not be able to harm you."

Oleksandr thanked the old woman profusely and ran to the church to buy a second cross. The priest looked surprised. "Why a second cross?" he asked. "Isn't one enough for you?" But Oleksandr said that there was no harm in having two, and he flashed his money before the priest's eyes. The deal was made.

Oleksandr did not go to the river immediately, but waited for the full moon. That was supposed to be the best night for seeing *rusalky,* and anyway, he reasoned, in the light of the full moon he could see better and protect himself.

When the night of the full moon came at last, Oleksandr went to the river. As he walked, his excitement filled him and all his senses seemed to expand. He took a deep breath and tasted the cool night air. In the moonlight the whole earth seemed to glow with a strange blue light. As Oleksandr approached the river, he heard the rushing water and above it—yes, a beautiful, mournful song, sweeter than anything he had ever heard before. Then he saw her. There on a dock at the river's edge sat a beautiful young woman clad in a flowing white gown. She was singing of lost love, and as she sang, she caressed and combed the long, dripping tresses that hung over her shoulders and down her back.

So this was a *rusalka*. Oleksandr's heart quickened as he slowly crept toward her. Closer and closer he came until he felt he could almost reach out and touch her. Then Oleksandr stepped onto the dock. Creak! The *rusalka* spun around, startled. She looked at Oleksandr with her large, sad eyes—strange eyes that seemed to be glazed over with a pale blue film. She smiled wanly and motioned Oleksandr to come to her. Oleksandr could not take his eyes off the beautiful maiden. He sat beside her until she finished combing her hair. Then she took the boy by the hand and led him up the stream. Oleksandr stumbled along, totally entranced.

The *rusalka* led the boy to a clearing in the woods not far from the river. There eleven *rusalky* danced in a circle. When they saw Oleksandr and his companion, they stopped and gazed at the two with the same sad, blue eyes and mournful smiles that Oleksandr's *rusalka* had. Then the circle opened and Oleksandr's *rusalka* stepped in, beckoning Oleksandr to join her in the dance. Without hesitation, the boy took the hands of two *rusalky* and made the circle complete once more.

The dance began slowly. Stepping and dipping in time, Oleksandr and the twelve *rusalky* moved and swayed, gradually increasing their pace. Oleksandr felt as though he were floating on air. He had never been so happy. His body throbbed with pleasure and excitement and he wondered if he was dreaming. Then the circle began to spin, faster and faster. Oleksandr looked about and saw a white blur as the *rusalky's* gowns trailed through the darkness in the blue light of the moon. Oh, it felt so wonderful, Oleksandr laughed aloud. He was in ecstasy.

Suddenly, they all stopped. Oleksandr felt the sad blue eyes of the *rusalky* upon him and he saw that they were all glazed over with the same pale blue film. His hand shot up to the crucifix around his neck—there were two there! All the fast dancing had made both crosses flop to his chest, and now his back was unprotected. The *rusalky* pounced.

 No one knows quite what happened next. The *rusalky* did not harm Oleksandr, but something strange happened, to be sure. When the villagers found him the next morning, there was not a mark on his body. In fact, he was home, sleeping in his own bed. Perhaps the *rusalky* had carried him there, or perhaps he had stumbled home on his own, but there he lay, his two crosses nested against his heart.

"Oleksandr, Oleksandr," they called to him. He stirred and opened his eyes—eyes that were glazed over with a faint blue film.

That's all—nothing else happened. Oleksandr did not sicken or lose weight. He went about his business and did all of his work just as before, but he was strange now. If spoken to, he always answered politely, but his eyes—those pale blue eyes—seemed always to be looking past to something beyond. And he sighed a lot, as though he were longing for something or someone far away.

Oleksandr never married. He grew to be an old man all alone, always going about quietly, always doing as he should. Always looking past you with those pale blue eyes. &

–Natalie O. Kononenko

Part IV

Legends and Fairy Tales

The Golden Slipper

ONCE UPON A TIME
there lived a man and a woman and their two daughters. Well, the oldest daughter favored her mother and the woman spoiled the girl, ignoring the younger. But the youngest daughter favored her father and he, in turn, doted on Hanna—the one who took after him. So things went along until the father took ill and died. The whole family grieved sorely, but especially young Hanna. She missed her father so! To make matters worse, the mother seemed to blame the girl for her husband's death. She became very aloof toward Hanna, as though she did not recognize the girl as her own.

Fortunately, Hanna's grandmother came to live with the family soon after the father's death. The old woman was quick to see the mother's unfairness and she tried to make up for it with the younger girl. When Hanna's mother scolded her or heaped her with household chores, Grandma would sneak a sweet bun into the girl's hand, or leave a pretty woven sash under her pillow.

But the grandmother was old and it wasn't long until she grew feeble and ill. One day as she lay sick in her bed, she called Hanna to her side. She handed the girl a tiny black seed, saying, "Take this

seed, my child, but don't tell the others of it. If anything bad happens, plant the seed and water it. From the seed will grow a willow tree. The tree will help you with whatever you need."

Silently, Hanna took the seed and put it in her pocket. Then the old woman closed her eyes and died.

From that time on, Hanna's mother and sister became even more haughty and cruel. They treated the girl like a servant, as though they themselves were royalty. Hanna worked hard trying to please them. Every day she cooked and cleaned from dawn till dusk, with never a cross word to her mother or her sister. She worked so hard that she didn't have time to comb her hair, or fix her own clothes, or even bathe properly, and she went about in tattered clothing. The townsfolk called her little rag-a-muffin.

Did this make Hanna's mother and sister pity her? No, it only made them hate her more. They told Hanna to sleep in the barn and they sat about the house gossiping, eating cakes, and getting fat while Hanna slaved.

One day the mother announced, "We're going to church today. While we're gone, I want you to husk this rye." With that she handed Hanna two huge bundles, adding, "and don't forget to clean the house and make dinner for us."

Hanna watched forlornly as her mother and sister dressed themselves for church in fine clothing. When they had gone, she went to fetch water for the husking. As she walked to the spring, she grew sadder and sadder. How could she manage all this work? She wished she could have gone to church with her mother and sister. Hanna's heart sank and by the time she reached the spring, she was weeping uncontrollably. Dropping her buckets, she fell to her knees. Tears streamed from her eyes. She was sobbing so hard she had to steady herself by wrapping her arms around her middle. As she did, her hand brushed across her pocket. She remembered the tiny seed and her grandmother's words: "If anything bad happens, plant it. . . . The tree will help you with whatever you need."

Sniffing back her tears, Hanna reached into her pocket and pulled out the tiny seed. Hurriedly she dug a hole, planted the seed, and poured spring water on it. Nothing happened and again the tears came. Hanna cried and cried until she fell asleep.

Who knows how long she slept, and whether or what she dreamed, but something certainly happened. Hanna awoke beneath a beautiful willow tree. Its branches waved gently in the breeze and beside it the spring bubbled gaily. As she stood marveling at it all, Hanna heard her name being called—first softly, then louder.

"Hanna, Mistress Hanna," the voices called. The tree branches parted and out stepped a dozen maidens, one by one. Cooing like doves, they gathered around the girl and touched her gently.

"Why are you crying?" they asked. "What is it you need?"

Hanna told them about her impossible chores, and the eldest of the girls took her by the hand and looked into her eyes.

"Don't worry about the rye or anything else. Just go to church and leave the rest to us. It shall all be done as you wish."

"But I can't go to church looking like this," Hanna protested. Then the maids began circling around her, washing her, brushing and braiding her hair, and draping her with fine clothes, ribbons, and jewels. All the while they laughed and chattered softly.

When they finished, Hanna was dressed in a beautiful gown as blue as the sky and as shimmering as the sea. Her hair was braided and pinned on top of her head and she wore tiny golden slippers on her feet. She twirled around and laughed softly. Then out of nowhere a bridled horse appeared. The maidens helped Hanna get on it and off she rode to church.

When Hanna stepped into the cathedral, all eyes turned to see the lovely lady, but no one recognized her, not even her own mother or sister. Murmurs rose as the townspeople speculated about her.

"Perhaps she is the princess from over the mountain," said one.

"Maybe she is a queen," said another.

All through the service, the villagers whispered this way, stealing glances at the girl from time to time. But there was one person who did not whisper, nor did he take his eyes from Hanna. The prince, who happened to be attending Mass in the village that day, was quite taken with the beautiful stranger.

When the service ended, Hanna was the first to leave, hurrying from the church to her horse and galloping away in a cloud of dust. As the crowds poured out, they searched in vain for the lovely young woman. No sign of her lingered.

Meanwhile, the horse brought Hanna back to the willow tree. Quickly she changed from the fine gown back into her old, tattered clothes and ran home. Inside, the husked rye lay neatly on the table, the house was spotless, and a pot of soup bubbled briskly on the stove.

Moments later, when Hanna's mother and sister arrived, they were astonished. Their mouths opened into little circles, but when their eyes fell on Hanna, the circles quickly closed and gave way to frowns.

"Where's dinner?" the old woman demanded, settling her huge bulk into a chair at the table.

"Dinner's ready," Hanna replied softly as she served the two.

As they ate, the mother and sister prattled on about the beautiful lady and the young prince who had been in church. Hanna listened quietly.

The next Sunday, the old woman and her eldest daughter again went to church, leaving Hanna behind to clean, husk barley, and cook dinner. As soon as they left, Hanna rushed to the willow tree. The limbs swayed and the spring bubbled, and again she heard her name being called. Then the twelve maidens stepped from the tree to ask her wishes.

After Hanna explained her chores, the maids set to dressing her in the beautiful blue gown and golden slippers. Then the horse arrived and carried Hanna to church.

As Hanna stepped into the church, heads turned and a flood of whispers arose. The prince, who had attended in hopes of seeing the maiden again, asked his courtiers who this young lady was and where she came from. No one knew.

After the service, Hanna raced back to the willow tree, changed clothes, and ran home. Meanwhile, the prince and his courtiers had begun questioning everyone in town as to who the beautiful maiden was. Everyone's answer was the same: "We don't know."

Finally, a young boy replied, "I don't know who she is, but I know how to find out." When the prince begged the boy to tell, the youngster explained that if pitch was put on the spot where the lady stood, her foot would get caught and she wouldn't be able to leave.

"Ah!" said the prince, and that's what he did.

The following Sunday, when Hanna arrived at church, everyone again gawked and stared. She stood in her usual spot with her head bowed in prayer. After the service, she turned to leave, but the pitch held fast and she could not budge. Panicked, she pulled and pulled, and finally wrenched her foot from the shoe. She was so distraught that she went running from the church without it. The prince's courtiers raced to the spot where Hanna had stood and pried the shoe from the pitch.

Well, the prince did not have his young lady, but he did have her slipper—a tiny golden slipper, more delicate than any shoe he had ever seen.

"Whoever fits into this slipper," he announced, "will be my wife." Then he and his courtiers began searching the village for the owner of the slipper. First they went to the nobles' houses, then they went to the houses of merchants and villagers, and finally they went to the homes of the peasants. Having heard the prince's promise, all of the young women tried their best to fit into the golden slipper, but none succeeded.

In the meantime, Hanna had gone home and served dinner to her mother and sister. Conversation once again settled on the prince and the young lady. "He said he would marry whoever might fit into that golden slipper," said the mother.

"Yes," agreed the older girl, "perhaps he'll come here and I'll have a chance to try it on."

"Me too," said Hanna brightly.

But her mother scowled, snarling, "You're not even fit to be seen by a prince!" Hanna's sister snickered and Hanna hung her head meekly.

When the prince and his courtiers arrived at the house, Hanna's mother ordered her to hide in the closet. "Royalty does not want to be bothered with the likes of you," she said haughtily, pushing the girl into the closet and closing the door. Hanna's sister again snickered. Then the mother ran to the door, all smiles.

The prince entered and asked if there were any young women in the household.

"Why, yes," the mother smiled, and she beckoned to her eldest daughter. The girl was only too eager to try on the golden slipper. She struggled and groaned, but no matter how hard she tried, she could not get her clumsy foot into it.

Just then Hanna, who was still in the closet, sneezed, "Ah-ah-ah-CHOO!"

"What was that?" demanded the prince.

"Oh, nothing, nothing." The mother and her daughter put on false smiles, but the prince saw through them and told his courtiers to search the house. They looked under furniture, behind curtains, and behind doors. When they opened the closet where Hanna stood, one of the men exclaimed, "Why, look here then!" And all gathered around.

"Don't pay any attention to that filthy thing," the mother tugged at the prince's sleeve, "she is just a servant." But the prince pulled away from the old woman, took Hanna by the hand, and led her to a chair. There her foot almost glided into the slipper, with no struggle at all.

Hanna's mother and sister stood with their mouths open. The prince took Hanna's hand in his and led her from the house, beaming with joy.

On the way to the palace, they stopped at the willow tree, and Hanna dressed once more in all her finery. When they reached the castle, they married, and a joyous wedding it was. The celebration lasted for weeks.

As for the willow tree, it's still there beside the bubbling spring. And if your heart saddens or life is unkind, you can go there as I do, for there really are happy endings and wishes are meant to come true.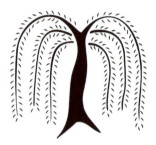

Oh! Lord of the Forest

IN DAYS LONG AGO,
when many strange things happened, there lived an old man and an old woman and their son Ivan. Now Ivan was a lazy fellow, and although he was nearly grown, he would not lift a finger to help his parents. While they slaved in the fields with their backs bent, day after day, Ivan sat by the fire dozing. Every so often he would open his eyes and stir the coals. In the evening, when his parents returned from their day's labor, Ivan would still be sitting there in front of the dying embers. If his folks made dinner, Ivan would certainly eat it, but if not, well, Ivan would go without.

Every day, Ivan's parents grew more distressed by their son's lack of ambition and his lazy behavior. As they worked in the fields, they grumbled to each other.

"Our son is worthless," the father would say. "Who will take care of us in our old age?"

The mother would shake her head and moan, "Oh, such a cross to bear. Is there nothing we can do to teach Ivan to work? It's not as if we're poor examples." And so the conversation would go.

Then one day the mother had an idea. "Maybe our Ivan should learn a trade in the village," she suggested. "Tailoring is not hard labor and surely our son could learn enough to make a living."

So the father and the mother went to town and spoke to the tailor. The tailor agreed to their proposal and took Ivan on as his apprentice. Ivan went to work for the tailor, but after three days in the village, the lad left. He went straight home and plopped himself into his favorite chair by the fire.

When his parents returned that evening, there was Ivan, in front of the fire as always.

"Why, you good-for-nothing fool!" the father shouted.

"How could you let us down like this?" the mother cried. But Ivan just shrugged and stared into the fire, stirring the coals as if nothing had happened.

The next day, Ivan's parents again complained to each other and tried to come up with a scheme to change Ivan's ways.

"Perhaps being a cobbler would be more to his liking," suggested the father. So the mother and the father went to the village again and arranged for Ivan to become a cobbler's apprentice. Then they brought him back to town.

Again Ivan stayed for only a short time and then ran home. His parents yelled and scolded, but Ivan paid them no mind. After some deliberation, they decided to try their son out as a blacksmith.

"It's more physical," said the father, "and not as complicated as being a tailor or a cobbler."

All the arrangements were made and Ivan was delivered to the blacksmith, but once again he returned home to sit by the fire.

"You ungrateful nincompoop!" his father roared, "This time I'll take you so far, you won't ever come back!" And he grabbed the boy by the scruff of the neck and dragged him down the road, while the mother stood at the door weeping.

Ivan and his father walked and walked and walked. They came to a forest so thick and dark that all they could see was the ground beneath their feet. By the time they reached the other side, they were very tired. Looking around for a place to rest, the father said, "Let's sit for a spell." He shuffled over to a burnt tree stump, lowered himself onto it and sighed, "Oh!"

No sooner had he spoken than a gnarled little man crawled up out of the stump. There he stood with his hands on his hips. He was only about knee-high and he was green as grass from head to toe, including his scraggly beard that hung to the ground.

"WELL, what is it you want?" the little man demanded.

"Wh-what? What do you mean?" the father stammered.

"You called me," scowled the little man. "I am Oh! Lord of the Forest, and you called my name. Now tell me what it is you want, but be quick about it because I have things to do."

The father sighed. "We want nothing from you. I am only looking for work for this lazy son of mine." He shook his head sadly.

"So where will you go?" asked Oh!

"Wherever the road leads us," said the father, "far enough that this lad won't come running home tomorrow." He told the little man how Ivan had left all his jobs, embarrassed his parents, and become a burden to them.

"Why not leave him with me, then?" said Oh!, "I'll teach him a thing or two, I guarantee it." And he gave a little laugh.

At this, the father brightened, but Oh! quickly became serious and shook his finger at Ivan's father, adding, "but I'll take him only on one condition."

"What's that?" Ivan's father asked.

"I will keep him for one year and no less. When you come back for him, if you recognize him, he's yours. If not, he's mine for another year."

Well, that sounded fair enough, and the two agreed, even shaking hands to seal the bargain.

Ivan's father turned homeward and Oh! led Ivan to his home in the other world beneath the earth. Oh!'s house was green and so was everything in it, even his wife and children. Wood sprites and nixies flew all around them, and they too were all green as green can be.

"Bring us some food," said Oh!, and the wood sprites and nixies set before them huge plates of green food. Ivan ate his fill, and when he had finished, Oh! looked him straight in the eye.

"Young lad, fetch me some wood from the wood pile now, and chop it," Oh! ordered.

Ivan walked off into the forest. Whether he did any work at all, no one knows, but after a time Oh! came looking for him. Ivan was lying by the woodpile, snoring. Oh! burst into a terrible rage. He ordered his servants to tie Ivan to the woodpile with ropes, and then he set fire to the whole lot of it. The flames shot up, and the fire blazed and blazed, till all had turned to ashes and been scattered by the four winds.

All, that is, except for one tiny cinder. Oh! took the cinder in his hand and sprinkled living water on it. *Whoosh*! Ivan came back to life, but now he was stronger, brighter, and more handsome.

"Now, go chop me some wood," Oh! commanded. So again Ivan left and again Oh! found the boy sleeping by the woodpile, and again Oh! burned it all to ashes to be scattered by the four winds. Then Oh! sprinkled living water on the one last cinder and brought Ivan back to life, even stronger, brighter, and more handsome than before. This happened one more time, and now the boy was as fine a man as can be imagined.

So Ivan worked for Oh! and time passed. At the end of the year, Ivan's father came to find his son. He journeyed though the forest, found the old tree stump, and sat upon it with a sigh, "Oh!"

No sooner had the word left his lips than Oh! climbed out of the stump.

"Well, well, what brings you here now, old fellow?"

"I've come for my son Ivan," replied the old man. Oh! winced and his eyes darted about nervously.

"Quite right, a year has passed. Follow me, then, but remember our agreement. If you recognize your son, he's yours, but if not, he will serve me another year."

"Of course," nodded the father and he followed Oh! into the nether world. As they approached Oh!'s hut, the little man took a handful of millet from his pocket and scattered it on the ground. Dozens of roosters ran up and began pecking at the grain.

"So then," Oh! smirked, "which of these roosters is your son?"

Ivan's father looked from one rooster to the next, but they all looked the same. He shook his head sadly. "I-I've no idea," he stammered.

"Ha! Then he's mine for another year." Oh! rubbed his hands together greedily. "Run along then, and don't come back till next year."

After the second year passed, Ivan's father came again. This time Oh! led the father to a flock of rams.

"Now do you recognize your son?" wheedled the little man. Ivan's father looked at the rams, but they all looked the same. Again he shook his head sadly.

"Aha! You see, you'll never recognize him. Your son will stay another year and another and another. Why keep coming back, old man?"

Ivan's father left with his head hanging low. But he did not give up, and after the third year had passed, he set out again to find his son. As he walked through the dark forest, he came upon an old, old man with white hair and a white beard and white clothes and pale, pale skin.

"Hello, good man," greeted the old one.

"Hello to you too, grandfather," replied Ivan's father.

"What brings you here?"

"I'm going to try to get my son back from Oh!"

"Ah," said the old one, "and how did Oh! manage to get your son from you in the first place?" Ivan's father told the old man the whole story about his lazy son, their journey, the bargain with Oh!, and how he had been tricked by the scoundrel for the past two years.

The old man shook his head, "You made a bad deal. Oh! will be turning you round and round for years to come."

Ivan's father agreed ruefully. "But isn't there anything I can do to get my son back?" he asked.

The old man cleared his throat. "Well, now that you ask, yes. This time, when Oh! leads you to his home, he will show you a flock of doves. As you might guess, they will all look alike and they will all peck at the grain Oh! throws to them—except one. That one will be sitting under the pear tree, cleaning its feathers. That one will be your son."

Ivan's father thanked the old man and went on his way. Soon he came to the clearing where the old stump stood. "Oh," he groaned as he lowered himself onto the stump, and up popped Oh! Lord of the Forest.

"Haven't you given up yet?" he grinned wryly. "Well, come on then." He led Ivan's father down into his green world and whistled three times. A flock of doves settled around the two men and Oh! began throwing wheat to the ground.

"Well, which is your son?" Oh!'s eyes glinted. Ivan's father looked and looked. All the doves looked the same, and all pecked at the grain Oh! threw. Then he saw the one sitting under the pear tree preening, just as the old man had said it would be.

He pointed excitedly, crying, "Why, that's him, underneath the pear tree. That is my son."

Oh! scowled. "So it is," he said, and immediately the dove changed into a man—a fine, strong, handsome young man. Father and son opened their arms to each other and embraced.

After a few moments, the father said to Ivan, "Come, let us go home, son." Oh! stomped into his little green hut, and Ivan and his father set out for the long journey home.

As they walked, they told each other of all the things that had happened in the past three years. "Your mother and I are getting so old now, we can hardly work any more," said the father. "We have no money at all. And you have nothing either, even after working three long years. I just don't know how we'll manage."

"Don't worry, father," replied Ivan, "I'll think of something." They continued walking in silence until they came to the edge of the forest, where they saw a fox being chased by a hound.

"The nobles are out fox hunting," said the father.

"Yes," Ivan replied, "and that gives me an idea. I will change myself into a hound and run down that fox. When the lords see me, they will offer to buy me from you. You can sell me for 100 *rubles**, but be sure to keep my leash." Before his father had a chance to reply, Ivan changed into a sleek greyhound. He ran down the fox, and when the noblemen came galloping out of the woods they saw the dog.

"Is that your dog, old man?"

"Yes, yes it is."

"What will you take for him?"

"100 *rubles** and not a *kopeck* less." The nobles talked amongst themselves and gathered the money together.

"Here you are, old man."

"And that doesn't include the leash," Ivan's father added.

But the nobles just laughed. "What would we want with your old leash anyway? We have many fine leashes of our own." They took the dog and galloped away. As soon as they sent the dog off after another fox, Ivan changed himself back into a man and ran to his father. They started off again, but it wasn't long till Ivan's father began complaining again.

"You know, 100 *rubles* won't go far, son," he said.

"Don't worry, father," replied Ivan. "I can always get more. See over there where those young nobles are gathered? They're hunting quail with a falcon. I can turn myself into a falcon, catch the quail, and then they'll want to buy me, just like the nobles wanted to buy the dog. You can sell me for 300 *rubles*, but don't take any less and be sure to keep my hood." So Ivan turned into a falcon and quickly flew to the place where the young lords were quail hunting. He swooped and soared and soon had caught a fat quail, which he carried back to his father. The nobles, seeing this amazing bird, came galloping up on their horses.

"Is that your falcon?" they asked.

"Why, yes."

"How much would you sell him for?"

---

* ruble (rouble)—*Russian (Ukrainian) monetary unit. 100 kopecks equals 1 ruble.*

"300 *rubles* and not a *kopeck* less," said the old man.

"Ooh, that's steep!" The lords talked among themselves and gathered money together.

"Here's 100 *rubles*, old man," they said.

"No, I won't take less than 300. And that's without the hood." So the nobles talked again and collected more money.

"We don't need the hood—we have our own, but here's the 300." So Ivan's father handed over the falcon and they rode off with it. As soon as they sent him after another quail, Ivan changed back to his human form and returned to his father. They continued walking.

Soon Ivan's father was grumbling again. "100 *rubles*, 300 *rubles*, what good will that do? We need at least 1,000," he said.

"I think I can manage that," said Ivan and then he was silent for a moment while he thought.

"See that town up ahead?" He pointed at the horizon. "The villagers are holding a fair. I'll turn myself into a horse and you can sell me there for 1,000 *rubles*. But don't take any less, and be sure to keep my harness." With that Ivan transformed himself into a fine steed. Ivan's father led the horse into the village and as they made their way to the fair, a crowd began to gather around them. No one had ever seen such a handsome and spirited animal before.

Then the bargaining began. One offered 500 *rubles* and next offered 600 *rubles*.

"I'll take 1,000 *rubles* and not a *kopeck* less," said the father, "and that's without the bridle." Some of the people began to leave. Just then a crusty old peddler joined the group.

"I'll give you 1,000," he called, waving his money in the old man's face.

"It's a deal, then." Ivan's father began removing the bridle.

"Oh no, I need the bridle," said the peddler.

"But it's not for sale. It's my wife's favorite," the father protested.

"How will I lead the horse without a bridle? Look—I'll give you five extra *rubles* for it."

Ivan's father thought and thought. True, his son had told him to keep the bridle, but five *rubles* was a good price for it. Why, it wasn't worth more than thirty *kopecks*!

"Come on, old man, I haven't got all day," the peddler badgered.

"Well, okay then," the father agreed and he handed the reins over to the old peddler.

Now, the old peddler wasn't really a peddler at all, but Oh! Lord of the Forest, who had disguised himself to get Ivan back into his clutches. As soon as Ivan's father turned his back, Oh! hopped on the horse and raced back to his kingdom. When he reached his hut, he tied the horse at the doorway and strutted into the house.

"That lad cannot escape me as easily as he thinks," he announced. Then he sat down at the table and feasted with his wife to celebrate his conquest.

Oh! took the horse to the river to water him, but as he bent to take a drink, Ivan turned himself into a perch and began swimming away. Without hesitating, Oh! turned himself into a pike and swam after the perch.

"Perch, perch, let's talk. Turn around and face me," the pike said.

But Ivan replied, "I can hear you just fine the way I am," and he continued swimming.

The pike swam closer to the perch and again he called, "Please turn around, perch. I really need to talk to you." The perch stuck out his bristly fins so the pike couldn't get near.

They swam and swam until the perch saw a beautiful princess sitting on the riverbank. In a flash he changed himself into a gleaming gold ring set with garnets.

The sparkle of the ring caught the princess's eye. Plunging her hand into the cool water, she plucked the ring from the river bottom. When she saw what she had found, the princess was overjoyed and she ran to show her father.

"Papa, look at the lovely ring I found in the river!" The king himself stood marveling as his daughter put the ring first on one finger, then the next, trying to decide where it looked best. As the king and his daughter stood admiring the ring, the servants rushed in and announced that a merchant was outside demanding to see the king.

"Oh well, tell him I'll be right there," the king sighed and tore himself away to attend to business. He met the merchant, who was really Oh!, once again in disguise.

"What is so important, then?" the king asked.

"I was sailing down your river with cargo for my king and I accidentally dropped a garnet ring. I wondered if any of your people had found it."

"Why, yes," the king replied, "my daughter has it," and he told the servants to call the princess. Moments later she arrived, wearing the ring. When Oh! laid eyes on it, he reached out for the princess's hand, but the girl shrieked and pulled back.

"What are you doing?" she cried.

Oh! recounted his story and said, "If I don't get the ring back, I will surely be put to death."

The princess frowned and fingered the ring. Then, pulling it from her finger, she threw it to the floor, exclaiming, "Well, if I can't have it, no one can!"

When the ring hit the floor, it shattered into hundreds of grains of wheat. They rolled this way and that over the floor. Oh! turned himself into a rooster and began pecking at the grains, but one had rolled under the princess's shoe and there it stayed. When Oh! thought he had eaten all the grain, he flapped his wings and flew out the window. The king and his daughter stood there, amazed at what they had seen.

Then the princess stepped back and the grain of wheat that had been under her shoe turned into a handsome lad who shone with the light of goodness. As their eyes met, Ivan and the princess fell in love, for neither had ever seen such beauty before. They begged the king and queen to let them marry.

"I will never be happy without him," said the princess. The king and queen looked at each other and smiled.

"Yes, you may marry with our blessing," they said. And so it was. There was a great wedding feast to which the whole world was invited. I tell you, it's true, for I was there eating and drinking with the rest of them, and what didn't make it into my mouth dribbled down my chin. &

The Frog Princess

LONG AGO,
when magic still roamed the hills and strange things happened, there lived a great king and queen with their three sons. These sons were their parents' pride and joy, and each day they grew taller, stronger, and more handsome. One day the king called them together and said, "My sons, my falcons, you are now grown men. It is time that you married. Shoot an arrow into the sky and where it lands you will find your bride."

With hearts surging, the young men ran for their bows and arrows, and then took turns shooting. The oldest son was first. *Zing!* His arrow soared high, high above the clouds, and finally dropped to the ground in a neighboring kingdom. The young man jumped on his horse and galloped off to find the arrow.

The arrow landed in a garden where a beautiful princess was strolling. Seeing something strange fall from the sky, the princess ran to see what it was. A delicate silver arrow lay among the roses. The princess picked it up and ran to find her father.

"Look, *Tato**, a silver arrow fell from the sky into our garden," she said.

Her father nodded wisely. "Ah, it's an omen. Save it for the one who will marry you."

When the prince arrived at the garden, he saw the lovely maiden with his arrow in her hand. He strode boldly up to her, saying, "I believe that's my arrow."

But the princess clutched the arrow to her breast. "The only one who can take it from me is he who will marry me," she replied.

"I will marry you," said the prince. And so they were engaged.

When the second son shot his arrow, *swoosh*, it flew over the treetops, just beneath the clouds, and landed in the courtyard of a wealthy merchant. The second son jumped on his horse and galloped off to find his arrow.

---

*Tato—*father, papa.*

The Frog Princess

His arrow landed at the feet of the merchant's beautiful daughter, who sat on the steps fanning herself. When she saw the arrow, she immediately reached for it. "Ah, pretty," she said, marveling at its delicacy. Then she took the arrow to her father and said, "Look what fell from the sky, father."

"It's a sign," said the merchant, "save it for the man who will marry you." The girl smiled and went skipping out to the courtyard. Just then the prince arrived and dismounted from his horse. He walked up to the maiden.

"That's my arrow," he said to the young woman, and he reached out for it. But the girl's fingers tightened around the arrow as she replied, "It belongs only to the man who will marry me."

"I will marry you," was the prince's answer. And so they were engaged.

Then the third son, whose name was Vasyl', shot his arrow. *Twang!* It spun around, zigzagged through the forest, and flew into a swamp. Vasyl' shrugged, jumped on his horse, and galloped off to find the arrow.

Now, it happened that there was a frog sitting on a lily pad in the middle of the swamp. As the arrow whizzed by, out went the frog's tongue to catch it. Seeing that this was not a dragonfly or anything else a frog could eat, she dropped it to the lily pad and placed two of her green, webbed feet over it. There she sat with her eyes bulging, smiling a strange frog smile, until the prince arrived. When Vasyl' saw his arrow on the lily pad, he waded through the swamp to get it, thinking, "What a bad shot! My next try will be better." But when he reached for the arrow, much to his surprise, the frog spoke.

"I will only give it to the one who marries me."

What? Vasyl' couldn't believe his ears. His head began to reel, but he picked up the frog and his arrow, put them in his pocket, and turned homeward. When he reached the castle he saw that his two older brothers were already there. Each had a fine maiden on his arm and when Vasyl' saw this, he hung his head in shame.

"What is it, son?" asked the king.

Vasyl' pulled the frog from his pocket and said, "Both of my brothers have found beautiful wives, but my arrow landed in the swamp and was snatched up by this wretched frog."

"Marry her," said the father, "for it is your fate."

So the king and queen held a triple wedding for their sons. The eldest walked proudly down the aisle with a beautiful princess on his arm. Behind him walked the second son with the merchant's lovely daughter on his arm. Last came Vasyl'. He walked down the aisle with a little satin pillow, upon which sat, well, a slimy green frog.

The king and queen gave each couple a home as a wedding gift, and peace, if not happiness, reigned in each household. Then one day the royal couple decided to get to know their new daughters-in-law. They called their sons together and said, "Let's see if your wives can spin and weave. Ask them to make us a piece of cloth."

When Vasyl' heard this, his heart sank. The two oldest sons hurried to their wives with the royal request, but Vasyl' stumbled home slowly and then sat by the fire weeping.

"What is it, my husband? Why do you cry?" the frog asked.

"Mother and Father want each of the new wives to weave a piece of fine cloth. How can I ask you to do this? You cannot weave. You have webbed feet—why, you're just a frog." Vasyl' began sobbing again.

"Don't fret, Vasyl'. Let's see what tomorrow brings." Vasyl' stopped crying, for he really had no choice, and went to bed. As soon as his head hit the pillow and his eyes fluttered shut, something strange happened. The frog rose on two legs, stepped out of her frog skin, and became a young maiden.

She whistled and a loom appeared. She snapped her fingers and piles of colored yarns and threads took shape. She clapped her hands and a dozen maids gathered together and began working. All night they worked together. They spun, they wove, they measured, they cut, they sewed, and they embroidered. By the time the dawn came, they had woven two beautiful shirts of the finest linen, embroidered with many bright colors. The frog wife quietly laid the shirts next to her husband's pillow and climbed back into her frog skin.

When Vasyl' awoke, he was truly amazed. Never had he seen such beautiful garments. He took the shirts to the king and queen, presenting them with a bow.

"I have never seen such exquisite handiwork," marveled the queen. The king too exclaimed and he put his shirt on, beaming.

"Your wife has done well," said the king. "Your older brothers' wives gave us only handkerchiefs." The queen shook her head sadly.

Vasyl' smiled, but his smile vanished like smoke with his father's next request.

"Now let's see how our new daughters-in-law can cook. We'll have the wives each bake a sweet treat for us and bring it to the castle tomorrow."

Again, the two older sons ran to their wives quickly, but Vasyl' dragged himself home slowly, stumbling and sighing. He sat on the stoop with his head in his hands until the frog came out and spoke to him.

"What now, dear?" her soft voice interrupted his thoughts.

"Father and mother want to find out which of their daughters-in-law is the best cook. How can you, a frog who eats nothing but mosquitoes and flies, cook for the king and queen?" Vasyl' shook his head sadly, but once again the frog comforted him.

"Oh, please don't worry, my husband. Let's see what tomorrow brings." Vasyl' took his wife's words to heart and went to bed.

Again the frog stepped out of her skin, whistled, snapped her fingers, and clapped her hands. Again the night maidens came, this time with buckets of cream, baskets of fresh eggs, flour as light as fairy dust, creamy butter, and the finest sugar. All night the maidens toiled. They stirred, they measured, they mixed, they poured, and they baked. By morning there stood a cake as tall as the king himself, decorated with little doves, pine cones, and garlands of periwinkle. The frog wife set it next to her husband's pillow and tiptoed away to find her frog skin.

When Vasyl' awoke, he gasped with delight. This was a cake like none he had ever seen. He carried it off to the palace, and the king and queen made no end of their praises. As for the sweets from the other daughters, well, the burnt *kalach* (that is, buns) and soggy *varenyky* (dumplings) were thrown to the dogs—and even the dogs turned up their noses and walked away.

Vasyl' was beginning to realize that his frog wife had talents, but just as his pride began to swell, his parents made a third request that crushed his heart.

"In honor of our sons and their wives, we are planning a royal dinner," said the queen. "We'll invite everyone in the kingdom to feast and dance with us. You and your wife will have the seats of honor, Vasyl'."

Vasyl' imagined how ashamed he would be sitting in the seat of honor next to his frog wife. How people would laugh, especially when she ate! And when they danced? Oh, it was too much to bear.

Disheartened, Vasyl' returned home, where once again he hung his head and cried.

"What's troubling you today, Vasyl'? Didn't your parents like my cake?" asked the frog.

Vasyl' explained what had happened, and the frog gave her usual answer: "Don't worry, let's see what tomorrow brings."

Vasyl' slept well, but the next day, as he prepared for the feast, he became sadder and sadder. Seeing her husband's grief, the frog spoke.

"You go ahead to the party," she said. "When it begins to rain, you'll know I am bathing. When the lightning flashes, I will be dressing myself in the finest garments. And when the thunder cracks, my carriage will arrive at your father's castle."

Well, what could Vasyl' do? He did as his wife told him, but when he arrived at the palace, his brothers and their wives began poking fun at him.

"Where's your frog?" teased the oldest brother.

"Ribbet, ribbet,* " mocked the second brother. Their wives tittered and blushed.

Now guests from all over the kingdom began arriving. When everyone was seated at the long banquet table, it began to rain.

"That is my wife washing herself," announced Vasyl'. The room grew quiet as everyone stared in amazement. The brothers and their wives looked at one another and rolled their eyes. The lightning flashed.

"And that is my wife dressing herself," said Vasyl'. Now the crowd began to whisper, and the brothers and their wives glanced at Vasyl' as though he had just taken leave of his senses. The thunder cracked.

"Ah, that will be my wife arriving," said Vasyl'. He stood up just as she entered—the most beautiful woman anyone had ever seen, draped in a golden gown embroidered with all the colors of the rainbow. Everyone gasped as she glided to the table and took her seat beside Vasyl'. Could this be the frog that the brothers had been joking about earlier?

As for Vasyl'—well, Vasyl' could not take his eyes off this lovely creature. He simply could not believe what he was seeing.

When the food was served, everyone fell to eating, and so did the princes and their wives. But as beautiful as she was, Vasyl' 's wife had strange table manners. She ate a piece of chicken and tucked the bones in her right sleeve. She took a sip of wine and then poured the rest down her left sleeve. The two other daughters-in-law noticed this and whispered between themselves. They

* Or, as frogs say in Ukraine, *kvak, kvak.*

did not want to be outdone by a frog again, so they did the same as she had done.

When everyone had finished eating, the musicians began to play. The king turned to his sons, saying, "You lead the dance with your wives!"

But the wives of the two older brothers backed away. "Let Vasyl' and his wife dance first," they said. As Vasyl' and his wife stepped out on the dance floor, they watched closely, hoping to mimic the frog-woman's every move.

The princess was as graceful as she was beautiful. Her tiny feet barely touched the ground as she and her husband swirled over the floor. Holding her close, Vasyl' stared rapturously at his wife. Could this really be the same frog he had married? Soon he told his wife that he was tired of dancing and sneaked away to wonder at his fate.

Now the princess danced alone, spinning and swaying with such grace that the crowd was hypnotized. She waved her right arm and a shimmering pond appeared. Then the princess waved her left arm and snowy swans glided upon the pond. Tiny stars fell from the sky to float on the placid water. Everyone gasped in amazement. Finally the princess took her seat.

"Bravo! Bravo!" bellowed the king. The queen clapped vigorously and beamed with joy.

Then the wives of the older brothers ran out to the floor and began dancing. They were so awkward that they tripped over their own feet, and people in the crowd turned away in embarrassment for the young women. Desperate for attention, the women began mimicking the beautiful princess. They waved their right arms and greasy bones tumbled from their sleeves. They waved their left arms and wine drops flew out, spattering right in the king's face. "Enough, you clumsy fools," he roared. "We'll all dance now."

So everyone from the king to the cook crowded into the courtyard and began dancing. Everyone, that is, except Vasyl'. He was hurrying home to solve the mystery of his wife's newfound beauty.

When Vasyl' reached the house, he immediately understood what had happened, for there in the middle of the floor lay a crumpled frog skin. "Never again will my beautiful wife be seen as a frog," he said to himself. With that he seized the skin and threw it in the fire, where it hissed and sputtered and burned. When Vasyl' was certain the skin had burned to ashes, he returned to the party, joyous at last.

All night long the people feasted and danced. Everyone was happy, from the poorest peasant to the king himself, and only when dawn peeked over the horizon did the guests depart from the great palace.

With their arms and hearts entwined, Vasyl' and his princess returned home. Vasyl' immediately climbed into bed, but the princess began searching for her frog skin.

"Have you seen my garment?" she called to Vasyl'.

"What? That ugly old frog skin? I threw it in the fire so you'd never have to wear it again," Vasyl' boasted. But the princess burst into tears.

"Oh, my Vasyl', you should not have touched it! My father has put a spell on me and without the frog skin, I cannot stay. Now I must leave for the crystal kingdom. Good-bye, my dear husband." As she spoke, the princess turned into a cuckoo bird, flew out the window, and disappeared, leaving Vasyl' alone in his misery.

For several days the young prince moped about, hoping his wife would return and wondering what to do. Every time a bird flew by or called out from a treetop, Vasyl' chased after it, but it was no use. When his grief became too heavy to bear, he packed his bow and arrows and set off in search of his beloved princess.

Vasyl' walked and walked. He trudged through a dark wood, he crossed a churning river, and he kept walking. He passed through many lands he did not know, but he asked everyone he met about the crystal kingdom. Not one person had even heard of it.

Then one day Vasyl' came upon a shriveled old man, so old that his skin was white as snow and his white hair and beard nearly reached the ground.

"Good day, my friend, and what brings you here?" greeted the old man.

"I'm going to the crystal kingdom to seek my wife," replied Vasyl'. "Can you tell me how to get there from here?"

The old man nodded solemnly. "I can tell you, but you'll never make it, son."

His heart leaped at the old man's words. "You must tell me, sir, for if I don't find my wife, I will surely die of loneliness."

A sad smile came over the old man's face as he handed Vasyl' a red ball of string. "Throw this ball of string before you," he said, "and follow it wherever it goes."

Vasyl' took the ball eagerly and rolled it before him. It led him into a forest so thick that no light could be seen—it was black as night. Two eyes shone in the dark and Vasyl' thought he felt the hot breath of a bear at his back. Fear seized his heart. Quickly he grabbed his bow and arrow. He was about to shoot when the bear spoke.

"Don't kill me, kind prince. I will be a friend to you some-  day." So Vasyl' put away his bow and arrow and went on his way. When he came to the edge of the forest, he heard the flap of great wings and the shriek of a large bird. Looking up, Vasyl' saw a majestic falcon sitting at the top of a tall pine, glaring down at him. Again Vasyl' reached for his bow and arrow. He was about to shoot when the falcon spoke.

"Don't kill me, kind prince. I will be a friend to you someday." Again Vasyl' put his bow and arrow away and continued his journey. Then he came to the edge of a sea and saw a large pike lying on the shore, gasping for air.

"This might make me a fine dinner," Vasyl' said to himself, as he reached for his bow and arrow. But once again, he stopped as words came from the pike's gaping mouth.

"Do not kill me, friend," said the pike, "for I can be of service to you someday." Once again Vasyl' put his weapons away. He threw the fish back into the sea and walked on.

After many days, Vasyl' reached the end of the string. He saw no crystal kingdom and no princess. The only thing he saw was a meager hut with foul-smelling smoke belching from its chimney. Vasyl' didn't know what to do, so he stepped up to the door and knocked.

"Who's there?" shrieked a voice from inside. Before Vasyl' could answer, the door swung open and there stood the oldest, ugliest woman he had ever seen. *Baba Yaha** stood about three feet high on crooked stick legs. Her skin was yellow, covered with knobby warts, and her thin hair hung in mats over a misshapen head. Her beady red eyes darted quickly over Vasyl' and then she smiled a toothless grin.

"What have we here? Could it be a handsome young prince paying me a call?" she said coyly, and then her face twisted into a hateful grimace. "What brings you here, lad? Are you hiding from someone or seeking someone? Answer me!"

"I'm seeking my beloved wife, the frog," Vasyl' answered earnestly. The old woman cackled and clapped her gnarled hands.

"You will never find her now," she taunted. "She belongs to my brother, the dragon in the crystal kingdom, and if he sets eyes on the likes of you, you're bound to be his dinner."

But Vasyl' was not deterred. "Please, grandmother, tell me how to get there."

*Baba Yaha—*a witch or hag figure common in Ukrainian, Russian, and Eastern European tales. Also known as* Baba Yaga.

The old hag smiled and her heart softened at the prince's sincerity. "The crystal kingdom is on an island in the middle of the sea. My brother lives in a great palace and it is there you will find your wife—*if* you ever get there, that is. No one in their right mind would even try to go to such a dangerous place. Everyone knows my brother is merciless. If he even so much as sees you, you will surely die." The old woman cackled again.

Vasyl' thanked the hag and retraced his steps to the sea. As he approached, he became dismayed. The sea was huge and he could barely even see the island. How would he ever get there? Vasyl' looked about for something to use as a raft, but the shoreline was empty. Suddenly a great splash interrupted his search. It was the pike.

"What troubles you, prince?" asked the fish.

"I must get to the crystal kingdom, but I haven't a way to cross the water," Vasyl' moaned.

"Don't worry—I'll help you," said the pike. He slapped his great tail against the water and up rose a shining bridge leading straight to the island. Vasyl' thanked the pike and hurried across the bridge.

When he reached the island, though, he saw that the castle was surrounded by a forest so thick he could not pass through the trees. Vasyl' tried to pry apart the thick branches, but he was weak with hunger. He sat down on a mossy rock and his eyes filled with tears. He had come all this way and now he would surely die of starvation.

Just then a rabbit hopped across his path and from out of the clouds swooped the falcon. The great bird pounced on the rabbit, carried it to Vasyl', and dropped it at the prince's feet. Vasyl' built a fire, cooked the rabbit, and ate it. Feeling better, he started toward the woods again, thinking, "There must be a way to get through it." Just then, the bear appeared.

"My friend, what brings you to this strange land?" asked the bear.

"My wife is held captive at the crystal kingdom," Vasyl' replied. "I want to free her, but I can't get through these woods."

The bear tossed his head to the side and roared. "I can help with that," he said. He put his huge arms around a tree, grunted, and pulled it out, roots and all. Then he pulled another out, and another until there was a clear path leading straight to the castle. Vasyl' thanked the bear and hurried down the path. By the time he reached the palace, he was weak and panting, but he pushed on the heavy gate and stepped through it. The gate slammed shut behind him.

When he entered the castle, all Vasyl' saw was winding halls lined with glass. He slipped up one hallway and down another, peeking in each door but seeing only his reflection in the glass walls. Deeper and deeper into the crystal kingdom he ventured. All the while he listened for the dragon and for the voice of his wife, but all he heard was the echo of his own footsteps. Finally he reached the heart of the castle, where there was one last door to open. Was that the faint sobbing of a woman he heard? Vasyl' held his breath and his hand trembled as he touched the door. As the door swung open, Vasyl' saw his wife. She sat spinning as though in a trance, pale and sorrowful. Still, she was more beautiful than ever.

"My beloved," Vasyl' spoke softly. The princess lifted her head and joy flooded the room like sunshine as they embraced.

"Because you have come for me, my father's spell is broken," she said. "Now we can be together."

Just then the heavy footsteps of the dragon thundered in the halls. The walls shone with the reflection of his fiery breath and the smell of smoke entered the room. The prince's heart pounded as he looked about, realizing that the gate had closed behind him and there was no place to hide!

"Hurry, my love," said the princess. As Vasyl' turned to her, she once again changed into a cuckoo. She took Vasyl' under her wing, flew up to the rafters, and escaped through a small window. As they left the crystal kingdom, Vasyl' and the princess saw forests go up in the flames of the dragon's wrath.

The cuckoo and the prince flew through the heavens for many days. When they reached home, the princess changed back to her true, beautiful form. That is how she stayed with Vasyl' for the rest of their days.

Vasyl' and his wife lived long, happy lives. They had many handsome sons and lovely daughters and each was brighter than the next. But there was one strange thing about these children: more than anything else they all loved to play in the frog pond behind the castle!

The Flute and the Whip

ONCE THERE LIVED AN OLD PEASANT
and his three sons. Year after year the family scraped by on practically nothing; meanwhile, the boys grew into young men. Now, two of the sons were clever and strong, but the third, Oferma by name, was a dreamer.

One day the old peasant called his sons together and said, "When I die, I want to be buried in the family plot, and I want each of you to come there and spend a night at my grave so I can give you my last advice."

"Oh yes, father, to be sure." All three nodded and they agreed to take turns going to their father's grave. First, the eldest son would go, then the middle, and finally Oferma.

Not long after this conversation, the old man took ill with fever. Although his sons nursed him, after several weeks he died. A funeral was held and the old man was buried in the family plot. Then came the time for the eldest son to spend the night at his father's grave.

"You know, I really don't have time for it," the oldest son told his brothers. "I have so much to do and I need my sleep. Why don't you go in my place, Oferma?"

"Why not?" Oferma shrugged. He certainly had nothing else to do.

That night Oferma ate heartily, bundled up in a sheepskin coat, and walked to his father's grave. Though the night was dark and cold, the stars shone brightly. Oferma lay down next to his father's tombstone and shivered. He looked up to the sky, thinking how peaceful it looked. He was about to doze off when suddenly a voice rumbled up from the earth.

"Who's there?" Oferma sat bolt upright. The voice was his father's voice.

"Why, it's me, father—Oferma," he replied.

"I thought my eldest son was to come first," said the voice. "Where is he?"

"Well, he is very busy," Oferma explained. "He didn't have time to come tonight."

The earth rumbled and groaned, "Too busy, too busy, yes, of course." After a long silence the voice continued, "Tell me, son, have you had anything to eat?"

"Oh yes, I had a good supper," the boy replied.

"Well then, are you warm enough?" asked the voice.

"Quite warm," said the boy, "I'm wearing my sheepskin."

Again there was a silence. Then the voice continued, loud and clear, "You are a good lad. Take this flute. When you play it, whatever you want will come to you."

Oferma found himself holding a small curved wooden flute. He turned it this way and that, and then said, "Why, thank-you, father."

He put the flute in his pocket and curled up to sleep for the rest of the night. When the sun rose the next morning, he went home and found his older brothers waiting for him.

"Well, how was your visit?" they asked. "Did father speak to you?"

"Yes," Oferma replied nonchalantly.

"What did he say?" the older brothers spoke in unison.

"He asked if I had eaten and wondered if I was warm enough."

The two brothers exchanged glances and laughed. "That's some dream you had, little brother," said the oldest boy. Oferma just shrugged and walked away.

Time passed, and the day came when the second son was to visit his father's grave. As night grew near, though, the lad began to fidget. "I can't do it," he said. "What if something should happen out there? Can't you go in my place, Oferma?"

Again Oferma shrugged, "I don't mind."

So Oferma ate a big meal, wrapped himself in his sheepskin, and went to his father's grave. This time he had no sooner sat down than the voice rose up from the earth.

"Is that you, son?"

"Yes, father, it's me—Oferma," replied the boy.

"And why didn't my second son come tonight?" asked the voice.

"He was afraid, father." A strange moan issued from the grave and then a long whip appeared at Oferma's feet.

"Take the whip, then," said the voice. "If you run into any danger, use it and you will be saved."

Oferma picked up the whip and admired it. It was shiny and long, and it smelled of fine leather. "Thank-you, father," he said.

"Now you can leave," said the old man's voice, "and you need not return a third time."

So Oferma rolled up the whip, tucked it into his belt, and went home. His brothers greeted him at the door. "Well, did our father talk to you again?" they asked.

"Yes," the lad replied.

"And what did he say this time?"

Oferma looked down and spoke slowly, "He said I was not to come to his grave again."

The older lads roared. "Only a fool could say such a thing," said the middle son. But Oferma just shrugged. Then he went to lie by the fire, where he fell asleep.

When he awoke, his older brothers were standing over him, glaring. "Listen, Oferma, we've had enough of your shenanigans," the older brother declared. "You don't contribute anything here and all you do is eat and sleep. Why don't you go and find some work?"

The young lad said nothing. He put on his raggedy jacket, stuck his flute in his pocket and his whip in his belt, and walked away.

From village to town Oferma journeyed. He spoke to everyone he met on the road, asking if they knew of work, but no one did. By and by, the boy came to a huge castle. The land around it stretched for many miles, green and bountiful. As he stood admiring it, an old man approached him.

"If you're looking for work, go to that castle," he said. "The king is in sore need of a shepherd. I heard that if you tend the royal flock for five years, the king will give you one of his daughters in marriage."

Oferma then made his way to the palace and asked to see the king. Two servants led him into a great hall where the king sat, his brow furrowed with worry.

"What is it?" the king said gruffly, without lifting his eyes.

Oferma stepped up to the throne and spoke, "Your majesty, I would like to tend your sheep."

The king's face brightened immediately. "Well, well, of course, lad. But remember that these sheep are like children to me. You must let them graze wherever they wish."

"All right," said Oferma.

So it was that Oferma became the king's shepherd. The servants showed him to his sleeping quarters in the barn and there he spent the night. The next day the young man woke early and drove the flock to the mountains. The sheep wandered this way and that, always climbing further up the mountainside, until they reached a beautiful meadow grown lush with silken grasses. There they stopped and began to graze. Exhausted by the journey, Oferma lay down in the shade of a large oak tree while the sheep nibbled away at the tender grasses. The wind stroked against his face, his eyes fluttered shut, and soon the lad was fast asleep.

Who knows how long Oferma slept, or what he dreamed? But he wakened with a start to the roar of a great dragon.

Now, this dragon was as ugly as it was huge. It had three heads, and each one was roaring with its mouth wide open and ready to swallow Oferma. The lad squinted at the dragon and asked, "Why are your mouths open like that?"

Oferma's boldness angered the dragon, and it stomped the ground so hard it trembled. "Because your sheep have ruined my beautiful silken grasses, and now I'm going to eat you, you fool!"

Before the dragon could even take a step toward him, Oferma pulled his whip from his belt and began thrashing the dragon. *Whoosh!* He struck the whip against the great beast's neck and a head tumbled to the ground. *Whoosh! Whoosh!* Oferma struck again and a second head rolled off. He lifted his whip a third time, but just as he was about to strike, the dragon began to cry.

"Please don't kill me," the creature begged. "Let me keep my last head. If you spare me, I will give you my marble house."

The lad's heart softened and he lowered his whip. "All right, then," he said, "take me to this marble house."

So Oferma and the dragon walked together, but the dragon kept throwing sly glances at the lad. Oferma could see that the dragon was up to no good and he kept his hand on the whip so the dragon wouldn't attack.

When they reached the marble house, the dragon said, "The key is in my ear. Why don't you take it out and unlock the door?"

"Why don't you do it?" the lad replied. The dragon muttered something, shook his head, and a key fell to the ground.

"Pick it up and use it," ordered the dragon, but Oferma resisted, for he knew the dragon would pounce on him as soon as he bent over.

"Why don't you pick it up?" he replied. "After all, you dropped it."

When the dragon stooped to pick up the key, Oferma struck him dead with a single blow. Then he took the key and let himself into the marble house.

Ah, how beautiful it was. Everything was made of marble and every surface sparkled and shone. Oferma walked up to a marble table, picked up a marble box, and opened it. Out jumped a shaggy dog who, much to Oferma's surprise, spoke.

"What is it you wish, master?" asked the dog.

"A pipe to smoke and a horse to ride," Oferma answered.

Immediately the dog delivered a pipe to Oferma. As the lad sat smoking, a marble horse appeared. The boy jumped from his seat and mounted the horse and together they soared out the window.

"Would you like me to fly above the clouds, then, or beneath them?" the horse asked.

Oferma replied quickly, "Beneath them, for I would like to survey my new property."

The marble horse bounded higher into the air and flew above the land like a bird. It took an entire year for Oferma to see all of it and when they returned, the horse asked if he could take the lad anywhere else.

"No, I must check on the king's sheep now," said Oferma. He dismounted from the great horse and walked back to the meadow.

When he arrived, there was not one sheep to be seen, for they had wandered hither and yon aimlessly, and now they were scattered to the ends of the earth. Oferma looked around, scanning the horizon from one end to the other, and scratched his head. Then he pulled his flute from his pocket and began to play.

Immediately the sheep came running, bleating as they flocked to him. There were twice as many sheep as before, because all the ewes had lambed. Oferma drove them back to the king's palace. As he entered the courtyard, he saw a beautiful princess in the window and he waved to her.

The young princess then ran to her father to tell him of the shepherd's return.

"Don't be silly," the king scolded, "you know that shepherd was killed long ago by the three-headed dragon."

But the princess took her father by the hand and led him to the courtyard where Oferma stood with the sheep. The king's mouth dropped open, but he quickly recovered from the shock to chide the lad. "What took you so long?

There had better not be any sheep missing," he said gruffly, "or you'll pay with your own life."

The king began counting his sheep and calling them by name, and when he finished he saw that there were many more in his flock than before.

"All right, then," he said to Oferma, "take them to pasture again tomorrow."

"I'd be glad to," said the shepherd. "That's why I'm here."

The next morning Oferma took a loaf of bread, a bag of onions, his flute, and his whip, and he drove the sheep to pasture. Again they surged ahead, higher and higher into the mountains. For three days they traveled, and only when they reached a beautiful meadow of silken grass did they stop to graze.

Oferma was exhausted. He sat beneath a sprawling oak tree and ate some bread and onions. When he finished eating, he fell asleep.

He woke with a start to find the ground beneath him trembling, the air filling with smoke, and a loud roar exploding in his ears. Before him stood a huge dragon—bigger and uglier than the last—and this one had six heads.

Oferma jumped to his feet, whip in hand. "What is it you want?" he demanded.

"Your sheep have destroyed my meadow of silken grass," roared the dragon, "and now you must die." The dragon opened all six of its mouths. Each was as big as a barn. Before the beast could blink, though, Oferma was trouncing it with the whip. One head after another shriveled and rolled to the ground, where they lay like huge old pumpkins. Finally there was only one head left on the dragon. This head began to cry and plead.

"Please don't take my life," the dragon slobbered. "Leave me my one last head and I will give you my crystal house."

Oferma lowered his whip and told the dragon to take him to the crystal house. The two walked together, but the dragon kept snapping at the lad. Again and again, Oferma had to use his whip to fend off the dragon.

When they reached the crystal house, the dragon said, "The key is under my tongue. Take it and unlock the door."

But Oferma was not to be fooled. "Do I look like a ninny?" he asked. "Spit it out!" Oferma waved his whip in the air and the dragon obeyed.

"Now pick it up and unlock the door," the boy commanded.

Smoke seeped from the dragon's ears as it hissed back, "Pick it up yourself!"

Without hesitating, Oferma struck his whip against the dragon's neck, and off rolled the last head. It landed on the ground with a loud thump. The key lay at Oferma's feet. He picked it up, unlocked the door, and entered the crystal house.

Inside, everything was made of crystal. The rooms glittered with light and rainbows played over every surface. Dazzled by the beauty of the place, Oferma walked slowly over to a crystal table. Upon it sat a crystal box. Oferma picked it up and opened it. Out jumped a shaggy dog.

"What is it you wish, master?" asked the dog.

"A pipe to smoke and a horse to ride," was the reply.

Immediately the dog brought Oferma a pipe. As he smoked, there appeared before his eyes a crystal horse. Setting the pipe on the table, Oferma strode over to the horse and mounted it. Then together they soared out the window.

"Would you like me to fly above the clouds or beneath them?" asked the crystal horse.

"Beneath them," Oferma replied, "for I would like to survey my land."

Off they went, skimming over fields and meadows and forests that stretched for miles. Oferma smiled as he rode, for the crystal house and its grounds were indeed beautiful. Two years passed as they toured the property. When they returned to the crystal house, the horse asked, "Is there anywhere else you would like to go?"

"No," Oferma replied as he dismounted from the horse, "I must go check on the king's sheep now."

So the shepherd returned to the silken-grassed meadow, but all the sheep had long since disappeared. No matter how hard he looked, not one could be seen. Quickly the lad plucked the flute from his pocket and began to play. It was a lovely tune and no sooner had he started than the sheep came running from all directions. There were many more sheep now, because all the ewes had lambed twice since he had left.

Oferma drove the sheep back to the castle. As he entered the courtyard, he again saw the king's youngest daughter sitting near her window. When she saw the young shepherd, she clapped her hands together with delight and ran to tell her father the news.

"That cannot be," insisted the king. "You know as well as I that the shepherd was destroyed long ago by the six-headed dragon." But the young girl insisted and finally led her father to the courtyard.

When the king saw Oferma, his face reddened with anger. "Curses on that good-for-nothing," he muttered, "will he never leave?" Then, stepping up to the lad, he said, "All my sheep had better be here or I'll sentence you to death." Oferma said nothing.

The king began calling to his sheep. He called each by name and counted them, and when he finished there were many left to be counted and named. Oferma glanced at the king's daughter and winked. She blushed, smiling, and lowered her eyes.

"Will I marry your daughter then?" Oferma asked boldly.

"Not so hasty, lad," the king glowered angrily. "You still have work to do. Tomorrow you must drive the sheep to pasture once again, and believe me, you have not seen the worst of it."

Oferma nodded and shrugged. "So be it," he said.

The next morning the lad woke at the crack of dawn. He loaded a bag with bread and onions and set off. Again the sheep ran higher and higher and further and further, until they reached a glade green with silken grasses. Oferma sat under an old oak tree and ate. Then he fell asleep.

Who knows how long he slept and what he dreamed? But he woke suddenly to a thunderous roar. Oferma opened his eyes and saw that all the leaves had fallen from the tree and lay scorched upon the earth. Before him stood a huge, menacing, twelve-headed dragon, flames pouring from each of its mouths and shooting in all directions.

"WHAT are you doing in my meadow?" roared the dragon.

"Resting," replied Oferma.

"You have ruined my silken grasses," thundered the dragon, "and for that you will die." He lunged toward the lad, but Oferma already had his whip in his hand and he thrashed with all his might against the dragon's shoulders. *Whoosh!* Off went one head, then another. In moments Oferma had lopped off all but one head, and that head began to plead and moan.

"Have mercy, lad, and spare my life," it sobbed. "For your kindness I will give you my golden house."

"Ha!" cried Oferma. "I know your dragon tricks. You offer me gifts when all you want is another chance to destroy me." The young man raised his whip high, waved it in the air, and wrapped it about the dragon's neck. With a loud crash, the dragon's head fell to the ground, making the earth shudder. Then Oferma took a key from under the dragon's tongue and walked up the mountain to the golden house.

He unlocked the door and stepped inside. For a moment he stood with his mouth open and his eyes wide, for the entire house was ablaze with light. Everything in it was golden and it was truly a beautiful sight. Oferma walked over to a golden table, picked up a golden box, and opened it. Out jumped a shaggy dog who spoke, "What is it your wish, master?"

This was all getting so familiar to Oferma that he replied, without thinking, "A pipe to smoke and a horse to ride." In a flash, the dog fetched the lad a pipe. As Oferma smoked it, a golden horse appeared before him. He set down the pipe, went to the horse, and mounted it. Together they sailed out the window.

"Would you like me to fly above the clouds or below them?" the horse asked.

"Below them," Oferma replied, "for I want to see my new property."

Up and away they flew, and by the time they returned, three years had passed. "Shall we go on?" asked the horse.

But Oferma answered quickly, "No, for I must check on the king's flock now." Then he dismounted and walked to the glade where he had left the sheep.

When he reached the meadow, Oferma saw no sign of the sheep, so he took out his flute and began to play. As though out of nowhere the sheep appeared, and there were many, many more of them, for all the ewes had lambed three times since he had left.

Oferma drove the flock back to the palace and the king's daughter greeted him with cries of joy when he arrived. She quickly ran to her father to tell of the shepherd's arrival.

"He's back, father," the girl cried as she threw her arms around the king's neck.

But the king turned white with rage. "So he wants to marry you, does, he?"

The princess lowered her arms to her sides and bowed her head. "Yes, father," she said quietly, "and I want to marry him, too."

What could he do? The king sputtered and fumed and finally consented to the marriage. There was a great wedding feast and all the people from all the nearby villages came to celebrate. They danced and sang and ate and drank for a full week, and the music never stopped playing.

After the wedding, Oferma took his bride to each of his houses. On the first day they stayed at the marble house. On the second day they stayed at the crystal house. On the third day they stayed at the golden house. But on the fourth day, Oferma turned to his wife and said, "Each of these houses is beautiful, but none of them feels like home." His wife agreed. So they returned to his village and built a house of wood and stone, where they lived together happily for many, many years. ❧

The Doll

Beyond the Dnipro and beyond the Dniester there lived a happy family—a mother, a father, and their daughter, Paraska. Together they prospered without a care in the world. Then one day the mother became sick. Pale and weak, she wasted away. They called the doctors and they called the wise women of the village, but no one could do anything for her. Soon everyone realized that the mother would die, and they all grieved sorely. But none grieved more than Paraska and her father.

As the mother lay on her deathbed, she called her daughter to her side. "Paraska," she said, "you are still a young girl. When I am gone, you will have no mother to protect you, but I will give you a mother's blessing. Remember, a mother's blessing can save you from the bottom of the sea, while a mother's curse brings nothing but trouble. Paraska, my blessing will always be with you."

Paraska stood silently, holding her mother's hand, tears streaming from her eyes. Then her mother handed her a doll. The doll looked just like Paraska's mother, with dark hair and round green eyes. As Paraska stood admiring the doll, her mother continued.

"Take care of this doll, Paraska. Feed her and care for her and always keep her with you. If you ever need anything, take your dolly from your pocket and tell her what you need. She will help you. Good-bye now, my love. Take the doll and go. Send your father to me, for I must talk to him too."

Paraska put the doll in her pocket, as her mother had told her, and went to fetch her father. When the father came and stood at his wife's side, she took her wedding ring from her finger and handed it to him.

"My beloved husband, we have been together only a short time. I am sorry I must leave you now, but it is the will of heaven. I know how hard it will be after I'm gone, but do not pine for me too long. The sorrow of the living weighs heavily on the dead and disturbs their eternal rest. Mourn for me for one year only. When the year is over, seek another wife. Take my wedding ring for the new wife you will find. The woman whom my ring fits will be the perfect bride for you. And she will bring you happiness as I have for this short time."

The mother closed her eyes. Her breathing became harsh and slow and finally it stopped. Her husband stood still, turning the ring over and over in his hands as tears poured from his eyes. Paraska rushed back into the room and threw her arms around her father, and together they wept. Then they laid out the body and buried it as was the custom in those parts. The two kept vigil at the mother's grave. Forty days passed and they celebrated her memory, her *molebin'** as it is called. Nine months passed and the mother's grave bloomed with flowers. Ever so slowly the sorrow began to lift from the hearts of Paraska and her father.

On the anniversary of her mother's death, Paraska's father remembered his wife's dying wishes. He took the wedding ring from the drawer and looked at it. Then he showed the ring to Paraska and told her of his wife's wishes.

"You know, Paraska, you look more and more like your mother each day. Try on the wedding ring and see how it looks on your hand." Paraska hesitated at her father's request, but did not want to disobey. She took the ring and slipped it on her finger. Lo and behold, the ring fit perfectly! Paraska's father was overjoyed.

"Paraska," he said, "look how well it fits! Your mother must have known. So, you see, I need look no further. You were meant to be my bride."

At first Paraska thought her father was joking and she laughed, but he kept insisting and Paraska's laughter changed into alarm. "Father, you can't mean this. You cannot marry me! I am your own flesh and blood. A father does not marry his own daughter. Who ever heard of such a thing?"

But Paraska's father had made up his mind. He was going to marry Paraska and that was that. He told his daughter that she would be very happy as his wife and that he would be happy too. Didn't she want to be happy? Then he started the wedding preparations. He brewed beer and ordered food, and

---

* molebin'—*A supplication, church service, or litany of gratitude celebrating the final rest of the dead.*

Paraska, seeing that her father meant to go through with it, worried desperately. What could she do? She could not marry her own father, but how could she get out of it? The more she thought about it, the worse she felt, and with her mother gone, Paraska had no one to talk to. Finally, she began to cry.

As Paraska wept, she felt something stirring in her pocket—almost as if it were tapping to get her attention. Then she remembered, "The doll!" Her mother's deathbed wishes had gotten her into this predicament. Maybe they could get her out too.

"Dolly, dolly, in my pocket," she whispered, "I need your help. Father wants to marry me and I don't know what to do—my own father, my own flesh and blood. It is wrong."

"I'm hungry," said the doll. "Take me out and feed me. Then we'll talk."

When Paraska went to dinner that night, she ate quickly and hid some of her food in her apron. Her father kept looking at her and smiling.

"Tomorrow's our wedding day, my love," he said. "After our wedding, we will not be just father and daughter, but also husband and wife." Paraska's heart shuddered.

"Please excuse me, father," the girl said. "I have so many things to do before tomorrow. May I go to my room?"

"Of course," her father agreed, again smiling.

Once she was in her room, Paraska took the doll from her pocket and the food from her apron. She fed the doll. Then the doll opened its round green eyes even wider and looked straight at Paraska as it spoke. "Tomorrow your father will come to take you to the church for the wedding. When he knocks on your door, tell him you're not quite ready. Tell him you need a few more minutes, then spit into each of the corners. Your spit will cover for us while we escape."

Paraska put the doll back in her pocket and went to bed. She woke early the next morning and had just gotten out of bed when she heard a knock on her door. It was her father.

"Come, my darling," he said. "Today is our wedding day. Come and I will take you to church."

"Just a minute, father," Paraska answered, "I'm not quite ready. Give me a few more minutes." Then she quickly spat into all four corners of the room as the doll had told her to do. She felt the doll stir in her pocket and took it out.

"Give me a piece of bread and put me in the middle of the room," said the doll. Paraska again did as she was told. The doll stamped three times and the floor opened to a dark, narrow staircase. Down, down, down it went. As Paraska stood with her mouth gaping, the doll spoke again.

"Hurry! Hurry down the staircase," it said. But the staircase looked so dark and foreboding that Paraska held back. Just then her father knocked again.

"Come, my darling. We must go to the church now."

To Paraska's surprise, the spittle answered him in her own voice, "Just a minute, father, I'm not quite ready. Give me a few more minutes." Paraska stood frozen in astonishment.

"Quick!" urged the doll. "We must escape before the spittle dries. Once it dries, it will not be able to speak."

So Paraska grabbed her doll and started down the stairs. She heard her father knock again and again the spittle answered, "Just a minute, father, I'm not quite ready. Give me a few more minutes." Paraska hurried on, her heart pounding and her feet clattering down the steps. When her father knocked the third time, Paraska could hear the impatience in his voice. The spittle tried to answer, but it was drying out and all it could say was, "M-m-m F-f-f."

Then Paraska heard her father burst into her bedroom. Of course, the room was empty. No Paraska there, only bits of dry spittle in the corners and a dark stain on the floor where the staircase had been!

So that was the last Paraska heard of her father. She continued down, down, down, and as she descended her eyes grew accustomed to the dim light and she became less afraid. When she reached the bottom, a horseman went by. He was all white: his saddle was white, his bridle and stirrups were white, and his whip was white. Even his face was a strange luminescent white. As he rode by, the darkness lifted and it became day. Paraska sighed and reached into her pocket to make certain her doll was still there. Yes, she felt better now. She went on.

Paraska had no idea where she was going; she just walked. She walked and she walked. She did not know how long she had walked and she did not know how far she had walked. Maybe it was far and maybe it was not, but after a time she heard hoofbeats and saw a plume of red dust in the distance. She saw as it got closer that it was another horseman. This one was completely red—as red as the first horseman had been white. He was dressed in red, his horse was red, and on the horse was a red saddle. Even his face was a ruddy, glowing red. When he galloped by, the sun rose to its highest point. It was high noon.

As the sun bore down upon her, Paraska grew tired. She was hungry and thirsty too, but there was nowhere to rest and nothing to eat. Soon the girl found herself surrounded by a dark, dense forest. On and on she walked, hoping to find something—a stream or a soft meadow perhaps—but every turn she made was like the last.

Still she walked on. Suddenly, and without warning, a third horseman rode by. He was as black as the others had been white and red. His horse was black and everything on his horse was black. He was black too, and so were all his clothes. He rode in silence and as he passed Paraska, the darkness fell and it became night.

Now Paraska began to worry. She had no idea where she was, except that she was in the middle of a forest in a strange land, and now it was nighttime. How had she gotten herself into this predicament? Had her doll misled her? Paraska shuddered. No, there could be nothing worse than having to marry her own father. Tears filled Paraska's eyes, but through them she glimpsed a light in the distance. Ah, she thought, maybe she was not going to perish after all!

Paraska hurried toward the light. The forest was so thick and overgrown that it was hard to stay on the path. As she approached the light, Paraska saw a small hut surrounded by a high fence. When she drew nearer, she saw that on each fence post was a strange beacon. Paraska strained to see. Could it be? Yes, they were human skulls! Their eyes glowed with an eerie light that illuminated the hut and its yard.

Paraska stopped dead in her tracks. Should she run? She looked about frantically. She wanted to leave, but there was nowhere to go, so she crept slowly toward the yard. The eyes of the skulls turned toward her and stared. Trembling, she opened the gate and entered the yard. With the eyes upon her, she was drenched in a strange light. As she crossed the yard to the hut, the eyes followed her. Finally she took a deep breath and knocked on the door.

A harsh, crackling voice answered, "Who's there? Who dares disturb my rest?"

"My name is Paraska," the girl replied. "I'm lost and I need food and shelter. Can I stay here for the night?"

"Why, yes," the voice said. "There is food on the stove. After you eat and sleep, we'll talk."

Paraska opened the door carefully and entered the cottage. Inside was a huge old woman. This woman was thin as a rail, but so tall that she had to hunch over and bend her knees to fit inside her own hut. She had a few wisps of white hair on her head and a few long hairs on her chin. Her wrinkled lips clung to her gums and her arms and legs seemed to have no flesh at all. Paraska stood silent before the old woman. This must be *Baba Yaha**, she thought to herself. Then the old woman spoke.

"There—the food is on the stove." She pointed a long, bony finger. "Take what you need, then rest till tomorrow." Paraska obeyed and ate from the pot. Then she curled up on a bench. She was still shaky and thought she would never fall asleep, but her eyes closed and the next thing she knew, she was waking to the sound of horses' hooves upon the ground. It was morning.

Paraska looked about. *Baba Yaha* was out in the yard puttering. The girl tiptoed to the door and stood watching quietly. Then the old woman turned around.

"Ah, awake at last!" she cried. "Now here is what you will do. You will work for me, my young one, and if you work, you will eat. And I will pay you as well. If you work hard, I will give you a spindle and a loom such as you have never seen."

"Thank you, grandmother," Paraska replied shyly, "I will do as you say."

Baba Yaha's eyes blazed. "And if you don't, your head will join the many on my fence, my precious." The hag pointed her chin to the skulls on her fence and cackled. Then she said, "My horses need oats. See that bag over there?" Paraska nodded and the old woman went on, "Take those oats and go to the field on your left. Plow it. Sow the oats. Reap the oats, thresh them, and roll the oats. You must have them ready for me when I return at sunset, for my horses will be hungry and so will I!"

The old woman then jumped into a huge mortar that stood by the gate. She grabbed the pestle and pushed herself off. The mortar lifted from the ground and flew up into the air, only to disappear behind the clouds. *Thump, swish ... thump, swish ...*" Paraska heard *Baba Yaha* row her mortar through the sky. When the old woman had disappeared from sight, the girl broke down and wept.

"I can't grow a field of oats in one day," she thought. "It's impossible, even in this strange land." Paraska sobbed and sobbed until she remembered her doll. She went to the stove and got some food, saying, "Dolly, dolly, in my pocket." Then she set the doll on the table and fed it. After the doll had eaten, Paraska told it what the old woman had said. The doll nodded as Paraska spoke.

---

* Baba Yaha—*a witch or hag figure common in Ukrainian, Russian, and Eastern European tales. Also known as* Baba Yaga.

"It can be done, it can be done," the doll repeated. "With a mother's blessing and good will and diligence, it can be done."

"But how?" Paraska whimpered.

"Don't worry," said the doll. "You clean and sweep *Baba Yaha's* house. Gather some wood, make a fire in the stove, and cook a meal. By the time you finish and the old woman returns, the oats will be ready."

Paraska did as she was told. In the meantime, the doll went outside. It turned to the left and looked at the field, then stamped its foot three times. Suddenly the soil began churning. It plowed itself into long, deep furrows. Then the doll walked over to the bag of oats and clapped its hands three times. The bag opened and oats flew into the furrows, covered themselves, and sprouted. The grain grew and grew, and then it turned yellow and lay on its side as though it had been mowed. The doll clapped its hands again. Stalks of grain lifted from the ground and gathered themselves into sheaves. The sheaves marched into the barn. There each sheaf beat itself till it was threshed and then swept the oats under the millstones to be rolled. Three empty bags glided up to the millstones and oats poured into each.

By the time Paraska had finished her chores inside the house, it was growing dark. Three bags of oats stood by the gate where the old woman parked her mortar and pestle. As the girl stood washing her hands, she heard hoofbeats, then the *thump* and *swish* of the mortar and pestle. Down from the clouds came *Baba Yaha*.

When the old woman saw the three bags of rolled oats, she did not know whether to be happy that the work was done or sad that she could not punish Paraska. After dismounting from her mortar she began to squeeze herself into the hut. First she stuck her head through the door, then her shoulders. Hunching her back, she bent her knees so they almost touched her chest. Then she squirmed inside. The old woman cast her eyes about the hut suspiciously. She could not believe what she saw! The house was spotless and a pot of soup was on the stove, ready to eat. *Baba Yaha* took a big slurp. Yes, it was good. Then she ate her fill, saying, "You eat too, my child. Eat and rest, for you will need your strength tomorrow. If you work, then you eat. That's how things go around here. You will have plenty to do tomorrow."

Paraska ate and stowed some food away for her doll. Then she curled up on the bench and slept soundly. In the morning, the old hag called to the girl through the window. "Wake up, wake up! Today you must work on the middle field. I need wheat and I need bread." Paraska stumbled outside, squinting in the light. The old woman pointed to a bag of wheat and said,

"Take that bag of wheat. Sow it in the middle field and have some fresh bread ready for me by the time I get home." *Baba Yaha* drew her long, red tongue over her mouth and smacked her lips. Then she got into her mortar and picked up her pestle. *Thump, swish,* she was gone.

This time Paraska did not cry. She took her doll out, fed it, and told it about the day's tasks. The doll said, "With a mother's blessing and good will and diligence, it can be done. You clean the house. Gather wood for the stove and build a fire. By the time the fire is ready for cooking, the loaves will be ready to bake."

Paraska got to work and the doll went outside. The doll looked at the middle field and stamped its foot three times. The soil plowed itself into furrows. Then the doll went to the bag of wheat and clapped its hands three times. The wheat flew into the furrows, covered itself, and sprouted. It grew, turned yellow, and lay on its side as though it had been mowed. When the doll clapped its hands again, the wheat gathered itself into sheaves and the sheaves marched to the barn. There the sheaves beat themselves till they were threshed and swept the grains between the millstones to be ground into flour. Three bags slid into place and flour poured into each one. The doll took one bag. It clapped its hands three times and the flour poured into a bowl with water, yeast, eggs—everything for the most delicious bread.

By the time Paraska had finished her chores, it was growing dark. Two bags of wheat stood by the gate where *Baba Yaha* parked and three loaves of bread were baking in the oven. As Paraska pulled the steaming loaves from the oven, she heard the sound of a galloping horse, then the *thump* and *swish* of *Baba Yaha's* mortar and pestle. She glanced out the door just in time to see the old woman descend to earth.

Baba Yaha looked at the bags of wheat. She sniffed the air and poked her nose into the hut and smelled the freshly-baked bread. Then she ate heartily, telling Paraska to eat, eat, and rest too. Again Paraska saved some of her food for the doll and then went to sleep on her bench.

The next morning, Paraska woke to the old woman's voice wheedling in her ear.

"Your task today, my precious," she said, "is to plow the third field—the field on the right. Sow it with flax seed. Mow the flax and soak it. Beat it and pull the fibers. Then cure them, spin them, and weave me a new *rushnyk.**"

* rushnyk—*An embroidered towel used as decoration and to adorn icons and holy images, as well as in engagement ceremonies and other rituals.*

Paraska rubbed her eyes and stretched. She watched the old woman fly off into the clouds, then fed her doll and told it the task. While Paraska worked in the house, the doll went outside. As before, the doll plowed and sowed the field. Then it marched the flax to the river to soak and clapped its little hands. The flax beat itself to fiber, combed itself, and presented itself to the spindle. At the doll's command, the spindle whirred, spinning the flax, and then the loom wove the *rushnyk*.

By the time Paraska had finished her chores, it was growing dark and a beautiful new *rushnyk* lay across the table. Then the girl heard the sound of horses and the *thump* and *swish* of the old woman's mortar and pestle. *Baba Yaha* was home.

The old woman again bent herself like a pretzel to get into the house. She hunched her back and lifted her knees and squeezed inside. There she saw the lovely *rushnyk* on the table. The house was clean and dinner was cooked and ready to eat. *Baba Yaha* turned to the girl and said, "I see you have earned your keep, but I must ask you how you accomplished this, for never before has a human done what I required."

"I will answer your question if you will answer mine," Paraska replied. The old woman nodded.

"When I was coming through the forest, three horsemen crossed my path—a white horseman, a red horseman, and a black horseman. Who were they?"

"Ah, those were my horsemen," said the witch, "morning, noon, and night. But young girls should not ask too many questions. So tell me, how were you able to do my tasks?"

Paraska looked down and then looked into the old woman's eyes. "I had my mother's blessing," she said, "and with a mother's blessing and good will and diligence, anything can be done."

"What?" *Baba Yaha's* eyes flared with anger. "A mother's blessing, eh? A mother's blessing?! No, no, no, we cannot have any blessings around here! Now you must go. Take your pay and leave. And ask no more questions."

The old woman handed the girl a spindle and a loom. Paraska checked her pocket to make sure the doll was still there, then headed back the way she had come. When she arrived at the edge of the forest, she found the stairs that led to the world above. Paraska stopped. What if her father was there, waiting to marry her? Still, the witch had told her she could not stay in the underworld. She touched the doll in her pocket and when she felt no objection, she headed up the stairs.

As Paraska emerged from the underworld, she was dazzled by the light. She found herself in a large field. Her old house was gone without a trace and her father was nowhere to be seen. Paraska did not know that she had been gone for a long, long time. What had seemed like days to the girl had actually been years. In that time, her father had married and moved away and their little mud and thatch hut, whipped by the winds and washed by the rains, had crumbled and become one with the earth. Paraska saw nothing but the field.

So she began walking again. She did not know how long she walked or how far. Perhaps it was far, or perhaps it was not, but after a time she saw a city in the distance. Paraska approached the city and entered it. She wandered into the poor section of the town, where she found an old widow woman. The woman had no children and was all alone. When Paraska asked her for shelter, the old woman agreed.

So Paraska lived with the old widow. Their lives were peaceful and routine and time passed; no one noticed how long Paraska stayed. The young girl did all the chores and whenever she had a free moment, she would take out her spindle and loom and spin or weave. The spindle produced the finest thread ever seen. It was thin and even and almost shone in the dark. The loom produced the most exquisite cloth—fine and strong and of the most beautiful white color.

Before long, Paraska had several measures of cloth. She called the old widow and said, "Take this cloth to the market, grandmother. Sell it and see what you can get. It is fine cloth. Perhaps it will make some money for us."

So the old widow went to the market and sat down near the stalls where vendors were selling cloth and fabric. Everyone who came by looked at the cloth and marveled. They touched it and rubbed it against their cheeks and sighed. "This is much too fine for us," they said. "We cannot afford such cloth. Only a king can have cloth like this. Take the cloth as a present to the king."

The old widow did not know what to do. True, the cloth was fine enough for royalty, but she had been hoping to get some money for it. Anyway, she was just a poor old woman. She did not know if she would even be allowed into the palace. But again and again people told her the same thing, until finally she set off to see the king. As she passed through the gates, she trembled. Almost instantly, two guards seized her.

"This is no place for the likes of you!" they shouted, and they were about to push her out when she managed to pull some of Paraska's cloth from the wrapper.

"Th-this is a gift for the king," she stammered, her hand trembling as she held the cloth before their eyes. The guards stared and then led her into the king's chambers.

The old woman bowed low and, without saying a word, laid the cloth at his feet.

"Where did you get this?" the king asked. "You didn't steal it, did you? Surely you did not make this yourself with your old, twisted hands!" At first the old woman was so frightened that she could not speak. Then she blurted out that the cloth was indeed hers, but this only confused the king and that in turn made the woman even more afraid. Finally she managed to tell him about Paraska, a poor orphan, a young woman who lived with her and did spinning and weaving in her spare time.

"Ah!" The king's face softened and his eyebrows raised. He touched the cloth to his cheek and caressed it. Then a hint of a smile crept across his lips. After ordering his carriage, he seated the trembling old widow in it beside him and told the coachmen to follow her directions to her home. As they approached the widow's house, they saw Paraska standing in the doorway. When the king saw the young woman, his smile broadened and he became almost cheerful. He stepped out of the carriage and bowed before Paraska. Then he kissed her hands and asked the old widow for Paraska's hand in marriage.

"If it is Paraska's wish to marry you, then so be it," answered the widow. "If my adopted daughter gives her consent, I will not stand in the way."

So Paraska and the king were married. They lived happily together and had no trouble and no sorrow, just beautiful children to bless their marriage. The doll stayed in Paraska's pocket till the end of her life, when Paraska gave her mother's blessing away to her own daughter. And so it is that the mother's blessing is passed from generation to generation. &

–Natalie O. Kononenko

The Stranger

FOR MANY YEARS IN UKRAINE
there were special harvest festivals. In some villages it is still so. In late autumn, after all the crops have been harvested, the young girls rent a house and go there to celebrate. They cook and bake and buy treats to eat, and then go to the house to spin or work on other handicrafts. In the evening, the boys join them and they eat together. That's when the fun really begins. The girls ask the boys riddles. They visit together and laugh; they sing songs, make music, and dance. Night after night the young people celebrate. Everyone has a marvelous time. This is the tradition and many have met their future husbands and wives at the harvest festivals.

So it was one autumn when Yaryna went to celebrate the harvest with her friends. Yaryna had been looking forward to the party. She was the only daughter of a poor, elderly couple and she enjoyed the company of other young people like herself. When she arrived, the other girls were already spinning and singing, but everyone stopped to greet her. Then they all began spinning and singing again, and Yaryna joined in. The girls had made enough food to feed the whole village for a week—*varenyky*, *holubtsi*,* and many other good things. Later, when the boys arrived, everyone began dancing. Yaryna danced too, just like all the others. The room was filled with music and laughter.

But the music and laughter stopped suddenly when a stranger arrived. This young man was not like the village boys. He was tall and thin and pale. His clothes were much finer than the others'. It was obvious that he had not worked long hours in a field as the local boys had.

* varenyky—*dumplings stuffed with meat, cheese, or mushrooms and other vegetables.*
* holubtsi—*cabbage rolls.*

The stranger bowed low before the group and greeted them. "Greetings, my good friends," he said. "May I join this merry company? I see you are a good and hospitable people."

"Of course, of course," everyone murmured their welcomes. Then the stranger bowed low again. He pulled a purse from his pocket and counted out gold coin after gold coin. He gave the money to one of the younger boys and told him to go buy nuts and candy and drinks for all. The boy left and soon returned with armloads of treats—all the things these young people could not normally afford. Everyone clapped with delight and helped themselves to the goodies. The celebration grew louder and merrier. Everyone danced and sang, but none as well as the stranger. He glided across the room with such grace and elegance that people could only guess that he had come from some great city. This dark-eyed man also sang with a voice sweeter and more melodious than anyone had ever heard before. Perhaps, some said, he had been schooled at a famous conservatory. Every time he sang, he turned and smiled at Yaryna, as if his song were just for her. And dance after dance, he chose Yaryna to be his partner.

When all the food and drinks were gone and it was time for the party to break up, the stranger turned to look at Yaryna with his deep, dark eyes. Then he said, "My dear young woman, may I walk you home?" Yaryna flushed deeply, but nodded her consent. Her friends whispered madly and tittered with excitement as Yaryna left with the stranger.

Once the two were outside, the stranger asked for Yaryna's name, which she told him. Then he took the girl's hand and they began walking. As they strolled along, the stranger asked many more questions, about Yaryna's family and her home and where she lived. Yaryna told him everything. She told him about her elderly father and mother and how they lived on the outskirts of the village. She told him how poor they were and how she often had to go to work on other people's farms to make ends meet. She also told him how she could not afford to buy fine clothes or even to mend the ones she already had. As she spoke, Yaryna giggled nervously.

"I don't know why someone like you would be interested in me," she said shyly.

"My darling child," replied the stranger, "you have other treasures much finer than fancy clothes. Now, what if I were to ask you to marry me? Yaryna, would you consider being my bride when the wedding season comes again next year?"

Yaryna's heart fluttered wildly, but she kept her composure. She thanked the stranger for his attention and for the great honor he had paid her by asking her to be his bride. "My parents and God willing, I will indeed marry you as you say," she said quietly. Then the stranger squeezed Yaryna's hand tightly and the two parted ways.

Yaryna ran home, her heart surging with excitement. When she entered the house, her mother greeted her and asked her about the celebration. "Did you have a good time, my little lark?"

Yaryna hugged herself and twirled around, smiling brightly. "Oh Mother," she exclaimed, "I had the most marvelous time. A handsome stranger came to our party and he only had eyes for me. He is very sophisticated and has lots of money. Why, he even bought treats for everyone! And you should see how he dances and sings." Yaryna went on and on about the wonderful stranger and told her mother how he had asked her to be his bride.

"Well," said the mother when Yaryna finished, "that is good news, but I wonder who this stranger is and where he lives." She thought for a moment and then said, "When you go to the festival tomorrow, take a spool of thin thread along. Then when the stranger asks to walk with you, slip a loop of thread around one of his buttons and let the thread unwind. Later you can follow the thread and see where it leads. That way we will find out where this mysterious man lives and who he is."

Yaryna did as she was told. She went to the party as she had the night before. As before, after the singing and dancing had begun, the stranger arrived. He proffered more money for food. The singing grew louder and the dancing grew faster. All the young people were enjoying themselves, but none more than Yaryna, for again the stranger had eyes only for her. He sang to her, he danced with her, and whenever the music stopped, he stood by her side, and smiled at her. When it came time to leave, the stranger again asked to escort Yaryna. She agreed.

As they walked, Yaryna slipped the thread over a button on the stranger's coat. When they parted, the thread began to unwind. Faster and faster it went, until it was slipping off the spool so fast that it burned against Yaryna's hand. It wasn't long until all the thread was gone and Yaryna had to run after the end of it so as not to lose it altogether.

Yaryna ran and ran. The thread led her down the road and then off the side of the road, across a fence and into a field. Then it went across a ditch and over another fence, through a graveyard, and right up to the church! Yaryna's

 heart pounded as she ran. Her mind raced too. Who could this stranger be? She grasped the church doors and pulled to open them, but they were locked. Quickly looking around, Yaryna saw a ladder lying by the side of the church. She picked it up, set it against a wall, climbed up, and peered inside through the church window. The church was dark, lit only by moonlight, but slowly Yaryna's eyes became accustomed to the dark. There in the middle of the church she saw a corpse laid out for burial the next day. The deacon who should have been reading the Psalter over the dead body was nowhere to be seen and all the candles had gone out, but there was a shadow moving near the coffin. Yaryna strained to see what the dark shape was. Then the moon cast a ray of light over the figure. Yes, it was the stranger—and he was eating the flesh of the corpse!

Yaryna gasped. She could not believe her eyes. Slowly she began descending the ladder, but she was shaking so hard that she lost her footing and the ladder fell to the ground with a loud clatter. Yaryna scrambled to her feet and ran. Fast as her legs could carry her, she ran, through the graveyard, across fences, through the field, and onto the road. All the while she felt that there was something right behind her, chasing her, breathing down her neck.

By the time she reached home, everything was dark. Yaryna collapsed into her own bed without even seeing her parents. Whether she slept or not, she did not know, but soon it was morning and everything from the night before seemed like a strange dream. Had it really happened? How could it be? Her wonderful stranger was a flesh-eater, a vampire! Yaryna felt so confused. Her head pounded and she could not make sense of it. Nevertheless, there were chores to be done and Yaryna threw herself into her work. Then evening came and it was time to go to the celebration.

"Aren't you going to the party, my little lark?" Yaryna's mother asked.

"I-I-I don't know," the girl replied, "I'm very tired."

But Yaryna's mother urged her to go. "Go while you're still young, my child. Enjoy yourself. It won't be long till parties and dancing are things you cannot do."

And so Yaryna went. Everything at the party was just as it had been on the previous nights. There was dancing. There was singing. The stranger came and bought food and drink. The party got louder and the stranger showered Yaryna with attention.

But Yaryna did not respond. She sat in a corner and hardly spoke, and she could not bring herself to look into the stranger's dark eyes. Over and over in her mind she kept seeing the dark figure in the church—hunched over the corpse, eating human flesh.

"What's wrong with you, Yaryna?" her friends asked. "You're ignoring the most handsome and cultured man at the party." But Yaryna just shrugged.

When it was time for the party to break up, again the stranger asked Yaryna to walk with him. Yaryna kept her eyes on the ground and shook her head no.

"What?" her friends cried. "Are you a baby or what? Be a proper young lady and accept the good man's invitation. Go with him."

So Yaryna went with the stranger. This time the stranger did not smile at Yaryna, nor did he engage her in small talk. Instead, a deep silence separated the two until abruptly the stranger spoke.

"Did you go to the church?" he asked. Yaryna shook her head from side to side.

"Did you see what I did?" he asked.

Yaryna gasped. "No!" she replied vehemently. Then the stranger took hold of her chin and looked straight into her eyes.

"Tomorrow your father will die," he said, and before Yaryna could respond, he walked quickly away.

Yaryna ran home with her heart pounding. She went straight to bed without saying a word to her parents. Whether she slept or not, no one knows, but the next morning she arose to do her chores, only to hear her mother weeping. In the night Yaryna's father had died.

Yaryna and her mother threw their arms around each other and wept. Then they prepared the body for burial. They did all the proper things, lamenting and grieving, and before they knew it, it was evening.

"Why don't you go to the party?" Yaryna's mother asked. "There is nothing else you can do here and it will do you good to get away for a while. You'll have enough time for lamenting when you get older."

Yaryna protested at first, but her mother kept coaxing, so finally she went. When she arrived at the party, Yaryna's friends began pestering her about her red eyes and her sad face.

"How can I not be sad?" said the girl. "Last night my father died." Then everyone felt sorry for her. During the party they let her sit alone in a corner, but when the party ended, they wouldn't let Yaryna leave without the stranger.

Again the stranger asked Yaryna to accompany him and again her friends badgered her into going. As soon as the two were alone, the stranger turned to Yaryna.

"Did you go to the church?" he asked.

"No," was her reply.

"Did you see what I did?"

Again she answered, "No."

The stranger cleared his throat and looked up at the moon. Then he said quietly, "Tomorrow your mother will die." Quickly he turned and walked away.

Yaryna stood frozen on the road for a long time, then she dragged herself home. She was so overwrought with fear and grief that she didn't remember getting home or going to bed, but the next morning she found herself in her bed. The house was deathly still.

Yaryna crept to her mother's room. There lay her mother, dead. She too had passed away, just as the stranger had predicted. Yaryna clutched her heart and wept bitterly. She prepared her mother's body for burial and did all that needed to be done. By the time she finished, night was falling.

There sat Yaryna, all alone in her house—no one to talk to, no one to touch. The house was getting darker and darker. Lonely and frightened, the girl set out for the party. At least she could see her friends there.

That night Yaryna told everyone that her mother had died. Again, they felt sorry for her and let her sit quietly in a corner. The girl looked strange now. Her eyes were swollen and glazed over and all night she stared straight ahead, not smiling or speaking to anyone.

When the party ended, the stranger again approached Yaryna. He took her elbow as though he knew she was going to walk with him again and Yaryna, blank-faced, stumbled after him.

As soon as they were alone, the stranger repeated his questions.

"Did you go to the church?"

"No!"

"Did you see what I did?"

"No!"

"Well, then, tomorrow you will die."

Yaryna turned away stiffly and stumbled home, her head slowly clearing. When she reached home, she gathered all her things and went to the next village where her old grandmother (her *babusia**) lived. As soon as she saw the

* babusia—*grandmother.* (Babusiu—*vocative form.*)

wizened woman, Yaryna burst into tears. Then she told her grandma everything that had happened: about the stranger, about the thread, about the corpse, and about her mother and father.

"And now he says I will die, *Babusiu*," the girl said.

The old woman nodded slowly as the girl spoke, then she sighed. "Do not be afraid, my child," the grandmother chided. "This stranger is indeed dangerous, but if you listen carefully and do exactly as I tell you, you will be safe." Yaryna nodded.

"First, you must go to the priest. Tell him that when you die you must be buried in a special way. They must dig a tunnel under the doorstep and your coffin must be removed through this tunnel. It must not be removed in any other way. They can take you for the church service, but when it's over they must not bury you in a graveyard. Do you understand?"

"I-I-I guess so," Yaryna stammered.

"No, it cannot be the graveyard. They must bury you near the crossroads, where the two main roads intersect. Remember this, my child, and repeat it to the priest exactly as I have told you."

Yaryna did as her *babusia* had told her. She went to the priest and repeated her grandmother's words to him. Then she went and bought a coffin, put it in her cart, and drove it home. The sun was setting as Yaryna dragged her coffin into the house. The girl ate her supper, lay down in the coffin, and died.

The next morning, neighbors came and found the poor girl. Ah, another death, they sighed. Then they went to get the priest.

The village priest did everything as Yaryna had instructed. Her coffin was removed through a tunnel under the doorstep and, after the church service, it was buried near the crossroads just outside the village. As time passed, the grave became overgrown with grass and the next spring a strange and beautiful plant sprouted from the place where Yaryna lay. The plant was a brilliant green. It had the most graceful and delicate leaves and from its center bloomed the most perfect and lovely flower anyone had ever seen.

One day a prince was riding past the village. He saw the flower on Yaryna's grave and he stopped to marvel at it. He smelled the flower and admired it again. Then he called to his servants and commanded, "Bring me a shovel and pot. I want this plant. Dig it up and plant it in the finest pot you can find. This plant will be kept in the palace on my bedroom windowsill and it must be watered and tended with care."

Everything was done just as the prince ordered. His servants dug up the plant and put it in a gilded pot. Then they carried it carefully to the palace and placed it on the prince's windowsill. There it flourished and grew.

Late one evening, just before the stroke of midnight, a servant who was walking through the palace heard a strange noise. He followed the noise to the prince's bedroom, but when he looked in, he saw nothing except the prince, who was sound asleep. Just then he heard the noise again. He hid behind a curtain and saw the plant on the prince's windowsill move. Then it moved again and he heard the same noise. How strange! There was no breeze to stir its leaves. What could be causing this?

The plant moved again and this time the servant saw that it was the flower that was moving. First it trembled, then it shook harder, then it lifted off the plant and fell to the floor. As soon as it struck the ground, the flower changed into a beautiful maiden. The servant stood in awe as Yaryna stretched her arms and legs, yawned, and walked to the kitchen. He followed the lovely girl in disbelief and watched as she rummaged through the cupboards for food and drink, ate and drank her fill, and walked back to the prince's bedroom. There she struck herself against the floor, turned back into a blossom, and ascended to her former position on the stalk.

As soon as the prince awoke the next day, his servant rushed in to tell what he had seen. "Let's both watch the flower tonight," said the prince.

That night both prince and servant hid behind the curtain and kept watch. Just before midnight the flower began to move. Again it trembled, shook harder, and lifted from its stalk. Then it dropped to the floor and turned into a lovely maiden. Yaryna wandered to the kitchen, ate and drank, and came back to the bedroom to return to her place on the plant. But just as she was about to turn herself back into a flower, the prince stepped out from behind the curtain, fell to his knees, and asked the girl to marry him.

Yaryna smiled and consented, saying, "I have watched you for a long time from my place on your windowsill and I have grown to love you deeply. Yes, I will marry you, but before we marry I must ask you for one thing."

"Just ask," replied the prince, "whatever your wish is, I am certain I can fulfill it."

The Stranger

"Well, then," continued the maiden, "after we marry, we cannot go to church for four years, for there is a curse on me. After four years the curse will be lifted, but before that time, it would be very dangerous for me to go there."

The prince agreed and he and Yaryna were married in the palace. The young couple was very happy and when a year had passed, Yaryna gave birth to a beautiful baby boy. The prince was so proud and happy. He ordered the servants to prepare a great feast and invited all his friends to celebrate with him. Everyone congratulated him and the prince bragged about his beautiful wife and child. At first the crowd nodded in agreement, but after a time they tired of his boasting.

"Yes, she is beautiful," they said, "but what kind of woman is she? We have not seen her at services once. Is she baptized? Will your son be baptized? Why don't you and your wife go to church?"

The bragging stopped and the prince grew sullen and cross. He resolved right then and there that the next week he and his family would go to church.

When Sunday came and the church bells rang to announce the service, the prince called to his wife, "Put on your finest robes, Yaryna. This morning we shall go to church!"

Yaryna pleaded and begged and cajoled and even became angry with her husband, but none of it dissuaded him. Finally she gave in, dressed, and went to church with her family. As they entered the sanctuary, Yaryna looked around fearfully. There by the window to the left sat the stranger, as big as life—and he was looking straight at Yaryna and smiling.

Yaryna sat quietly through the service, but afterward, as she was leaving with her family, she felt a tug on her sleeve and a familiar voice whispered in her ear.

"Did you go to the church?" the stranger asked.

Yaryna answered as before, "No!"

"Did you see what I did?"

"No!"

"Then your husband and your son will die."

When Yaryna heard this she went running down the road. She went straight to her old grandmother and told her what had happened. The old woman handed Yaryna a small vase filled with water.

"Take this holy water," she said. "It was blessed in the church on the day of St. John the Baptist. When that vampire asks his questions, tell him the truth. After that your heart will tell you what to do."

 Yaryna thanked her grandmother and hurried home. There she was met with long, dark faces and mourning, for as soon as her husband and child had returned from church, they had died. Yaryna ran to her bedroom. There the corpses of her husband and son were laid out for burial. At the head of their bier stood the stranger, gloating and rubbing his palms together. Yaryna tightly clutched the vase of holy water in her hand.

"Ah, the lovely Yaryna!" he exclaimed, "I've been expecting you. And tell me, did you go to the church?"

"Yes!" Yaryna answered. The vampire hesitated a moment and stepped backward.

"Did you see what I did?"

"Yes!" Yaryna screamed and she threw holy water into the vampire's face. The vampire grimaced and groaned as his face contorted. Then his head and body shriveled and he crumbled into a pile of ashes.

Yaryna took what was left of the holy water and sprinkled it on the bodies of her husband and son. They stirred and stretched and opened their eyes. Then they threw their arms around Yaryna and covered her with kisses. So it was that Yaryna and her family lived on into a ripe old age, and the stranger was never seen in those parts again. 🦢

The Sorceress

A LONG TIME AGO,
in a village that has long since turned to dust, there lived an old priest
and his daughter Lesia. Lesia was a clever girl and her father thought
she might make something of herself some day, so he sent her to a
school in the next village. An old woman there gave her reading and
writing lessons.

Every morning the priest's daughter set out with her arms full
of books, and every night she returned with her head filled with
hundreds of thoughts and ideas. It was a long walk, but Lesia
amused herself by naming the flowers and trees, or singing, or
talking to the animals in the pastures. Most of all, she liked to look
at the king's castle as she passed by, always hoping to catch a glimpse
of the king or his beautiful daughter.

One day Lesia studied late and by the time she made her journey
home, darkness had fallen. As she passed the king's castle, she heard
a strange sound, like a terrible caterwauling. The girl stopped and
looked around. She peered intently through the darkness until her
eyes fell on a lighted window of the castle. There sat the king's
daughter.

The princess was holding her hands against her ears as she
pushed, pushed, pushed. Then a strange expression twisted across
her pretty face. Was she in pain? But no, now with eyes clenched
shut she lifted and pushed up with her hands. Suddenly—off
popped her head!

"Oh!" Lesia gasped and clutched her books tightly to her chest.
But this was not the end of it. The princess placed her head in a basin,
washed her hair, and rinsed it. Then she set it on the table next to
her and brushed and braided the hair. Her hands moved deftly and
the stub of her neck swayed to and fro as she worked. When she

finished, the princess set the head back on her shoulders and stood up to leave the room. Just before leaving, she glanced out the window.

As the princess's gaze swooped over the landscape, Lesia's heart skipped a beat. Had the princess seen her? She couldn't tell. For a moment she stood rooted to the ground, afraid to make a move. Then, hugging her books tightly to her chest, she ran all the way home. She went straight to bed without telling her father about the king's daughter or even saying goodnight, for she knew quite well he would say she had been imagining things. That night Lesia slept a restless sleep. The princess's head floated through her dreams and she kept hearing a strange wailing sound off in the distance.

The next day Lesia told some of her friends in the village what she had seen. As she spoke, their eyes widened and they began whispering, "Sorceress. A sorceress. The princess is a sorceress." The story spread quickly and soon the whole village buzzed with gossip and speculation.

A few days later the news came that the king's daughter was gravely ill. The king, heartsick with grief, had locked himself in the castle and refused to leave. At this news, the rumors stopped and the villagers fell silent. A pall washed over the entire town as the beautiful girl wasted away.

Day after day passed and the princess grew thinner and paler. Her eyes became sunken and dark, and her lips became cracked and thin. Then, just before dying, the princess called her father to her bedside.

The old king bent close to her as the princess whispered hoarsely, "Please let the priest's daughter say the prayers of the dead over me before I am buried, lest the evil ones take my soul." Blinded by his tears, the king nodded in agreement. Then the mourning began, for the princess was dead.

The princess's body was placed in a coffin and carried to the church. The king himself followed the funeral procession, and when they reached the church, he knocked on the priest's door. "Father," he asked when the priest appeared, "do you have a daughter?"

"Why, y-yes," stammered the priest.

"Then let her say prayers over my dead daughter. This was the princess's final wish."

"Of course, your majesty." The old priest bowed deeply and went to tell Lesia to prepare for her duties.

"The king wants you to say prayers over the dead princess. He says it was his daughter's dying wish."

The girl began stammering, "B-b-but, father, you d-d-don't understand. The princess is wicked. She's a sorceress."

"How many times do I have to tell you? There is no such thing as a sorceress, or magic, or curses," the old man replied. "Now, don't argue with me—we must obey the king's request."

The girl hung her head. "Yes, *Tato**," she said.

That day at her reading lesson, Lesia sat moping over her books. She twirled her hair between her fingers and stared out the window listlessly.

"What's bothering you?" asked her teacher.

The young girl poured out her story. "And now my father says I must read prayers over the sorceress. Surely I will die!"

But the old woman comforted the girl. "Come, come. I've known this all along. What you say is true, but you need not be afraid." Then the old teacher handed Lesia a small piece of white chalk. "Take this chalk. When you go to read the prayers, draw a circle around yourself. Stay within that circle, no matter what happens. Keep reciting the prayers and do not stop. If you're saying the prayers inside the circle, you will be safe."

So the girl took the chalk and the old woman's advice. That evening she went to the church with a prayer book in one hand and a piece of chalk in the other. As she entered the dark nave, she thought of her teacher's words. Stationing herself next to the coffin, she drew a circle around herself, opened her prayer book, and began reading.

Night fell. Against the darkness, tiny candles flickered, and against the silence, the young girl's voice quavered in prayer. Only that and the smells of incense and hot wax filled the old cathedral.

Lesia stood rooted to the cold stone floor, her eyes fixed on the prayer book, but she was constantly aware of the heavy coffin just an arm's length away. Sometimes, as she watched out of the corner of her eye, the coffin seemed to be moving, getting bigger. With her hands trembling, the girl read on into the night.

At the stroke of midnight, a strong wind swept through the church. It blew all the candles out and howled into the corners where the darkness was deepest. Lesia prayed faster, her heart pounding.

* Tato—*Father.*

Cre-e-e-a-k.

The coffin lid opened and then slammed shut with a great crash. A horrible wailing filled the room, the cries of many souls who beseeched the girl, drawing shivers and shudders from her flesh.

"Come with us ... help us," a chorus of hollow voices entreated. Lesia wanted more than anything to run from the church, but she remembered the old woman's words: "If you're saying your prayers inside the circle, you'll be safe." Only a sliver of moonlight that slipped through the church window allowed her to read the words before her, and read she did, for she knew not what else to do.

All night long the spirits howled and cried out. The princess called too. By the end of her vigil, Lesia's eyes fluttered with weariness, her hands could barely hold the book, and her voice cracked like a crow's. Still she kept reading.

When the sun finally seeped up over the horizon, the wind ceased and once again the girl heard the coffin lid creak open and slam shut. Then the priest's footsteps echoed through the church.

"Come," he said, "it's time to go to bed." But although she was very tired, Lesia insisted on going to her lesson, for she wanted to tell her teacher what had happened. She ran all the way to the next village and arrived at the teacher's doorstep exhausted.

As soon as the old woman saw the girl, she threw her arms around her. Then she looked deep into Lesia's eyes.

"Was it a frightful night?" she asked.

"Oh yes," Lesia replied. Then she recounted all the horrors she had endured, adding, "but I did as you said, and here I am to tell of it."

The old woman slowly shook her head. "Tonight will be worse, you know. Here, take these mustard seeds. When the sorceress appears, scatter them on the ground. The seeds will protect you. And whatever happens, stay in your circle and keep reading."

So Lesia took the basket of seeds and went back to the village. That night, when she went to the church to pray over the dead princess, she carried the basket with her.

Again, Lesia found her place next to the coffin and again she drew a circle around herself. Then she set the basket of seeds at her feet and began reading. As she read, the sky darkened and the wind began to howl.

Before long, a great storm came over the village. As the priest's daughter read, she heard thunder crash closer and closer, louder and louder. Lightning bolts cut like great blades through the darkness. Then the first rain spattered

 on the roof. As the rain grew stronger, it poured through every crack and crevice of the church, winding over the floor in dark rivulets. The girl read on.

When the clock struck midnight, the coffin began to tremble. Again the lid creaked open and slammed shut. Suddenly the floor was swimming not only with rainwater, but also with all manner of vermin—rats and mice, lizards and snakes, maggots and worms. Lesia gasped in horror. The stench of death filled the church and the girl began to choke. Stammering and shaking with fear, she raised her voice.

It was then that the dead princess appeared. Crawling on all fours, she thrashed her head from side to side and clutched at her throat. Her hair hung in snarled mats that draped over her shoulders and dragged down to the floor. Her body was covered with vermin—maggots hung from her hair, snakes slithered around her arms and legs, and rodents scampered upon her back. Her eyes rolled in their sockets, dark and wild.

"I'm drowning, I'm drowning," she wailed as she reached her bony hand toward the priest's daughter.

Lesia jumped back and almost stumbled out of the circle. Not only had she lost her footing, but she had also lost her place in the prayer book, and she began stammering. The evil princess laughed.

Lesia took a deep breath and gave a big kick to the basket at her feet. Suddenly the air was thick with thousands of tiny seeds. As they settled to the floor, the princess and all the vermin began to scramble for them in a sea of writhing motion.

All night the rats and mice, the lizards and snakes, the maggots and worms, and the dead princess picked at the tiny seeds that covered the church floor. The rats squeaked, the princess moaned, and there was a scuffling noise as the creatures scrambled over each other to get at the seeds. But Lesia continued reading. When dawn came, the vermin melted into the shadows and the dead princess crawled back to her coffin.

Lesia stood dizzy and blinking in the morning light. As her father ushered her out of the church, he again ordered her to rest, but Lesia refused, saying that she must go to her reading lessons. Again she told her teacher of her experiences.

"Yes, yes," the old woman nodded as the girl spoke. When the story had been told, the old woman solemnly handed Lesia a hammer and four long nails. Then she said, "Take these with you, for this, the last night of your vigil, will be the worst. Before nightfall, pound one nail into each corner of the coffin and put the hammer in front of you. Remember to stay in the circle and keep reciting the prayers, no matter what happens."

That evening, when the girl went to the church, she once again did as her teacher had instructed her. Carefully, she nailed the coffin shut, stood in the circle, and laid the hammer at her feet. Then, as the sky darkened, she began to read.

Knock, knock, KNOCK, KNOCK, KNOCK. A terrible pounding came from inside the coffin. The princess began to scream and curse, and smoke oozed from under the lid of the coffin, filling the room with a thick haze. Lesia's eyes burned with tears as she read. By midnight thick clouds of smoke hovered among the rafters, and as the clock struck the hour, out from them flew small demons. They circled silently, then suddenly began shrieking and diving at the girl with their sharp teeth bared. Startled, Lesia jumped and ducked, almost falling. Again and again the demons dove, but they could not get beyond the circle's edge.

"THIS is what you get for spying on me and spreading vicious rumors," a voice hissed, and a huge ball of flame hurtled toward the girl. Lesia spoke louder and faster as the fireball came flying toward her, certain she would meet her death. But when it hit the edge of her circle, the fireball shattered, sending flames everywhere.

Just then the door opened. The old priest stood at the doorway, a dark silhouette in his long robes. Lesia looked up. "*Tato,* go back!" she cried—but it was too late. Her father went up in flames and an evil laugh issued from the coffin.

Lesia could hardly see through her tears to read. She wanted to run to her father, but she knew she could not leave the circle or she too would die. "Amen, amen," she kept repeating. Sobbing and reading, she stood her ground, never leaving the circle while flames leaped all about her and the building around her burned to ashes.

When the cock crowed, all that remained was the girl, the hammer, the prayer book, and a dark, silent coffin. As the villagers emerged from their houses, they rubbed their eyes and stared in disbelief. No one dared enter the circle where the priest's daughter stood.

Then the king himself arrived and, seeing the young girl, he ran to her and grabbed her by the shoulders. "What's happened, girl?" he demanded.

Lesia did not reply, her face blank and ashen. But the king kept asking and asking until finally, speaking in a low monotone, she told him everything. She told him about the night when she saw the princess in the window, about her terrifying vigils at the church, and about this last night, when she had witnessed her father being consumed by fire.

As the king listened to the girl, he bowed his head. His eyes filled with tears and then he embraced the girl. "I am your father now," he said. He picked up the hammer and walked over to the coffin. The priest's daughter followed silently.

The nails were solidly set, but, using all his strength, the king managed to pry open the coffin. Everyone watched with bated breath, and as the lid fell to the ground, they gasped as one. The princess, serene and rosy-cheeked as a newborn child, sat up, rubbed her eyes, and stretched.

"Oh, what a dream I have had," she said. She looked around for a moment, confused by the crowd. Then, seeing the priest's daughter, she smiled brightly and threw open her arms. "Sister," she cried, and it was as though they had always known one another. Lesia ran to her and they embraced, crying tears of joy.

The villagers shook their heads and slowly shuffled back to their huts and their fields. The king, the princess, and the priest's daughter returned to the castle, where some say they lived peacefully for the rest of their lives. ॐ

Pea-Roll-Along

ONCE THERE WAS AN OLD COUPLE.
Through the years they loved each other dearly, but although they longed for a child, they had none. They wished and hoped and prayed, but year after year passed and no child was born. They told each other that life was fine without children and that they had been blessed in many other ways. Still, whenever they saw a little girl or a little boy, they would sigh and hope and dream.

One day the wife was washing clothes by the river. Across the way a group of children played in the shallows, giggling and splashing gaily. The woman watched them and sighed. "I know I am too old to have a child now," she said to herself, "but if only ... if only ..."

Just then, something small and green caught her eye. It was a tiny pea rolling about in the water, just where she was doing her wash. For some reason, a pang of hunger took hold of the woman and she grabbed the little pea and popped it into her mouth. It tasted sweet and delicious, and although it was small, the pea satisfied her craving. The woman went home, cheerfully humming a children's song.

"You seem happy today," the husband said to his wife after she returned.

"Oh yes," she replied, and she told him about the children at the river and the marvelous little pea.

That night, the woman slept as never before and she had the most blissful dreams. The dreams were filled with beautiful children—playing in fields, playing in streams, swinging on swings, running about the village, and laughing, always laughing. When she awoke the next morning, she told her husband about the dreams, and he confessed to having had the same marvelous dreams. Then he looked at his wife and said, "Oh, look, we have been dreaming and talking about children so much that your stomach has begun to swell. Do you suppose ...?" The man's face brightened for a moment, but then he shook his head. "No, we are too old to have children. Better just to dream about the dear little lambs. Better not to get our hopes up."

But the woman's stomach continued to swell and swell. After five weeks had passed, she was heavy with child. After nine weeks had passed, there was no denying that she was about to have a baby at any moment. Sure enough, nine weeks, nine hours, and nine minutes from the moment she had swallowed the pea, the woman was overcome with the pangs of birth—and out came a little boy.

This little boy was the most beautiful child the couple had ever seen, and not just because he was their own. As big as a young child, he was fair and tall, with a handsome face, strong limbs, and thick blond hair, even right at birth. On his back was a strange little birthmark in the shape of a peapod.

"We will call him Pea-Roll-Along," said the wife, "for surely it was the pea that helped us have this child."

 Pea-Roll-Along had grown quickly in his mother's womb, but he grew twice as quickly in the light of day. Within hours he could crawl. Within days he had learned to walk and talk. Within weeks he had grown as tall as his father. After a month he was the tallest, strongest, and handsomest boy in the village. His parents were as proud as could be. They could not get their fill of admiring their son.

Then one day Pea-Roll-Along went to his parents and said, "Mother, Father, I must leave now and go to seek my fortune."

His parents protested, "No, please don't leave. Why, you have only been here a short time and we have not had our fill of loving you. We longed for a child for so many years, please don't go. Besides, you are still young. You may look big, but it has only been a year since you were born."

Pea-Roll-Along felt sorry for his parents, but he was a child of fate, and fate had called him. He had to follow. His parents knew this and eventually they gave him their blessings for the journey. "May fate be kind to you, son," they said, "may fate protect you."

"Wait," said Pea-Roll-Along, "before I leave I must have a weapon—a weapon that matches my power and strength." So he went to the smithy and told the blacksmith to craft the biggest, strongest club that he could.

"I have been called by my fate," he said. "Make my club as powerful and compelling as fate."

"Come back tomorrow and you will have your club," said the blacksmith. Then he set to work. He fanned the flames and tempered the steel. When he had finished, he had a club that came up to his chest. It was so heavy that he could not lift it. When Pea-Roll-Along arrived the next morning, the blacksmith had to drag the club along the ground to deliver it to the boy.

"This is indeed a fine club," Pea-Roll-Along said, looking it over from top to bottom, "but let me test it." So the hero took the club and threw it up in the air. It flew up, up, and up, disappearing behind the clouds. Pea-Roll-Along lay down to rest, saying, "Wake me when the club returns to earth."

The club continued its flight for hours, and then finally turned around and descended to earth. Exactly one day after being thrown into the air, the club emerged from the clouds. When he saw the club falling, the blacksmith roused Pea-Roll-Along. Quickly the boy reached for the club. As he grabbed hold of it, the club shattered. Fine metal dust covered Pea-Roll-Along, the blacksmith, and the smithy.

Pea-Roll-Along shook his head. "I'm afraid this will not do," he said. "Please try again, sir."

"Come back in two days," replied the blacksmith. Then the blacksmith worked and worked. He pumped the bellows and fanned the flames. He added more and more steel. He tempered the steel and tempered it again. After two days he had a club that was as big as he was tall, and he could not even lift it. When Pea-Roll-Along came to pick up his club, the blacksmith and his apprentice together had to drag it outside.

"This is indeed a fine weapon," Pea-Roll-Along said, admiring the club, "but let me test it." Again Pea-Roll-Along threw the club up into the air, and again it flew up, up, and up, disappearing behind the clouds. Again Pea-Roll-Along lay down to rest, telling the blacksmith to wake him when the club reappeared. For three days Pea-Roll-Along rested. On the morning of the fourth day, the blacksmith heard a terrible whistling as the club descended from the clouds. He woke Pea-Roll-Along and quickly the lad grabbed the club just before it reached the ground. The weight of the club made Pea-Roll-Along sink into the earth up to his ankles, but the club was not strong enough to withstand Pea-Roll-Along's grasp. Almost as soon as it was in his hands, it shattered, sending small pellets of metal all around the smithy and throughout the village.

"That was better," said Pea-Roll-Along, "but I'm afraid it still will not do. Please try again. Make me another club that is stronger."

The blacksmith told Pea-Roll-Along to return in a week. Then he set to work. Day and night he worked without stopping. He worked as he had never worked before. When he finished, he had a club bigger than he was. Even standing on his toes with his arm outstretched he could not reach the top of it. Nor could he lift the club, either alone or with the help of his apprentice. So when Pea-Roll-Along came to get the club, he himself had to drag it into the light of day.

Pea-Roll-Along tossed the club from hand to hand as though it were a matchstick. "This is a fine, fine club," he said, "but let me test it."

Again Pea-Roll-Along threw the club up into the air, and again it disappeared behind the clouds. After asking the blacksmith to wake him when the club returned, Pea-Roll-Along lay down to rest. This time he rested for a whole week. After a week had passed, a terrible whistling filled the whole village. The townspeople came out from their houses to see a red fireball coming down from the sky. It was the club, heated red hot from the friction of its long, long flight. The panicked villagers began to scream and bolt about looking for shelter. The noise woke Pea-Roll-Along and he jumped up and seized the club just before it hit the ground. The impact of the club on his hand drove Pea-Roll-Along into the earth up to his knees. The hero held the club in his hand and tossed it from one hand to the other like a hot potato. Finally, the club cooled down—but it did not shatter. Pea-Roll-Along just smiled.

"Now, THIS is a fine club," he said.

Then Pea-Roll-Along pulled his legs out of the earth. He thanked the blacksmith and paid him. Carrying his club on his shoulder, he went to say good-bye to his parents. Once more they begged him to stay, and once more they blessed him. Then off he went on his journey.

Pea-Roll-Along had not traveled far before he heard a terrible noise. It sounded as though the forest were being torn asunder. The noise got louder and louder as Pea-Roll-Along got closer and closer, until he saw a man with his arms around a tree. The man twisted the tree and uprooted it, then grabbed another and twisted and uprooted it. Pea-Roll-Along watched the man uproot trees for awhile and then greeted him.

"Hello, my good man," said the hero. "Tell me who you are and what you are doing in the forest."

"My name is Twist-a-Tree," said the man. "It is my fate to travel through forests, twisting and uprooting trees to make a path for others to follow."

"How did you come by this fate?" Pea-Roll-Along asked.

"Well, my parents were wishing and wishing for a child, but had none. Then one day my mother saw a rowan berry—the reddest, prettiest berry she had ever seen. She ate it, and not long after that, I was born."

"Then we are brothers!" exclaimed Pea-Roll-Along, and he told Twist-a-Tree his own story. When he finished, he asked Twist-a-Tree to join him on his journey.

The two men traveled on together, but they had not traveled long before they heard a terrible noise. It seemed to be coming from the bowels of the earth and it sounded as though the ground itself was being torn asunder. Just then they saw a man on the horizon. He was squatting with his back against a mountain and his hands under the mountain's edge. The man grunted and groaned and strained so hard that the veins on his neck bulged and sweat poured from his forehead. Then he straightened his knees and, lo and behold, with a great rumble the mountain moved.

Pea-Roll-Along stepped up to the man. "Greetings, my good man," he said. "Tell us who you are and what you are doing with that mountain."

"My name is Move-a-Mountain," came the answer. "It is my fate to move mountains and change the landscape."

"How did you come by this fate?" asked Pea-Roll-Along.

"Well, my parents had no children and for years they wanted a baby more than anything. Then one day my mother saw a mushroom on the side of a mountain. It was the whitest, most perfect mushroom she had ever seen. So she ate it, and not long after that, I was born."

"Then we are brothers!" exclaimed Pea-Roll-Along, and he told Move-a-Mountain his own story and the story of Twist-a-Tree. When he finished, he asked Move-a-Mountain to join them on their journey.

So the three men traveled together, but they had not traveled long before they heard another terrible noise. It sounded as if all the waters of the earth were being sucked from the streams and rivers and lakes. Just then they saw a man up ahead. He had long whiskers and he was dipping them in the river. After he drenched the whiskers, he twirled and whirled them, and the waters parted with a terrible sucking sound.

Pea-Roll-Along approached the man. "Greetings, my good man," he said. "Tell us who you are and what you are doing with the river."

"My name is Whirly-Whiskers," came the answer. "It is my fate to part the waters and make passage through streams and rivers possible for those who follow."

"And how did you come by this fate?" asked the hero.

"Well, for many years my parents had no children, but they wanted a baby more than anything. Then one day my mother saw a clear, blue stream. It was the clearest, bluest stream she had ever seen. So she drank from it, and not long after that, I was born."

"Then we are brothers!" Pea-Roll-Along again exclaimed. He told Whirly-Whiskers his own story, followed by the stories of Twist-a-Tree and Move-a-Mountain. When he finished, he asked Whirly-Whiskers to join them on their journey.

So the four traveled together. The journey was easy for the four men. Every time a tree stood in their path, Twist-a-Tree removed it. When they came up against a mountain, Move-a-Mountain squatted down beside it and moved it out of the way. And whenever they came upon a river, Whirly-Whiskers twirled his whiskers so the waters parted for them.

Toward dusk, the four came upon a strange little hut that stood beside a huge lake. It looked well maintained and in good repair, but it seemed to be deserted. The four men walked around the hut. The fences were all neat and new. Then they went inside the hut. The walls were freshly painted and the *rushnyky** on the walls were cleaned and ironed.

"Hello! Hello? Anybody home?" they called out as they searched the hut. Yet no matter how loudly they called, no one answered them.

"Our destiny has led us here," said Pea-Roll-Along. "We must settle in this hut and see what fate will bring." So the four brothers cooked themselves supper and bedded down in the hut: Twist-a-Tree and Move-a-Mountain next to the stove, Whirly-Whiskers on a bench near the icon corner, and Pea-Roll-Along on a bench near the door.

After their long journey, everyone slept soundly—everyone except Pea-Roll-Along. All night he was troubled by strange dreams. He dreamed of a land of dragons and gnomes. In the middle of the land sat a beautiful maiden, crying. She seemed to be calling out to the hero, but Pea-Roll-Along could not understand what she was saying.

---

*rushnyky (plural of rushnyk)—*Embroidered towels used as decoration and to adorn icons and holy images, as well as in engagement ceremonies and other rituals.*

The next morning, when the brothers awoke, Pea-Roll-Along told them about his dream. "Surely we are in a strange land," he said, "so we must explore it. Twist-a-Tree," he continued, "you are the eldest brother. Stay here and mind the hut. Perhaps you could even cook us a dinner. The rest of us will see what we can find. We'll do some hunting too, and maybe we'll bring home something a bit more substantial for tomorrow's supper."

The brothers all agreed. Twist-a-Tree gathered some roots, mushrooms, and berries. Then he chopped some wood. He set a pot to boil on the stove, put all he had gathered into the pot, and soon the smell of a delicious vegetable stew filled the air.

"This will be a tasty supper," Twist-a-Tree said to himself. Then he lay down to rest and wait for his brothers. He had just nodded off to sleep when he heard a loud knocking on the door.

RAP-TAP-TAP! RAP-TAP-TAP!

"Who's there?" Twist-a-Tree called.

"Let me in!" came the answer. "I'm hungry. I want my stew." Before Twist-a-Tree could answer, the door flew open and there stood a wee little man. He stood only about one hand tall, no bigger than a doll, but he had a loud voice and a haughty demeanor. But the strangest thing about him was his long, long beard. It stretched out behind him so far that Twist-a-Tree could not see its end.

"What a rude little man!" said Twist-a-Tree. "Let yourself in!" The little man clambered over the threshold and entered the house.

Then he stood by the table. "Lift me up to the table," he demanded. "I'm hungry. I want to eat!"

"Lift yourself up," replied Twist-a-Tree. "Why should I help you to a supper that is not even yours?"

At this, the little man flew into a rage. He vaulted onto the table, grabbed Twist-a-Tree by the hair, and swung him around and around. Then he hung Twist-a-Tree by the belt on a nail in the wall. After that, he lifted Twist-a-Tree's shirt, tore a strip of skin from the helpless man's back, rolled it up, and put it in his pocket. Finally, he took the pot from the stove, set it on the table, and ate the whole stew, even the roots meant only for seasoning.

As quickly as he had appeared, the little man was gone. So there was Twist-a-Tree, hanging on the wall with a strip of skin missing from his back and no supper to feed his brothers. What was he to do? Twist-a-Tree's back stung horribly and his eyes watered ferociously. Finally he did the one thing he knew how to do—he twisted. He twisted and pulled, and twisted and turned, and somehow he managed to free himself. But just as he was about to start dinner again, he heard the singing of his three brothers as they returned from their hunt. They walked in and threw the game they had caught on the floor by the stove.

"We're famished!" they said in unison. "Give us some food, brother, and then you can tell us about your day and we can tell you about ours."

"But there is no food," Twist-a-Tree answered sheepishly. He was about to tell them about the little man when he stopped in embarrassment. How could he admit that a little man only a hand high had beaten him? "I-I-I must have overslept," he stammered.

"What?" The brothers grumbled, but they all helped Twist-a-Tree fix supper. As they ate, they talked about the hunt and the forest. Only Twist-a-Tree was silent, but in their excitement none of the others noticed. Soon it was time for bed and Twist-a-Tree went to sleep without revealing his secret.

The next morning Pea-Roll-Along suggested that Move-a-Mountain take his turn at the hut while the others went out to hunt and further explore the fields and forest. Move-a-Mountain agreed. After the others left, he too chopped wood and set a pot on the stove. Then he too gathered roots and berries and added them to the meat left from the previous day's hunt. As everything began to simmer on the stove, the smell of a delicious stew filled the air. Move-a-Mountain was quite proud of himself, and he lay down to rest while he waited for his brothers. He had just nodded off to sleep when he heard a loud knocking on the door.

RAP-TAP-TAP! RAP-TAP-TAP!

"Who is it?" Move-a-Mountain called.

"Let me in!" came the answer. "I'm hungry. I want my stew." But before Move-a-Mountain could answer, the door flew open and there in the doorway stood the wee little man with the long, long beard.

"Let yourself in," Move-a-Mountain grumbled and he turned over to go back to sleep. The little man clambered over the threshold and entered the house.

"Lift me up to the table," he demanded. "I'm hungry. I want to eat!"

"Lift yourself up," replied Move-a-Mountain. "Why should I help you to a supper that is not even yours?"

Again the little man flew into a rage. He vaulted onto the table, grabbed Move-a-Mountain by the hair, and swung him around and around. Then he hung Move-a-Mountain by the belt on a nail in the wall. The little man lifted Move-a-Mountain's shirt, tore a strip of skin from the helpless man's back, rolled it up, and put it in his pocket. Finally he took the pot of stew from the stove, set it on the table, and ate it all up, even the bones.

As quickly as he had appeared, the little man was gone. So there was Move-a-Mountain hanging on the wall, with a strip of skin missing from his back and no supper to feed his brothers. What could he do? Move-a-Mountain could hardly think. The pain of his back and the pain of his humiliation were almost unbearable. Finally he did the only thing he knew how to do. He pushed and pushed against the wall with his hands and his feet, and somehow he freed himself from the nail. But just then he heard the singing of his three brothers as they returned from their hunt. When they entered the hut, they threw the game they had caught onto the floor near the stove.

"We're famished!" they all said in unison. "Give us some food, brother, and then you can tell us about your day and we can tell you about ours."

"But there is no food," Move-a-Mountain replied.

"What? Again?" exclaimed Pea-Roll-Along and Whirly-Whiskers. But Twist-a-Tree was silent. He understood all too well what had happened when Move-a-Mountain stammered, "I-I-I must have overslept."

The brothers grumbled, but they all helped Move-a-Mountain fix supper. Again they ate and talked, but the tale of the little man was left untold. The next morning Pea-Roll-Along suggested that Whirly-Whiskers be the one to stay at the hut while the others went out to hunt and explore the land. Whirly-Whiskers agreed and did just as his brothers had done before him. He put a stew to simmer on the stove and lay down to rest. Just as he was nodding off, the wee little man appeared and did to Whirly-Whiskers exactly what he had done to the others. When evening came and the brothers returned, only Pea-Roll-Along was surprised that supper was not ready. The others just set about helping Whirly-Whiskers as best they could.

The next day, of course, it was Pea-Roll-Along's turn to stay at the hut while his brothers went out to hunt and explore. As soon as his brothers had left, Pea-Roll-Along chopped wood and set a pot on the stove. He gathered roots and berries and mushrooms, and added these to the leftover meat. Then he put it all in a pot to cook on the stove, and soon the smell of a delicious stew filled the air. Pea-Roll-Along lay down to rest and wait for his brothers. He had just nodded off to sleep when he heard a loud knocking on the door.

RAP-TAP-TAP! RAP-TAP-TAP!

"Who's there?" Pea-Roll-Along called.

"Let me in!" came the answer. "I'm hungry. I want my stew." Before Pea-Roll-Along could answer, the door flew open and there in the doorway stood the wee little man with the long, long beard.

"Do come in, sir," said Pea-Roll-Along. The little man clambered over the threshold and entered the house.

"Lift me up to the table," demanded the little man. "I'm hungry. I want to eat!"

"Here, let me help you," said Pea-Roll-Along as the little man vaulted onto the table. Pea-Roll-Along set a plate before the little man and filled it with stew. The little man slurped up the stew, then grabbed Pea-Roll-Along by the hair and swung him around and around. Then he hung Pea-Roll-Along by the belt on a nail in the wall.

"What an ungrateful and impolite little man!" Pea-Roll-Along thought to himself, and then he said aloud, "What a rude way to treat someone who has welcomed you and fed you supper!"

Just then the little man lifted Pea-Roll-Along's shirt, intending to tear a strip of skin off the hero's back as he had done to the other brothers. But when he saw the mark of the peapod, he hesitated just long enough for Pea-Roll-Along to grab his club and hit the little man upon the head. The little man grabbed his head with both hands and staggered backward. Pea-Roll-Along used his club to push against the wall, lift himself off the nail, and set himself free. Then Pea-Roll-Along grabbed the little man by the beard and dragged him to the backyard. He split a tree stump with his club and wedged the little man's beard in the cleft. The little man struggled furiously, but his beard was caught fast in the tree stump.

"Whew!" Pea-Roll-Along sighed and wiped his brow. He had just stood up and straightened his back when he heard his brothers returning from their day in the forest. Pea-Roll-Along ran to meet them and started to tell them about the little man, but as he spoke, he realized that his brothers did not seem at all surprised by the story.

"Did any of you see the little man?" he asked. The three brothers silently lifted their shirts, turned their backs, and showed their wounds to Pea-Roll-Along.

"What an evil little man," gasped Pea-Roll-Along. "We had better go punish him so that he learns not to hurt people. I have him trapped by his beard in the backyard. Come with me—I'll show you."

Pea-Roll-Along and his brothers went outside, but when they came to where the little man had been trapped, there was no tree stump and no little man. Unable to free his beard, the little man had pulled the tree stump out, with his beard still caught in it, and dragged it after him as he walked. He had left a clear trail—a deep rut cut into the earth where he had dragged the stump—so the four brothers followed it. Through the backyard, down the hill, and right into the lake it went.

"We must catch him," said Pea-Roll-Along. "It is our fate to rid the world of this evil demon! Whirly-Whiskers, part the water so we can follow the trail."

Whirly-Whiskers did as he was told. He dipped his whiskers into the water and whirled and twirled them until the waters parted. There they could all see a trail that led down along the lake bottom. Further and further it went. The four brothers followed the trail, hoping to catch sight of the little man, but the trail seemed to stretch before them as they walked.

As they ventured deeper, the walls of water rose higher and higher, blocking out the light from above. It grew darker, darker, and darker still. It was so dark that they had almost lost sight of the trail, when suddenly it began to grow light again. The brothers looked up, but the walls of water at the sides of the path were so high that they could no longer see the heavens. Where was the light coming from? They squinted and looked all around. Yes, now they saw—it was coming from within the waters. There, ahead of them, was a glowing castle, shining with copper, silver, and gold.

The brothers approached the castle cautiously and pushed against the huge gates. The gates swung open and the brothers entered. They looked to the left and they looked to the right. All around them were gold, silver, and precious stones, but there was not a soul in sight. No one greeted them and no one stopped them, so they walked further and further inside. Then they heard a muffled sound coming from behind closed doors. Pea-Roll-Along gently pushed on the door and peered into the room. There, in the middle of the room, sat a beautiful princess, sobbing.

"Why are you crying?" Pea-Roll-Along asked.

"Why should I not cry?" she replied. "I have been held prisoner in this underworld for many years and now some fool has gone and trapped the little man's beard in a tree stump. He's so angry that when he frees himself, I know he will punish me. I will be the one to suffer."

"Don't cry, beautiful princess," Pea-Roll-Along said. "It was I who trapped the man's beard, and it was not foolishness but fate. Fate has sent me here and surely fate will show me what to do next."

"Yes," agreed the princess, "it is always good to follow fate, but it is also good to know what you are up against. This little man is no ordinary man. You must know that his strength is in his beard and that his soul is in a walnut shell at the top of the world tree. Only if you control his beard can you control the little man. And only if you find his soul can you kill him."

No sooner had the princess finished speaking than Pea-Roll-Along heard a terrible noise. It was the little man approaching. He threw open the door and when his gaze fell on Pea-Roll-Along, his eyes blazed like bonfires. Truly, the little man's rage knew no bounds. He flew at Pea-Roll-Along, dragging the stump at the end of his beard. They fought long and hard. Pea-Roll-Along kept trying to strike the little man with his club, but the little man was so quick and agile that every blow fell on the floor or the furniture instead. Even the stump did not seem to slow the little man down.

"Brothers! Brothers!" Pea-Roll-Along called. "Help me! Can't you see I'm in trouble?"

The brothers could see well enough, but being confronted by the horrible little man again had set fear in their hearts and they stood frozen in the doorway, doing nothing.

"Move-a-Mountain! You must trap his beard!" yelled Pea-Roll-Along. "Grab something heavy as only you know how and set it on his beard. Only when his beard is trapped will we be able to control him."

Only then did Move-a-Mountain come to his senses. He saw a huge cooking pot in the hallway—a black, iron pot that surely weighed a ton. Move-a-Mountain squatted and put his hands under the pot. Then he straightened his knees and lifted. The pot fell squarely on the little man's beard, trapping it so that the little man could not move. Swiftly Pea-Roll-Along swung his club and hit the little

 man on the head as hard as he could. The blow stunned the little man but did not kill him. As the princess had said, the little man's soul was outside his body and no attack on his flesh could destroy his life force.

Even in the heat of battle, Pea-Roll-Along remembered the princess's words. He called to Twist-a-Tree. "Twist-a-Tree, you must find the world tree and break the walnut on top of it. Only then can we defeat this demon!"

Now Twist-a-Tree sprang into action. He looked around, but where to find the world tree? The princess, seeing his confusion, called out, "There,

there, see over there? The roots of the world tree grow into this lake. The walnut is at the top. You must get to the top and break the walnut. Only then can you defeat the little man."

Twist-a-Tree ran to the roots of the world tree. He twisted and pulled and twisted and pulled again. The tree creaked and bent. Twist-a-Tree grunted and groaned and kept pulling. Slowly he pulled the trunk beneath the waters. Then he pulled the branches beneath the waters too. And there in the branches sat one shiny walnut about the same size as the little man's head. Twist-a-Tree could not hold the tree down and grab the walnut at the same time, so he called to Whirly-Whiskers.

Whirly-Whiskers reached for the walnut, snapped it off the branch, and threw it as hard as he could in the direction of Pea-Roll-Along. Just then Twist-a-Tree let go of the tree. *WHOOSH*! It sprang back up, and the force of its motion propelled the walnut into the castle and right into the room where Pea-Roll-Along was trying to keep the little man at bay. The walnut rolled and rolled, stopping just inches from the little man's chin. The little man's eyes grew wide and he began trembling with fear. Seeing this, Pea-Roll-Along felt sorry for a moment, but then the little man tried to kick Pea-Roll-Along and he knew that it was his fate to destroy the little man. He lifted his club and struck. When it hit the walnut, the club shattered and so did the walnut. The pieces of walnut turned into sparks of light that drifted upward, while the body of the little man melted into a pool of dark, vile-smelling oil that seeped into the earth.

Pea-Roll-Along ran to free the princess. Taking her by the hand, he told his brothers to gather all the gold, silver, copper, and precious stones they could carry. Each filled a bag and slung it over his shoulders. Off they went.

When the four brothers emerged from the lake, they passed by the little hut and went into the forest the way they had come days before. Soon darkness and fatigue overcame them and they bedded down for the night, each brother with his head on a sack of gold and Pea-Roll-Along with his head in the lap of the princess.

Morning came and Twist-a-Tree awoke, then Move-a-Mountain, then Whirly-Whiskers. But Pea-Roll-Along did not wake up, nor did the princess. They slept a hero's sleep, the sleep of relief, the sleep of accomplishing one's fate. The three brothers waited and waited, but Pea-Roll-Along did not wake up. Then the brothers started to grumble.

"Why should he have the princess while we have only money? Could he have beaten the little man without us?" said Whirly-Whiskers.

Move-a-Mountain joined in, "What if he tells people about the hut? What if people find out that a little man no bigger than a doll beat three mighty champions?"

"I will twist a tree about him," said Twist-a-Tree.

"And I will move a mountain and set it on top of him," agreed Move-a-Mountain.

"And I will twirl my whiskers and part the waters and let them flood over him," said Whirly-Whiskers.

So the three brothers did just as they said they would. They lifted Pea-Roll-Along's head, took the princess from under him, and trapped him with a tree, a mountain, and water. Then they left.

When Pea-Roll-Along awoke, he did not know where he was or what had happened. All he knew was that he was surrounded by darkness. He reached for the princess, but all he felt was tree bark. Still groping, he touched the soil. Slowly he struggled from the grasp of the twisted tree and slowly he dug through the soil of the mountain, only to find himself deep underwater. As he swam to the surface, he realized what had happened to him.

"So that's how my brothers repay me!" he thought. He emerged from the water and walked in search of the others.

Pea-Roll-Along walked and walked until he heard a great tumult. He saw a city in the distance, decorated with ribbons, streamers, and bright lights. Music was playing, people were dancing and singing, and everyone seemed to be celebrating a great occasion. "What's going on here?" he asked an old man who passed his way.

"Oh, three great champions are visiting our town. They say they have rid the world of a great evil and they have sacks of silver, gold, copper, and precious jewels. And they have a princess too. They say when she awakens, she will choose our next ruler from among them. The other two will serve as generals or councilors."

Pea-Roll-Along thanked the old man for the information and hurried toward the center of the city. As he approached the square, he saw that a crowd had gathered. Many were standing on tiptoe, straining to see.

"What's going on here?" he asked an old woman standing at the edge of the crowd.

"Oh, the princess has awakened," she replied. "Now she will choose her husband, our next king."

Pea-Roll-Along pushed his way to the front of the crowd just in time to see the princess being led onto a balcony of the palace. Twist-a-Tree, Move-a-Mountain, and Whirly-Whiskers were all lined up on a stage that had been erected in the square below.

The princess looked and looked. "But there were four of you," she said. "Where is the fourth champion?"

"Here I am!" Pea-Roll-Along stepped onto the platform to join his brothers. The three brothers looked nervously at one another, but quickly regained their composure.

"Choose!" they demanded.

The princess looked from one hero to the next. All had been conceived by fate, so they all looked the same. There was no way to tell them apart.

"Why don't you look at our backs, fair princess?" shouted Pea-Roll-Along. The princess did not understand, but told all four to turn their backs to her and lift their shirts. Then she understood. In the middle of the three brothers' backs were the red scars where the little man had torn flesh from them. But in the middle of Pea-Roll-Along's back was the birthmark in the shape of a peapod.

So the princess chose Pea-Roll-Along and they were married. All the people of the city rejoiced at their new king and queen.

As for the three brothers, for awhile Pea-Roll-Along thought to banish them from the city, but he soon realized that the four of them were bound together by fate. So he called them to his chamber and talked with them. The three brothers apologized for trying to leave Pea-Roll-Along. Then they all agreed to work and live together as they had before they met the little man.

Thus they lived together, as fate had decreed. Pea-Roll-Along also brought his parents, and the parents of his brothers-in-fate, to the city. The old folks were overjoyed to be reunited with their beloved children and the four brothers lived happily together, using their special talents, heroes all. &

–Natalie O. Kononenko

The Magic Egg

W HEN THE LARK WAS KING
and the shrew mouse was queen and the
whole world belonged to them, everything
was peaceful and good. For many years the
world and all its creatures prospered, without
wars or crime or hatred. Then one year, the
mouse and the lark decided to plant a field of
wheat. Together the royal couple planted the

seeds. All through the summer they tended their crop. They watered,
they weeded, they cultivated, and they kept it free from pests. The
wheat flourished. At the end of the season, the mouse and the lark
harvested their crop, piling it high in their storehouse. Then they
carefully divided the harvest between them, grain by grain. But when
all had been divided, there was one tiny grain of wheat left over.
That's when the trouble began.

"It's mine!" claimed the mouse.

"Mine, mine," shrieked the lark, flapping his wings. And so
they fussed and quarreled all day long, for there was no higher
authority to settle the dispute. Finally the mouse shrugged her tiny
shoulders and said, "Well then, I'll bite the grain in two and we'll
each have half." The lark agreed to this and the mouse quickly seized
the grain of wheat, but instead of biting it in two, she swallowed it
whole!

Oh dear! The tiny lark was beside himself. He strutted back and
forth upon a tree branch with his feathers ruffled high, and then he
shouted for all the world to hear, "This means war!"

He called together all the birds of the heavens as his troops and
began training them as soldiers. The shrew mouse, not to be outdone,
assembled all the beasts of the earth and started shouting orders to
them. They marched to and fro. Then the war began.

At first it seemed the birds would win—they could fly, and they attacked from above at will. When the poor earthbound animals tried to defend themselves, the birds simply flew to the trees. Some animals tried to climb the trees to get at the birds, but as soon as the animals drew near, the birds simply flapped over to the next tree, hooting and cackling raucously.

The birds celebrated victory after victory and the animals grew more and more discouraged, but the haughty shrew mouse refused to give up. One night, as she inspected her troops, the mouse noticed that there were no ants among them.

What? Not a single ant? This is unacceptable!" she shrieked. She summoned all the ants to report for duty at once. As the ants filed into rank, the little queen strutted and fumed, her tiny paws clenched behind her back. What could she do with these worthless ants? She thought and thought. Then she had an idea. Her eyes sparkled with glee as she addressed the ants.

"Attention, attention please," she said, "I want you to listen carefully now." The ants fell silent as the mouse gave instructions. "After the sun sets and the birds have fallen asleep, I want you to climb the trees and gnaw all the feathers from the birds' wings. Tomorrow when they try to fly, hee-hee, they will have a big surprise!"

 So the ants did as they were told. They waited till dark, quietly marched over to the trees, and climbed them. Then they chewed all the feathers from the sleeping birds. By the time they finished it was nearly dawn, so they hurried back to camp. The shrew mouse met the ants as they entered. She fidgeted and paced, and paced and fidgeted, but she could not wait for the sun.

"Up, up, soldiers. It's time to fight again—and this time we will win!" she shouted. The animals staggered groggily from their sleep and prepared for battle. When the lark saw the animals assembling, he called to his troops, ordering them to attack immediately.

"Let's beat them once and for all," he called out. The lark and all the birds rose from the trees, but without feathers, their wings could not carry them. One by one they tumbled to the ground, where they lay helpless until the beasts pounced on them and tore them to pieces.

❧ ❧ ❧

All the birds perished in this final battle, except one eagle, who saw what was happening to his comrades and decided to stay on his perch. There he sat, pondering his fate, when a young *cossack** appeared. Now this *cossack*, whose name was Bohdan, was out hunting, but he'd had no luck. When he saw the eagle, he thought to himself, "Ah, perhaps my luck has changed." The *cossack* raised his bow and took aim, but before he could shoot, the eagle called out, "Please don't shoot me. I can be of service to you."

The startled hunter lowered his bow, wondering if he had really heard what he thought he had just heard.

"Oh, I must be imagining things," he told himself. Again he took aim.

Again the eagle cried out, "Don't shoot me. Take me home with you and feed me. I will repay your kindness." The *cossack* lowered his bow and shook his head as though to clear it. Then a third time he raised his bow.

"Stop!" This time the eagle's voice was loud and clear, and he looked straight into the hunter's eyes. "Do not kill me. Take me with you and you'll see how much I can help you."

"This is no ordinary eagle," the *cossack* said to himself. He walked over to the tree, gently lifted the eagle from the perch, and carried him home.

The eagle lay quietly as Bohdan carried him. He did not make a peep, nor did he struggle to get free. But when they reached the *cossack's* home he spoke again, saying, "I will need meat to regain my strength." Now, Bohdan owned two cows and a steer and upon hearing the eagle's words, he slaughtered one of the cows. Every day he gave the eagle a large piece of meat and slowly the bird grew stronger. A year passed and the meat was gone, but by this time the eagle's feathers had grown back. The eagle asked Bohdan to set him free so he could fly. The man released him and the great bird went soaring into the air. He flew and flew.

After a time the eagle returned. "I'm still weak," he said, "I need more meat." So the *cossack* slaughtered the second cow and fed its meat to the eagle. Another year passed and again the eagle asked to be set free. This time he flew faster and higher. He flew the entire day, and only when the sun dropped below the horizon did he return.

"I am still not strong enough," he told Bohdan. "Kill the steer and feed it to me."

---

* cossack—*warrior; a Ukrainian soldier.*

Now Bohdan hesitated. Should he do as the eagle said? He had already sacrificed two cows, and for what? He was not a rich man. "Oh well," he thought, "what good is a steer without the cows?" So he slaughtered the steer and continued to feed the eagle.

The eagle grew stronger and stronger. By the end of the third year, he was bigger and more powerful than ever before. His eyes shone fiercely, his feathers glistened, and when he spread his wings, the leaves on all the trees trembled. Once again he asked to be set free and Bohdan did as he wished. Up to the clouds he flew, soaring over rivers and mountains. Then he returned to the man and said, "Now jump on my back."

At first Bohdan refused, but the eagle fixed his eye on the man and demanded, "Jump on my back." Bohdan hemmed and hawed, then mounted the bird as he would a horse.

So the eagle took the *cossack* into the heavens. With the breeze licking his cheeks, Bohdan took the ride of his life. But just when he was beginning to enjoy the ride, the eagle dropped him. Tumbling through the air, Bohdan quickly said his prayers, for he was certain he would die. Just before he hit the ground, the eagle swooped under him and lifted him back into the sky.

"How did that feel?" asked the eagle once they were high in the sky again.

"It felt as though all the life had drained from me," the man replied.

"Ah—that is how I felt when you first raised your bow and took aim at me." Then the great bird flew high above the clouds and once again dropped the man, catching him just before he hit the ground.

As the eagle flew up to the clouds with the *cossack*, he asked, "And how did that feel?"

"It felt as though my bones had turned to sand," Bohdan replied.

"Ah—that is how I felt when you raised your bow the second time and took aim at me."

Then the eagle flew so high that the earth was tiny beneath them. Again he dropped the man. This time as the *cossack* fell, he saw the earth rise up beneath him and his heart almost stopped. Just before he hit the ground, the eagle swooped under him, caught him, and flew back up to the heavens.

"Now how did that feel?" the eagle asked.

"I felt I was no longer of this world," Bohdan said.

"Ah—that is how I felt when you raised your bow against me the third time. But now we are even and all is forgiven. Hang on and I will take you to the land where I was born." The *cossack* wrapped his arms around the eagle's neck as together they flew far and away.

When they reached the eagle's homeland, they stopped at the house of the eagle's uncle. As Bohdan dismounted, the eagle instructed him, "Go knock on their door. If they ask if you have seen their nephew, tell them you can bring him before their eyes, but only if they give you the magic egg."

Bohdan had no idea what this meant, but he had become accustomed to obeying the eagle, so he went straightaway to the door and knocked.

"Are you here of your own free will or by the will of another?" asked a gruff voice from behind the door. Bohdan was not afraid.

"Why, a true *cossack* never goes anywhere but of his own free will," he answered. The door opened and the bird's old uncle greeted his visitor.

"Welcome, welcome," he said. "Tell me, in your travels have you seen our poor nephew? He left for the war three years ago and we haven't seen him since." The old uncle shook his head ruefully and stroked his beak.

"Seen your nephew?" Bohdan replied brightly. "Why, I'll bring him before your eyes if you give me the magic egg."

The uncle stepped back and eyed the man suspiciously. Then he shook his head.

"Oh, no. No. We can't do that. It's better that we never see him again," he said. Then he slammed the door in the *cossack's* face.

Bohdan went back to the eagle and told him what had happened, but the eagle just shrugged. "Let's fly farther then," he said, and Bohdan hopped onto the eagle's back as they took to the air.

It wasn't long before they reached the home of the eagle's brother. Again they landed. "Go up to that house and knock. When they ask if you've seen their brother, say that you'll bring him before their eyes if they give you the magic egg," said the eagle. Bohdan walked up to the door and knocked.

"Are you here by your own free will or by the will of another?" a voice boomed from behind the door.

Bohdan replied without hesitating, "A true *cossack* goes nowhere but of his own free will." The door swung open and there stood the eagle's brother.

"Traveler, have you heard of our own poor brother who went to war? He's been gone three years and we haven't had a word from him."

Bohdan smiled, "Heard of him? Why, if you give me the magic egg, I will bring him before your eyes."

At this the brother paled and began stammering, "The m-m-magic egg? Wh-why, no. No, indeed. We cannot give you the magic egg. It would be better never to see him again." And once again a door was slammed in the *cossack's* face.

So Bohdan turned on his heels. When he reached the eagle, he recounted what had happened. The eagle just sighed.

"Let's fly farther, then," he said. Back in the air, they flew and flew until they came to the house of the eagle's father.

"Go up to that house, and when they ask if you've seen their poor son, tell them you will bring him before their eyes if they give you the magic egg." The *cossack* did as he was told.

"Are you here of your own free will or by the will of another?" thundered a voice from inside.

"A true *cossack* goes nowhere except by his own free will," Bohdan replied, and the door opened. There stood the eagle's father, as strong and beautiful as the eagle himself, but older and wiser too.

"Have you seen or heard from our poor son who left for the war three years ago?" asked the eagle's father. "Or perhaps you have heard about him."

"I'll bring your son before your very eyes if you give me the magic egg," Bohdan replied. The eagle's father stepped back in surprise.

"The magic egg? Why, what good would that do you? The lucky penny would suit you better." He patted the *cossack's* shoulder and repeated, "Yes, I will give you the lucky penny."

But Bohdan insisted, "No, it's the magic egg I want."

The old eagle rolled his eyes and said, "Well, we could give you three sacks of gold . . ." But Bohdan interrupted before he finished the sentence.

"Excuse me, sir, but only the magic egg will do."

The eagle's father sighed, "So be it. Bring our son back to us and you shall have the magic egg."

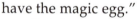

Bohdan ran back to the eagle and together they approached the father's house. So overjoyed were the eagle's parents that they immediately gave the *cossack* the magic egg, and then they gave him their blessings. As Bohdan prepared to leave, the eagle's father turned to him.

"Take care in your travels that the egg does not break," he said and Bohdan nodded in agreement. "And when you reach home, build a high fence around it lest you lose everything." Again the *cossack* agreed. Then he set out on his journey home.

Bohdan walked and walked. The day wore on and the sun rose high and beat down upon his head, and the dust rose up from the road to parch his throat with thirst. When he saw a spring, he quickly hurried to it and bent to drink, but as he did, the magic egg dropped to the ground and shattered. Herds of cattle and sheep and pigs sprang from the egg, stampeding around the man. Bohdan ran after them, but the cattle went one way and the sheep went another. The faster he ran, the faster they ran, and just as he got the cattle together, the sheep would go off in another direction. It wasn't long till the man tired. As he stood panting and scratching his head, a huge old she-dragon slithered up next to him. Her skin was scaly and her beady eyes locked upon him as she spoke.

"What will you give me if I get the animals back in the egg?" she wheedled.

Exasperated by his own efforts, Bohdan wiped his brow and replied, "What is it you want?"

"I want whatever's new at your house," the she-dragon replied.

Well, the *cossack* was not a rich man, and for his life he could think of nothing new he might have that the she-dragon would want, so he agreed. The dragon waved her huge tail and breathed smoke and fire, and soon all the animals had been herded back into the egg. Then with her sharp talons she patched the egg so cleverly that it looked as though it had never been broken. Bohdan sighed with relief when it was finished. He put the egg back in his pocket and returned home.

As he entered his house, Bohdan's mouth dropped open and his heart sank. There sat his wife, rocking a newborn child. In agony, he realized that he had promised his own son to the she-dragon.

Bohdan's wife looked up. "This is our son, Taras," she said. "Why do you look so sad?" The *cossack* told his wife all that had happened. Then they threw their arms around each other and wept bitterly.

క్ష   క్ష   క్ష

The *cossack* and his wife realized that there was really nothing they could do to change their fate, and they went on with their life together. They built a fence around the egg and broke the shell, releasing all the herds of animals. Over the next years the two of them worked hard, the herds multiplied, and the *cossack's* family flourished. Little Taras grew; fine and strong he grew.

When the boy came of age, his father told him about the promise that had been made to the she-dragon. The brave young Taras took it in stride.

"Don't worry," he said, "I will go to the dragon as you have promised. I'll be all right—you'll see." And with that he walked away.

When Taras reached the she-dragon's house, he found her pacing impatiently.

"It's about time!" she fumed. "Don't you realize there's work to be done?" Taras removed his hat and made a little bow.

The she-dragon snorted. "If you ever want to leave this place, you had better listen carefully. There are three tasks you must complete, and you must follow my directions carefully." Taras nodded.

"See that forest over there?" The dragon gestured to a clump of trees at the horizon. "I want you to clear that forest, plow the field, and plant it with wheat." Again Taras nodded.

"THEN," the dragon continued, "I want you to reap the wheat and put it in storage. And I want you to thresh the wheat and mill it, and bake me a tasty *kalach**, that is to say, a bun."

The old dragon looked slyly at the boy to see how he would react, but Taras simply replied, "Yes, ma'am, I understand."

So she continued, "AND I want that bun to be at my bedside when I awaken tomorrow morning." Taras's eyes grew wide, but he said nothing. He just turned and walked out to the forest.

When he reached a stone pillar at the edge of the woods, Taras stopped and leaned against it to ponder his fate. He thought and thought, but no matter how hard he thought he could not figure out how to accomplish his first task. Realizing that it was impossible, Taras buried his face in his hands and wept. His tears fell to the ground, soaking the soil.

"Why are you crying?" The gentle voice of a maiden greeted him. Now, Taras did not know it, but this was the she-dragon's daughter, Olena, who had been banished from the house for her kindness. Held captive by the land, Olena had been released from the soil by the boy's tears.

"How can I help crying?" Taras sniffled. "The she-dragon has asked me to do something that cannot be done, and I must do it in one night."

"What is it that is so impossible?" asked the girl. Taras told her.

"If you promise to marry me, I'll do all that she has demanded," said Olena. Taras stopped his crying and gladly agreed. "Better get some sleep now so you can bring her the roll before dawn," the girl cautioned.

*kalach—*a bread or bun, often made with twisted or plaited dough.*

Taras did as Olena said. As soon as he laid his head on the grass he was fast asleep. Then the girl clapped her hands and the land began to snap and crackle. Quick as the blink of an eye, she cleared the forest and plowed the field and sowed the wheat and reaped it and put it into barns. In another eyeblink, she threshed the wheat, milled it, and baked a fine *kalach*. As she pulled it from the oven, she called to Taras.

"Wake up now, it's almost dawn. Take this *kalach* to the she-dragon and place it at her bedside." Taras did not question the girl, but simply took the bun and brought it to the dragon, who lay snoring in her bed.

When the she-dragon opened her eyes, she was at first amazed to see all that had been done. But as she chewed her *kalach* and surveyed her land, she began scheming. Placing a gnarled hand on her hip, she spoke haughtily, "It's true that you have done as I asked, but that was just the first task. Let's see how you do with the second!" Taras spoke not a word, but waited for the dragon's instructions.

"See that mountain?" She pointed to a snowy peak in the distance. "You must dig a passage so the Dnipro River can flow through it. AND you must build a storehouse on the banks of the river and fill it with the wheat you have harvested. AND, as merchants sail through the mountain, you must sell all the wheat to them, collect the money in a bag, and give it to me." The old dragon pointed to her chest, gave a sideways glance at the boy, and snorted. "This you must do by sunrise tomorrow."

Again Taras walked silently away. When he reached the stone pillar, he leaned against it and cried, for this task was even more impossible than the first. As his tears ran down the pillar and soaked the earth, he again heard the voice of the maiden.

"Crying again? Now what is wrong?" Taras lifted his head and told the girl of his predicament, but Olena just smiled. "I will do everything," she said, "go to sleep now." So Taras lay down and fell fast asleep as the she-dragon's daughter set to work.

In a heartbeat she tunneled through the mountain and set the Dnipro River flowing in a new direction. Then she erected a huge storehouse and filled it with wheat. As merchants sailed through, she sold the wheat to them. When all the wheat had been sold, she held in her hands a heavy sack of gold.

Again Olena called to Taras, saying, "Wake up now and take this gold to the she-dragon's bedside." So Taras did as she said and just as light stepped over the horizon, he set the bag of coins next to the sleeping she-dragon.

The she-dragon opened her eyes and blinked. She lifted the bag and shook it. The coins clinked. She looked inside and saw gold. Her beady eyes widened. When she looked outside and saw the Dnipro River running through the mountain, her eyes widened even more. Everything she had asked for had been done. But lest the boy notice her pleasure, she put on a grave face.

"Oh-ho, you think you are so clever," she scolded. "Those were the easy tasks. Now you must accomplish the difficult task. Yes, now you must catch the golden hare!" The she-dragon's eyes flashed and she gave a wicked laugh. "See how you do with *that* one!"

Taras walked out to the field and stood at the stone pillar thinking. He did not even know what the golden hare was. How on earth would he be able to catch it? As he thought thus, he began to weep, his tears once more spilling to the earth.

"Why do you weep now?" Again it was the she-dragon's daughter. Taras was relieved to see her and he quickly recounted his conversation with the dragon and her instructions for the third task. Olena shook her head in disbelief.

"That IS a difficult task," she said. "To accomplish this I will need your help." The young girl pointed to a rock in the distance.

"See that rock? We will go there and I will drive the hare from his burrow. When he comes out, you must catch him. Whatever comes from the hole, grab it and don't let go."

Taras agreed and went to stand at the entrance of the burrow. The girl went into the burrow and began beating the ground. When a snake slithered from the hole, Taras grabbed it, but the snake began to writhe and hiss, and the boy let go. The snake quickly slithered back into the hole.

Meanwhile, Olena continued her beating. After a time she emerged. "Have you seen anything yet?"

"Only a snake," replied Taras, "but it tried to bite me, so I had to let it go."

Now the girl frowned and stamped her foot. "Oh no! That was the golden hare!" she said. "Listen, I'll try again. This time, grab *whatever* comes out and hold onto it no matter what." Then she scrambled back into the burrow and began beating. After a time, an old woman crawled out and said to Taras, "What are you looking for, son?"

"I'm trying to catch the golden hare," he replied.

The old woman chuckled and shook her head. "There's no golden hare here," she said, "only snakes." Then she hobbled down the road, laughing softly to herself and shaking her head. Taras watched her disappear over the horizon.

Again Olena emerged and asked, "No rabbit yet? Haven't you seen anything?"

Taras looked at the girl disdainfully. "Only an old woman, and according to her there are no hares at all in this hole—only snakes!"

"What?! You were tricked again!" Taras felt his face grow warm with embarrassment as the girl scolded, "That was the golden hare disguised as an old woman. Why didn't you listen to me? Now he's gone."

The girl fell silent as she thought. Then she continued, "There's only one thing we can do now. I'll turn myself into a rabbit and you can set me on the she-dragon's table. She'll think I'm the golden hare." With that, the girl became a golden rabbit and Taras carried her to the she-dragon. He plopped the hare on the table and said, "There's your golden hare. Now I'm leaving." While the she-dragon stood with her mouth gaping, Taras walked away. The dragon turned to call her husband. But as soon as she turned her back, the hare changed back into a girl and went running after the boy.

When the she-dragon discovered that she had been fooled, she flew into a rage. She screamed and threw pots against the wall and created a terrible ruckus. When her husband came running to see what was wrong, she bellowed at him, "They're gone! Find them!" So the dragon's husband took off down the road.

As for Taras and Olena, they ran and ran. When they felt the earth tremble beneath their feet, Olena said, "He's coming after us. Soon he'll overtake us." Taras scowled with worry and the girl continued, "I'll change myself into a field of wheat and you into an old farmer. When my father asks if you have seen us, tell him that a young man and woman passed by when you were sowing the field."

The two had no sooner transformed themselves than the he-dragon arrived. "Have you seen a young man and a young woman pass by?" he asked the farmer.

The farmer (who was really Taras in disguise) took off his straw hat and gazed into the distance. "Well, yes, I believe I have. I believe they passed by when I was sowing this wheat. They headed east."

"Hmmph!" grunted the dragon, "that can't be them—they just ran away today and this wheat is ready for harvest." He turned on his heels and thundered home. When he arrived, his wife screeched at him, "What are you doing back here empty-handed? Did you see no sign of them?"

"I only saw an old farmer tending a field of wheat," he shrugged, "and when I asked about a young man and a young woman, he said only that he had seen two people pass by when the wheat was being planted."

Now the she-dragon's eyes blazed and she shouted, "You fool—that was them! Why didn't you tear the farmer to shreds and burn his field?" She pointed a long claw toward the door, ordering, "Go back and find them. FIND THEM!"

So the he-dragon ran down the road again, his eyes roving the land in search of the young pair. By then Taras and Olena were growing tired and although they ran, they ran slower. They were panting with exhaustion and sweat poured from their bodies. It was not long till the earth shook and the dragon was again at their heels.

Olena turned to Taras, her eyes wide with fear. "It's him again! I'll change myself into an ancient monastery and you into a monk. When the dragon asks if you've seen us, tell him a young man and woman passed by when the monastery was being built."

Almost as soon as they had transformed, the dragon thundered over the horizon. He saw a shimmering sight almost like a mirage. As he approached, he saw that it was an old, old building. When he reached the monastery, he spotted the monk and stomped up to him.

"Have you seen a young man and a young woman?" he roared. "If you value your life, you'll answer truthfully!" The old monk shrugged and squinted and scratched his bald head.

"It is told," he began, "that a fine lad and a lovely maid passed this way when the monastery was being built." He shrugged again and said, "Apart from that, I know nothing."

The dragon snorted, "Why, that must have been a hundred years ago! These two have been gone only a day." So he turned and went home, only to be greeted by his angry wife.

"What?! No young maid? No young man? Didn't you see anything at all?"

"All I saw was an old monk standing near a monastery," he sulked.

"AND?" The she-dragon snorted a thick plume of smoke.

"He said that a young man and a young woman had passed by when the monastery was being built," the he-dragon replied, adding, "and you know that monastery was at least a hundred years old."

"You ignoramus!" roared his wife. "That was them! You should have killed the monk and trampled the monastery to rubble." Then she stomped to the door, muttering, "You can't do anything right. I'll have to catch them myself." And with that she hurled her huge body into the air and flew off.

Soaring over the mountains, the she-dragon searched the land for the boy and girl. She breathed fire and smoke as she flew and her wings beat the air like thunder. The sky darkened beneath her huge shadow and the trees bent to the ground as she flew.

Meanwhile, the young couple ran on. When they heard the sky rumble and felt the earth shudder, Olena put her hand to the ground. The earth was hot as coals.

"Now we really are doomed," she wailed. "The she-dragon herself comes for us." The girl changed herself into a stream and the boy into a perch, but the she-dragon was not to be fooled.

"You think you can escape me with such a flimsy trick?" she screeched. She turned herself into a pike and began chasing the perch. Up the stream they swam, but every time she got close, the perch puffed out his prickly fins so that she could not get near. On and on went the chase. When the dragon finally realized that she would never be able to grab hold of the perch, she began drinking the stream. She drank and drank, but the stream would not run dry. She drank more and more and more until finally she burst. Dragon flesh scattered like ashes over the entire earth.

Then Taras and Olena resumed their human forms and the girl said, "Now that we are safe, you must return to your family." Taras nodded in agreement. The girl continued, "When you greet them, though, beware not to kiss your uncle's newborn daughter. If you do, you will lose all memory of me."

"But what will you do?" asked the boy.

"Don't worry about me," Olena assured him, "I will find work in the village. Once you are settled, you can come to find me."

So Taras went to his village. His parents were so happy to see him that they wept with joy. All his family and friends came to greet him with kisses and open arms. Then his uncle stepped forward with a baby girl in his arms. Taras flushed with embarrassment. "What will they think if I do not kiss the baby?" he thought. Everyone was looking at him, so he put his lips to the baby's forehead, planting there the tiniest and gentlest of kisses. Of course, as soon as he did, he forgot about Olena, the maiden who had saved him, and about all of their adventures together, and most of all, about his promise of marriage.

Meanwhile, Olena found work with a family in town and waited for Taras to arrive. Time passed, but Taras did not come for her. In fact, so empty were his thoughts that after a year he decided he should marry. His family found a village girl and made the arrangements with her family, and they were betrothed. Everyone in the village was invited to the wedding, including Olena, although the villagers barely knew her.

As was the custom in those days, the night before the wedding, a group of young women gathered to bake the *korovai* (wedding bread) and play games. The forgotten maid was among them.

The young women mixed and kneaded the dough for the bread, then divided it for shaping. With her dough, Olena fashioned a pair of larks. She placed them carefully on top of the bread.

The next day everyone gathered together for the big event. They were all laughing and cheering and celebrating. Only Olena was quiet. She kept to herself and said nothing, but in all the excitement, no one seemed to notice. Suddenly, when the wedding bread was set upon the table, the larks came to life, strutting and chirping. Then the female lark spoke softly to her mate, saying, "Have you forgotten the forest I cleared for you and the field of wheat I planted and sowed, and the bread I baked for the she-dragon?"

And the male lark cocked his head and chirped, "Forgotten, forgotten."

So the female lark circled round the male and asked, "Have you forgotten the mountains I moved and the ports I built so the wheat might be sold? Have you forgotten the sack of gold?"

And the male lark fluttered his wings and replied, "Forgotten, forgotten, all forgotten."

So the female lark walked up to the male, nestled her head on his shoulder, and implored, "Then have you forgotten the golden hare and your promises to me? Have you forgotten me entirely then?"

And the male lark cocked his head to one side and repeated softly, "Forgotten, forgotten."

As the birds spoke, the veil lifted from Taras's mind and he remembered everything. His eyes filled with tears and when he looked up from the birds his gaze met the gaze of his beloved Olena. Gently they embraced as he repeated, "Now I remember. I remember it all. I remember."

So it was that Taras's engagement to the village girl was broken, and he and Olena were married. Everything was as it should be and the whole village celebrated for days with feasting and merriment. And Taras and Olena lived the rest of their lives in complete happiness, for that was what was meant to be. &

Glossary and Pronunciation Guide

Note: In addition to the vowels a, e, i, o, u, Ukrainian has the vowel "y," which is pronounced like the "y" in *system*. Apostrophes indicate soft pronunciation of the preceeding consonant. For example, the "l" in *maladjusted* is soft, while "l" in *mall* is hard. Alternate spellings (usually Russian) are given second. Attempts have been made for the easiest pronunciation, without the use of complex linguistics standards.

Baba Yaha/Baba Yaga (bah - bah - yah - HAH)—a witch or hag figure common in Ukrainian, Russian, and Eastern European tales. There are many variations of the *Baba Yaha* character, but she is usually described as very old and ugly, living in a house surrounded by skulls in the middle of a dark forest. Rather than flying on a broom, *Baba Yaha* flies in a mortar, rowing the air with a pestle. See "Introduction to Ukrainian Folktales," "The Frog Princess," and "The Doll."

babusia (bah - BOO - syah)—a variation of the word "baba," which means grandmother. See "The Stranger."

bandura (bahn - DOO - rah)—a unique, asymmetrical stringed instrument similar to a mandolin and often used to play or accompany traditional Ukrainian folk songs. See "Old Dog Sirko" and photograph in "Introduction" (page xxxii).

Bolshevik (bol - sheh - VYK)—a Russian term, this word refers to a member of the extreme left wing of the Russian Social Democrat party, which advocated the violent overthrow of capitalism. The *Bolsheviks* seized power in Russia in the 1917 revolution. The philosophy of the *Bolsheviks* is called *bolshevism*. See "Introduction" (page xxix).

borshch/borscht (BORSHCH)—a hearty beet soup made with meat and vegetables, and a common peasant meal in Ukraine as well as other Eastern European countries and Russia. See "Pan Kotsky, Sir Puss O'Cat."

chumak (choo - MAHK)—carters or those who drive a cart to transport salt and other goods. See "Further Adventures of Fox and Wolf."

Chornobyl/Chernobyl (chor - NOH - byl)—site near Kyiv of a nuclear reactor meltdown in 1986.

cossack/kozak (koh - ZAHK)—independent frontiersmen who settled in the lower Dnipro Valley and
other territories north of the Black Sea in the mid-
sixteenth to late eighteenth centuries. The *cossacks*
formed a military brotherhood and became well
known for their bravery and fighting skills. They fought against Turkish
and Tatar invasions and they fought for Ukrainian independence against
the rulers of Poland and Russia. In Ukraine, *cossacks* are generally considered heroes (similar to American cowboys). See "Introduction,"
"Dovbush's Treasure," and "The Magic Egg."

détente (day - tahnt)—a policy promoting relaxation of strained or tense
relationships

didus' (dee - DOOS')—grandfather, grandpa.

Dnipro/Dnieper (D'NEE - proh)—a large river in Ukraine.

domovyk (doh - moh - VYHK)—a house spirit, one of the many supernatural
beings in Ukrainian folk belief. See "Introduction to Ukrainian Folktales"
and "How Evil Came into the World."

Dunai/Danube (doo - NAHY)—a river in Ukraine.

Dovbush, Oleksa (DOHV - bush, Oh - LEK - sah)—Oleksa Dovbush is a
historical figure. This *cossack* (independent warrior, frontiersman) was
the leader of the *opryshky* (a band of outlaws) and, like Robin Hood, he
fought against injustice and robbed from the rich to give to the poor. But
he purportedly also ambushed and killed many people, keeping a lot of
the riches for himself.

glasnost' (GLAHS - nost)—a Russian word that means "openness," this term
refers to the Soviet policy that lifted censorship in favor of public discussion of political and social issues and freer dissemination of the news.

het'man (HET - mahn)—an elected political and military leader of the *cossacks*.
The *het'man*'s domain is called a *het'manate*.

Hohol'/Gogol' (HOH - hol)—the devil or Satan. See "How the Earth Was Made."

holubtsi (HOH - loob - tsee)—cabbage rolls stuffed with meat and rice. See
"The Stranger."

horilka (hoh - RILL - kah)—vodka. See "Dovbush's Treasure."

Hutsul (HOO - tsoohl)—member of an ethnic group from the Carpathian Mountains. *Hutsuls* are know for their colorful dress and elaborate handicrafts such as woodcarving and embroidery. Other ethnic groups in Western Ukraine include the *Lemkos* and the *Boikos*. See "The Stolen *Postoly* and the Boiled Eggs."

kalach (kah - LAHCH)—a yeast bun. See "The Little Round Bun" and "The Frog Princess."

kystka/kystky, pl. (KYST - kah/KYST - keh)—a writing tool, similar to a batik stylus, used in making *pysanky*. It has a wooden handle and a copper funnel to hold and dispense melted wax into intricate designs. See color plates.

klad (KLAHD)—one of the many spirits of Ukrainian folk belief, this manifestation was identified as a treasure spirit, usually the guardian of a buried treasure. See "Dovbush's Treasure."

kobzar/kobzari, pl. (Kohb - ZAHR/Kohb - zah - REE)—professional *bandurists* and other folk musicians. Before Stalin professional *kobzari* were blind mendicants who belonged to church-affiliated guilds and sang religious and historical songs including *dumy*, Ukrainian heroic poetry about the *cossacks*. They roamed the Ukrainian countryside, sometimes entering cities, especially to visit churches or monasteries during religious holidays. *Kobzari* of today are folk musicians and usually are not blind.

kopeck/kopiika (KOH - pek/ko - PEE - kah)—a unit of Russian money that was also used in Ukraine for many years. 100 *kopecks* are equal in value to one ruble. See "Oh! Lord of the Forest."

korovai (koh - roh - VAHY)—Ukrainian wedding bread elaborately decorated with dough figures of birds, leaves, flowers, and so forth. See "The Magic Egg."

krasanka/krasanky, pl. (KRAH - san - kah/KRAH - san - keh)—eggs boiled and dyed a solid color, eaten on Easter morning. See "Introduction to Ukrainian Folktales."

Kyiv/Kiev (KY - yeev/KEE - yev)—ancient city in Ukraine.

mara (MAH - rah)—the specter, one of the many spirits in Ukrainian pagan belief. Mara torments and oppresses people, causing illness, misfortune, and sometimes even death. See "Introduction to Ukrainian Tales" and "How Evil Came into the World."

mavka (MAHV - kah)—a term interchangeable with *rusalka* (see page 204).

molebin' (moh - LEH - beehn)—a supplication, church service, or litany of gratitude, celebrating the final rest of the dead. Also called *vichnaia pamiat.* See "The Doll."

opryshky (oh - PRYSH - keh)—bands of outlaws, sometimes with as many as 30 or 40 members, that roamed the Ukrainian countryside. These people were often social bandits, like Robin Hood, who robbed from the rich and gave to the poor. See "Dovbush's Treasure."

Paraskovia Piatnytsia (Pah - rahs - KOH - vy - ah/PYAT - ny - tsyah)—also known as Mother Friday, the patron saint of cloth and fiber arts. She was a protectoress of women and their work, especially their work with thread and textiles. See "Introduction to Ukrainian Folktales."

perestroika/perebudova, pl. (peh - reh - STROY - kah/peh - reh - boo - DO - vah)—a word used to described the Soviet economic reform plan instituted by Gorbachev in the late 1980s. In Ukraine this policy was called *perebudova*. See "Introduction."

pol'ovyk (poh - loh - VYK)—the field demon, one of the many spirits in Ukrainian folk belief. The *pol'ovyk* brings harm to those who work in the fields when they should not. See "Introduction to Ukrainian Folktales" and "How Evil Came into the World."

postoly (poh - STOH - leh)—everyday shoes, cheap peasant footwear. See "The Stolen *Postoly* and the Boiled Eggs."

pysanka/pysanky, pl. (PYH - sahn - kah/PYH - sahn - keh)—Ukrainian Easter eggs exchanged as gifts or buried under houses or fields to bring good luck. They are made with raw eggs, decorated with layers of wax and dye. See "Introduction to Ukrainian Folktales" and color plates.

ripka (REEP - kah)—a turnip. See "The Turnip."

ruble/rouble (ROO - buhl)—a unit of Russian money, this currency was also used for many years in Ukraine. It is equal in value to 100 *kopecks*. The Ukrainian currency today is called *hryvnia*.

rusalka/rusalky, pl. (roo - SAHL - kah/roo - SAHL - keh)—a water nymph or mermaid, usually the spirit of a dead woman or child. See "Introduction to Ukrainian Folktales" and "The Man Who Danced with the *Rusalky*."

rushnyk/rushnyky, pl. (roosh - NYK/roosh - NY - keh)—embroidered towels used as decoration around icons and windows and for sacred ceremonies, such as weddings and baptisms. See "Introduction to Ukrainian Folktales," color plate, "The Doll," and "Pea Roll-Along."

russify (ROO - sih - fī)—an English term meaning to impose the Russian language and culture on non-Russian people. Usually instituted by political edict, the process is called *Russification*. See "Introduction."

Spas—a harvest festival celebrated in August, that includes the blessing of fruit, nuts, and honey.

tata/tato (TAH - tah/TAH - toh)—Father, papa. See "The Sorceress."

varenyky (vah - REHN - ny - keh)—dumplings stuffed with meat, cheese, potatoes, or other fillings. A favorite food of Ukrainians, this is often considered the national dish. See "The Frog Princess" and "The Stranger."

vodianyk (voh - dyah - NYK)—the water dweller, one of the many spirits of Ukrainian pagan belief. The vodianyk supposedly punished people who fished out of season and sometimes married the *rusalka* or *mavka*. See "Introduction to Ukrainian Folktales" and "How Evil Came into the World."

Wooden church. (Photo by N. Kononenko)

Bibliography

Folktale Collections

Afanasev, Aleksandr. *Russian Fairy Tales*. 1945. New York: Pantheon Books.

Bain, R. Nisbet. *Cossack Fairy Tales and Folk Tales*. 1975 Kraus reprint. New York: Frederick A. Stokes.

Bilenko, Anatole, and Olga Shartse, eds. *Ukrainian Folk Tales*. 1974. Kyiv: Dnipro Publishers.

Bloch, Marie Halun. *Ukrainian Folk Tales*. Translated from the Original Collections of Ivan Rudchenko and Maria Lukiyanenko. 1964. New York: Coward-McCann.

Courlander, Harold, ed. *Ride with the Sun: An Anthology of Folk Tales and Stories from the United Nations*. 1955. New York: McGraw-Hill.

Franko, Ivan. *When the Animals Could Talk: Fables*. 1987. Kyiv: Dnipro Publishers.

Lottridge, Celia Barker. *Ten Small Tales*. 1994. New York: Maxwell Macmillan International.

Manning-Sanders, Ruth. *A Book of Princes and Princesses*. 1969. New York: E. P. Dutton.

A Mountain of Gems: Fairy Tales of the Peoples of the Soviet Land. 1975. U.S.S.R.: Raduga Publishers.

Oparenko, Christina. *Ukrainian Folk-tales*. 1996. Oxford: Oxford University Press.

Yashinksky, Dan, ed. *Tales for an Unknown City: Stories from One Thousand and One Friday Nights of Storytelling*. 1990. Montreal and Kingston, Canada: McGill-Queen's University Press.

Ukrainian Folk Tales. 1986. Kyiv: Dnipro Publishers.

Picture Books

Bilenko, Anatole, transl. *Pan Kotski, the Puss-o-Cat: Ukrainian Folk Tale.* 1987. Kyiv: Veselka Publishers.

Brett, Jan. *The Mitten: A Ukrainian Folktale.* 1989. New York: Putnam.

de la Mare, Walter. *The Turnip.* 1992. Boston: David R. Godine.

Kismaric, Carole. *The Rumor of Pavel and Paali.* 1988. New York: Harper & Row.

Lewis, J. Patrick. *The Frog Princess.* 1994. New York: Dial Books.

The Mitten. 1975. Moscow: Malysh Publishers.

Morgan, Pierr, illus. *The Turnip.* 1990. New York: Philomel Books.

Tresselt, Alvin. *The Mitten.* 1964. New York: Lothrop, Lee & Shepard.

Vladov, Serhiy, transl. *The Witch-Princess: Ukrainian Folk Tale.* 1989. Kyiv: Dnipro Publishers.

Historical, Language, and Cultural Information Sources

Andrushyn, C. H., and J. N. Krett, comps. *Ukrainian-English Dictionary.* 1955. Toronto: University of Toronto Press.

Kardash, Peter. *Ukraine: Its History and Its Arts.* 1991. Melbourne: Fortuna.

Kubijovyč, V., ed. *Encyclopedia of Ukraine.* vol. 1. 1984. Toronto: University of Toronto Press.

———. *Ukraine: A Concise Encyclopaedia.* vol. 1. 1963. Toronto: University of Toronto Press.

Magocsi, Paul Robert. *History of Ukraine.* 1996. Toronto: University of Toronto Press.

Pawliczko, Ann Lencyk. *Ukraine and Ukrainians Throughout the World: A Demographic and Sociological Guide to the Homeland and Its Diaspora.* 1994. Toronto: Shevchenko Scientific Society and University of Toronto Press.

Subtelny, Orest. *Ukraine: A History.* 2d ed. 1994. Toronto: University of Toronto Press.

Sources on Folklore and Folk Belief

Andriievs'skyi, O. *Bibliohrafiia Literatury z Ukrains'koho Fol'kloru,* 1. 1930. Kyiv: Universytets'ka typohrafiia.

Berezovs'skyi, I. *Ukrains'ka Radians'ka Fol'klorystyka.* 1968. Kyiv: Universytets'ka typohrafiia.

Chubyns'kyi, Pavol. *Mudrist' Vikiv: Ukrains'ke Narodoznavstvo*, in 2 vols. 1995. Kyiv: Mystetsvo.

Dovzheniuk, H. *Ukrains'kyi Dytiachyi Fol'klor*. 1981. Kyiv: Nankova dumka.

Hnatiuk, Volodymyr. *Znadoby do Halyts'ko-Rus'koii Demonologiii*. Vol. XV. 1904. L'viv: Etnografichnyi Zbirnyk Naukovoho Tovarystva imeni Shevchenka.

———. *Znadoby do Ukraiins'koii Demonolgiii*. Vols. XXXIII and XXXIV. 1912. L'viv: Etnografichnyi Zbirnyk Naukovoho Tovarystva imeni Shevchenka.

Ivanits, Linda J. *Russian Folk Belief*. 1989. New York: M. E. Sharpe.

Klymasz, R. "Folklore Politics in the Soviet Ukraine: Perspectives on Some Recent Trends and Developments," in *Folklore, Nationalism, and Politics*, ed. F. J. Oinas. 1978. Columbus, Ohio: Slavica.

Kolessa, F. *Ukrains'ka Usna Slovesnist'*. 2d ed. 1983. Edmonton, Canada: Canadian Institute of Ukrainian Studies.

Lintur, Petro. *A Survey of Ukrainian Folk Tales*. Transl. B. Medwidsky. Edmonton, Canada: Canadian Institute of Ukrainian Studies Press, 1994.

Ukrains'ka Narodna Poetychna Tvorchist'. Radians'kyi Period. vols. 1 and 2. 1958. Kyiv: Vyshcha Shkola.

Zelenin, D. K. *Ocherki po Russkoi Mifologii: Umershie Neestesvennoiu Smertiu i Rusalki*. 1995 (reprint of the 1916 original with a new introduction by N. I. Tolstoi). Moscow: Indrik.

Other Sources

In addition to using the print sources listed previously, I have retold some tales from versions given to me by people from Ukraine or of Ukrainian descent. This includes tales that my editor, Natalie Kononenko, contributed. Some of these are stories she heard as a child from her mother and grandfather, but several of these are her own conflations, using traditional themes and plots to create new tales. In addition, Larysa Onyshkevych provided me with her unique version of *The Turnip*, one of the versions on which I based my retelling. For further details on contributions, refer to the preface.

For those who wish to learn more about Ukrainian culture, the list below offers a sampling. Readers are encouraged to check their own communities for other resources.

Bookstores, Gift Shops, and Catalogs

Kalyna Bookstore
952 Main St.
Winnepeg, MN
Canada R2W 3P4
phone: (204) 582-2832

Surma Book & Music
11 E. 7th St.
New York, NY 10003
USA
phone: (212) 477-0729

Ukrainian Bookstore
2315 W. Chicago Ave.
Chicago, IL 60622-4723
USA
phone: (773) 276-3733

Ukrainian Bookstore
P.O. Box 1640
10215 97 St.
Edmonton, AB T5J 2N9
Canada
phone: (403) 422-4255
fax: (403) 425-1439

West Arka Bookstore
2282 Bloor St. W.
Toronto, ON M6S 1N9
Canada
phone: (416) 762-8751
fax: (416) 767-6839

Yevshan Ukrainian Catalog
Yevshan Corporation
Box 1075
Champlain, NY 12919-1075
USA
phone: (800) 265-9858
fax: (524) 630-9960
e-mail: www.yevshan.com

Cultural Centers and Organizations
Ukrainian Cultural Center
2247 Chicago
Chicago, IL 60622
USA
phone: (773) 384-6400

Ukrainian National Museum
2453 W. Chicago Ave.
Chicago, IL 60612
USA
phone: (312) 421-8020

Ukrainian Women's League and
    Museum
108th 2nd Ave.
New York, NY 10003
USA
phone: (212) 533-4646

Publishers and Research Organizations

Canadian Institute for Ukrainian
  Studies (CIUS)
352 Athabasca Hall
University of Alberta
Edmonton, AB T6G 2E8
Canada
phone: (403) 492-2972

Shevchenko Scientific Society
63 Fourth Ave.
New York, NY 10003
USA
phone: (212) 254-5130

Ukrainian Academy of Arts and
  Sciences
206 W. 100 St.
New York, NY 10025
USA
phone: (212) 222-1866

Ukrainian Research Institute
Harvard University
1583 Massachusetts Ave.
Cambridge, MA 02138-2801
USA
phone: (617) 495-1000

Vydubytsky monastery is situated on the Dnipro River.

Index

About the Author

Barbara J. Suwyn is a professional copywriter and published poet. She has taught creative writing and journal-keeping classes in an adult education program and is a member of the Voices of Women (VOW) writers' group. Her interest in storytelling and in Ukrainian culture and history motivated her to write this book. She has a B.A. in Comparative Religions from the University of Michigan in Ann Arbor and she currently resides in Denver, Colorado.

(Photo by Mary Taber)

About the Story Editor

Natalie O. Kononenko is Associate Professor at the University of Virginia, where she teaches folklore courses that are very popular with both undergraduate and graduate students. Her interest in Ukrainian tales goes back to her childhood when she heard some of the stories in this book from her mother and grandfather. She became committed to the study of folklore while studying at Harvard University under the famous folklorist Albert Lord. Her other work includes studies of Ukrainian and Turkish folk performers and writings about ritual and ethnography. Her book *Ukrainian Minstrels: And the Blind Shall Sing* has been awarded the Kovaliv prize.